# 15 MINUTE
# ITALIAN
## LEARN IN JUST 12 WEEKS

FRANCESCA LOGI

**DK** Penguin Random House

**Senior Editors** Angeles Gavira, Christine Stroyan
**Project Art Editor** Vanessa Marr
**DTP Designer** John Goldsmid
**Jacket Design Development Manager** Sophia MTT
**Jacket Designer** Juhi Sheth
**Pre-Producer** David Almond
**Senior Producer** Ana Vallarino
**Associate Publisher** Liz Wheeler
**Publishing Director** Jonathan Metcalf

**Language content for Dorling Kindersley by g-and-w publishing.**

**Produced for Dorling Kindersley by Schermuly Design Co.**

First published in Great Britain in 2005.
This revised edition published in 2018 by
Dorling Kindersley Limited
80 Strand, London WC2R 0RL.

Printed in China

A WORLD OF IDEAS:
SEE ALL THERE IS TO KNOW

www.dk.com

# CONTENTS

How to use this book     4

**WEEK 1**
**INTRODUCTIONS**
Hello     8
Relatives     10
My family     12
To be and to have     14
Review and repeat     16

**WEEK 2**
**EATING AND DRINKING**
In the café     18
In the restaurant     20
To want     22
Dishes     24
Review and repeat     26

**WEEK 3**
**MAKING ARRANGEMENTS**
Days and months     28
Time and numbers     30
Appointments     32
On the telephone     34
Review and repeat     36

**WEEK 4**
**TRAVEL**
At the ticket office     38
To go and to take     40
Taxi, bus, and metro     42
On the road     44
Review and repeat     46

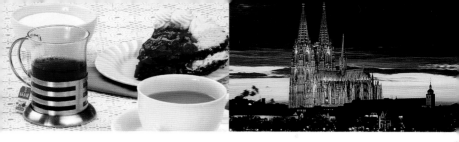

### WEEK 5
**GETTING ABOUT**

| | |
|---|---|
| About town | 48 |
| Finding your way | 50 |
| Sightseeing | 52 |
| At the airport | 54 |
| Review and repeat | 56 |

### WEEK 6
**ACCOMMODATION**

| | |
|---|---|
| Booking a room | 58 |
| In the hotel | 60 |
| At the campsite | 62 |
| Descriptions | 64 |
| Review and repeat | 66 |

### WEEK 7
**SHOPPING**

| | |
|---|---|
| Shops | 68 |
| At the market | 70 |
| At the supermarket | 72 |
| Clothes and shoes | 74 |
| Review and repeat | 76 |

### WEEK 8
**WORK AND STUDY**

| | |
|---|---|
| Jobs | 78 |
| The office | 80 |
| Academic world | 82 |
| In business | 84 |
| Review and repeat | 86 |

### WEEK 9
**HEALTH**

| | |
|---|---|
| At the chemist | 88 |
| The body | 90 |
| At the doctor's | 92 |
| At the hospital | 94 |
| Review and repeat | 96 |

### WEEK 10
**AT HOME**

| | |
|---|---|
| At home | 98 |
| In the house | 100 |
| The garden | 102 |
| Pets | 104 |
| Review and repeat | 106 |

### WEEK 11
**SERVICES**

| | |
|---|---|
| Post office and bank | 108 |
| Repairs | 110 |
| To come | 112 |
| Police and crime | 114 |
| Review and repeat | 116 |

### WEEK 12
**LEISURE AND SOCIALIZING**

| | |
|---|---|
| Leisure time | 118 |
| Sport and hobbies | 120 |
| Socializing | 122 |
| Review and repeat | 124 |
| Reinforce and progress | 126 |

| | |
|---|---|
| **MENU GUIDE** | 128 |
| **ENGLISH–ITALIAN DICTIONARY** | 132 |
| **ITALIAN–ENGLISH DICTIONARY** | 146 |
| Acknowledgments | 160 |

# How to use this book

The main part of the book is devoted to 12 themed chapters, broken down into five 15-minute daily lessons, the last of which is a revision lesson. So, in just 12 weeks you will have completed the course. A concluding reference section contains a menu guide and English-to-Italian and Italian-to-English dictionaries.

**Warm up**
Each day starts with a warm up that encourages you to recall vocabulary or phrases you have learned previously. To the right of the heading bar you will see how long you need to spend on each exercise.

**Instructions**
Each exercise is numbered and introduced by instructions that explain what to do. In some cases additional information is given about the language point being covered.

**Cultural/Conversational tip**
These panels provide additional insights into life in Italy and language usage.

**How to use the flap**
The book's cover flaps allow you to conceal the Italian so that you can test whether you have remembered correctly.

**Revision pages**
A recap of selected elements of previous lessons helps to reinforce your knowledge.

**la brioche**
*lah breeosh*
croissant

**la crema**
*lah kremah*
custard cream

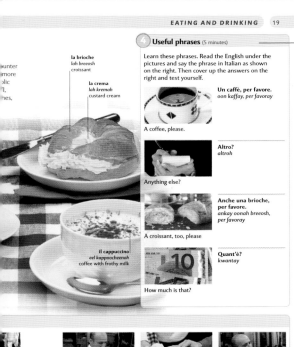

**il cappuccino**
*eel kappoocheenoh*
coffee with frothy milk

4 **Useful phrases** (5 minutes)

Learn these phrases. Read the English under the pictures and say the phrase in Italian as shown on the right. Then cover up the answers on the right and test yourself.

A coffee, please.

**Un caffè, per favore.**
*oon kaffay, per favoray*

Anything else?

**Altro?**
*altroh*

A croissant, too, please

**Anche una brioche, per favore.**
*ankay oonah breeosh, per favoray*

How much is that?

**Quant'è?**
*kwantay*

**Useful phrases**
Selected phrases relevant to the topic help you speak and understand.

**Sì, certo.**
*see, chertoh*

Yes, certainly.

**Allora, prendo una brioche. Quant'è?**
*allorah, prendoh oonah breeosh. kwantay*

I'll have a croissant, then. How much is that?

**Quattro euro, per favore.**
*kwattroh ayooroh, per favoray*

Four euros, please.

**Text styles**
Distinctive text styles differentiate Italian and English, and the pronunciation guide.

**In conversation**
Illustrated dialogues reflecting how vocabulary and phrases are used in everyday situations appear throughout the book.

**Say it**
In these exercises you are asked to apply what you have learned using different vocabulary.

6 **Say it** (2 minutes)

Do you go to the train station?

The Vatican, please.

When's the next coach to Rome?

**Dictionary**
A mini-dictionary provides ready reference from English to Italian and Italian to English for 2,500 words.

**Menu guide**
Use this guide as a reference for food terminology and popular Italian dishes.

## Pronunciation guide

Many Italian sounds will already be familiar to you, but a few require special attention. Take note of how these letters are pronounced:

**c**   an Italian **c** is pronounced _ch_ before **i** or **e** but _k_ before other vowels: **cappuccino** kappoo_cheen_oh

**ch**   pronounced _k_ as in _keep_

**g**   pronounced _j_ as in _jam_ before **i** or **e** but _g_ as in _get_ before other vowels

**gh**   pronounced _g_ as in _go_

**gn**   pronounced _ny_ like the sound in the middle of _onion_

**gli**   pronounced _ly_ like the sound in the middle of _million_

**h**   **h** is always silent: ho oh (I have)

**r**   an Italian **r** is trilled like a Scottish _r_

**s**   an Italian **s** can be pronounced either _s_ as in _see_ or _z_ as in _zoo_

**sc**   pronounced _sh_ as in _ship_ before **i** or **e** but _sk_ as in _skip_ before other vowels

**z**   an Italian **z** is pronounced _ts_ as in _pets_

Italian vowels tend to be pronounced longer than their English equivalents, especially:

**e**   as the English _lay_

**i**   as the English _keep_

**u**   as the English _boot_

After each word or phrase you will find a pronunciation transcription. Read this, bearing in mind the tips above, and you will achieve a comprehensible result. But remember that the transcription can only ever be an approximation and that there is no real substitute for listening to and mimicking native speakers.

# How to use the audio app

All the numbered exercises in each lesson, apart from the Warm ups at the beginning and the Say it exercises at the end, have recorded audio, available via a free app. The app also includes a function to record yourself and listen to yourself alongside native speakers.

To start using the audio with the book, first download the **DK 15 Minute Language Course** app on your smartphone or tablet from the App Store or Google Play. Open the app and scan the QR code on the back of this book to add it to your Library. As soon as the QR code is recognized, the audio will download.

There are two ways in which you can use the audio. The first is to read through your 15-minute lessons using the book only, and then go back and work with the audio and the book together, repeating the text in the gaps provided and then recording yourself. Or you can combine the book and the audio right from the beginning, pausing the app to read the instructions on the page as you need to. Try to say the words aloud, and practise enunciating properly. Detailed instructions on how to use the app are available from the menu bar in the app.

Remember that repetition is vital to language learning. The more often you listen to a conversation or repeat an oral exercise, the more the language will sink in.

Menu, Help/How to Use, Your Library

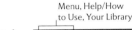

**1 Getting started**
The list of weeks will open when the audio has been downloaded. From here you can tap into each week's lessons.

When all the lessons in a week have been completed, the week button will be filled with colour and show a check mark, so you can track your progress.

**2 Lessons week by week**
Each numbered exercise in a lesson is listed in the app as it appears in the book. Tap on an exercise to start.

A check mark indicates when an exercise has been completed.

**3 Audio for exercises**
Tap the play button to hear instructions, then the exercise. You can pause the audio at any point, and return to it.

You can tap any part of the exercise to play the audio from that point.

**4 Record yourself**
When you are in the *Your recordings* screen, you can record yourself reading the words or participating in the conversations with native speakers, then listen back (and rerecord if desired).

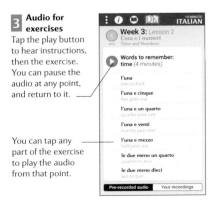

Add recording

Play recording

## 1 Warm up (1 minute)

The Warm Up panel appears at the beginning of each topic. Use it to reinforce what you have already learned and to prepare yourself for moving ahead with the new subject.

# BUONGIORNO
## Hello

In Italy a firm handshake usually accompanies an introduction or meeting in a formal situation. Italians greet relatives and friends with a kiss on each cheek but only when they haven't met, or are not going to see each other, for a while. Men often greet each other with a hug.

## 2 Words to remember (2 minutes)

Say these polite expressions aloud. Hide the text on the left with the cover flap and try to remember the Italian for each. Check your answers and repeat, if necessary.

| | |
|---|---|
| **Buongiorno.** <br> *bwonjornoh* | Hello/Good day. |
| **Piacere.** <br> *peeahcheray* | Pleased to meet you. |
| **Come si chiama?** <br> *komay see keeamah* | What's your name? |
| **Buonasera/Buonanotte.** <br> *bwonasayrah/* <br> *bwonanottay* | Good evening/ Good night. |

Ciao!
*chow*
Hi!

**Conversational tip** Italians tend to use *sir* (**signore**), *madam* (**signora**), and *miss* (**signorina**) more than English-speakers would. These titles are also used with surnames.

## 3 In conversation: formal (3 minutes)

**Buongiorno. Mi chiamo Suzi Lee.**
*bwonjornoh. mee keeamoh soozee lee*

Hello. My name's Suzi Lee.

**Buongiorno. Marco Paoletti, piacere.**
*bwonjornoh. markoh pa-olettee, peeahcheray*

Hello. Marco Paoletti, pleased to meet you.

**Piacere.**
*peeahcheray*

Pleased to meet you.

## 4 Put into practice (3 minutes)

Join in this conversation. Read the Italian beside the pictures on the left and then follow the instructions to make your reply. Then test yourself by concealing the answers with the cover flap.

**Buonasera.**
*bwonasayrah*

Good evening.

**Buonasera signora.**
*bwonasayrah seennyorah*

Say: Good evening madam.

---

**Mi chiamo Marta.**
*mee keeamoh martah*

My name is Marta.

**Piacere.**
*peeahcheray*

Say: Pleased to meet you.

## 5 Useful phrases (3 minutes)

Familiarize yourself with these phrases. Read them aloud several times and try to memorize them. Hide the Italian with the cover flap and test yourself.

| | |
|---|---|
| Goodbye. | **Arrivederci.** <br> *arreevederchee* |
| See you soon. | **A presto.** <br> *ah prestoh* |
| See you tomorrow. | **A domani.** <br> *ah domanee* |
| Thank you. | **Grazie.** <br> *gratseeay* |

## 6 In conversation: informal (3 minutes)

**Allora, a domani?**
*allorah, ah domanee*

So, see you tomorrow?

**Sì, arrivederci a domani.**
*see, arreevederchee ah domanee*

Yes, goodbye, see you tomorrow.

**Arrivederci. A presto.**
*arreevederchee. ah prestoh*

Goodbye. See you soon.

# I PARENTI
## Relatives

In Italian the word for *the* varies depending on whether the word it refers to is masculine or feminine - for example, **il cellulare** (*mobile phone*) is masculine, but **la riunione** (*meeting*) is feminine. You will sometimes find **lo** used with masculine words. **Il**, **la**, and **lo** change to **l'** before a vowel.

**2 Match and repeat** (5 minutes)

Look at the numbered family members in this scene and match them with the vocabulary list at the side. Read the Italian words aloud. Now, hide the list with the cover flap and test yourself.

**❶ la sorella**
*lah sorellah*

**❷ il nonno**
*eel nonnoh*

**❸ il padre**
*eel padray*

**❹ il fratello**
*eel fratelloh*

**❺ la nonna**
*lah nonnah*

**❻ la figlia**
*lah feelyah*

**❼ la madre**
*lah madray*

**❽ il figlio**
*eel feelyoh*

grandfather ❷        ❸ father

sister ❶        ❹ brother

❺ grandmother        ❻ daughter        ❼ mother        ❽ son

**Conversational tip** In Italian the word **nipote** means four different things: *nephew*, *niece*, *grandson*, and *granddaughter*. For *nephew* and *grandson* you use the masculine **il nipote**, for *niece* and *granddaughter* you use the feminine **la nipote**.

## 3 Words to remember: relatives (4 minutes)

**il marito**
*eel mareetoh*
husband

**la moglie**
*lah molyay*
wife

**Sono sposato/sposata.**
*sono spozatoh/spozatah*
I'm married (male/female).

Look at these words and say them aloud. Hide the text on the right with the cover flap and try to remember the Italian. Check your answers and repeat, if necessary. Then practise the phrases below.

| | |
|---|---|
| uncle | **lo zio** *loh tzeeoh* |
| aunt | **la zia** *lah tzeeah* |
| cousin | **il cugino/la cugina** *eel koojeenoh/lah koojeenah* |
| in-laws | **i suoceri** *ee swocheree* |
| I have four children. | **Ho quattro figli.** *oh kwattroh feelyee* |
| We have two daughters. | **Abbiamo due figlie.** *abbeeahmoh dooay feelyeeay* |
| I have a sister. | **Ho una sorella.** *oh oonah sorellah* |
| I have two brothers. | **Ho due fratelli.** *oh dooay fratellee* |

## 4 Words to remember: numbers (5 minutes)

Memorize these words and then test yourself using the cover flap.

The word for *a* or *one* changes to match gender: **un fratello** (*a brother*, masculine); **una sorella** (*a sister*, feminine). **Un** changes to **uno** in front of **z** or **s** plus consonant: **uno zio** (*an uncle*), **uno sport** (*a sport*). **Una** changes to **un'** before a vowel: **un'amica** (*a female friend*). To make a plural, a final -**a** usually changes to -**e**: **figlia/figlie** (*daughter/daughters*). A final -**o** or -**e** usually changes to -**i**: **fratello/fratelli** (*brother/brothers*). *The* also changes in the plural: **le** for the feminine; **i** or **gli** for the masculine.

| | |
|---|---|
| one | **uno** *oonoh* |
| two | **due** *dooay* |
| three | **tre** *tray* |
| four | **quattro** *kwattroh* |
| five | **cinque** *cheenkway* |
| six | **sei** *say* |
| seven | **sette** *settay* |
| eight | **otto** *ottoh* |
| nine | **nove** *novay* |
| ten | **dieci** *deeaychee* |

## **1** Warm up (1 minute)

Say the Italian for as many members of the family as you can. (pp.10-11)

Say "I have two sons". (pp.10-11)

# LA MIA FAMIGLIA
## My family

There are two ways of saying *you* in Italian: formally and informally. **Lei** is the formal version and **tu** is for family, friends, and young people. This means there are also different words for *your* (see below). It's a good idea to use the formal version until you are addressed by the other person as **tu**.

## **2** Words to remember (5 minutes)

There are different words for *my* and *your* in Italian, depending on whether they precede a masculine, feminine, or plural word.

| | |
|---|---|
| **mio/mia**<br>*mee-oh/me-eah* | **my** (masculine/feminine singular) |
| **miei/mie**<br>*mee-ayee/mee-ay* | **my** (masculine/feminine plural) |
| **tuo/tua**<br>*too-oh/too-ah* | **your** (informal masculine/feminine singular) |
| **tuoi/tue**<br>*too-oh-ee/too-ay* | **your** (informal masculine/feminine plural) |
| **suo/sua**<br>*soo-oh/soo-ah* | **your** (formal masculine/feminine singular) |
| **suoi/sue**<br>*soo-oh-ee/soo-ay* | **your** (formal masculine/feminine plural) |

**Questi sono i miei genitori.**
*kwaystee sonoh ee mee-ayee jeneetoree*
These are my parents.

## **3** In conversation (4 minutes)

**Lei ha figli?**
*lay ah fillyee*

Do you have any children?

**Sì, ho due figlie.**
*see, oh dooay feellyay*

Yes, I have two daughters.

**Queste sono le mie figlie. E Lei?**
*kwestay sonoh lay mee-ay feellyay. ay lay*

These are my daughters. And you?

**Conversational tip** The Italians generally ask a question by simply raising the pitch of the voice at the end of the statement: **Vuole un po' di vino?** (*Do you want a little wine?*). Some questions are introduced by a question word (*what, where, how,* and so on): **Quant'è?** (*How much is it?*), **Dove va?** (*Where are you going?*).

## 4 Useful phrases (3 minutes)

Read these phrases aloud several times and try to memorize them. Conceal the Italian with the cover flap and test yourself.

| | |
|---|---|
| Do you have any brothers? (informal) | **Hai fratelli?** *ahee fratellee* |
| Do you have any brothers? (formal) | **Ha fratelli?** *ah fratellee* |

| | |
|---|---|
| This is my husband. | **Questo è mio marito.** *kwestoh ay mee-oh mareetoh* |
| This is my wife. | **Questa è mia moglie.** *kwestah ay mee-ah molyay* |

| | |
|---|---|
| Is that your sister? (informal) | **Quella è tua sorella?** *kwellah ay too-ah sorellah* |
| Is that your sister? (formal) | **Quella è sua sorella?** *kwellah ay soo-ah sorellah* |

## 5 Say it (2 minutes)

**No, ma ho un nipote.**
*noh, mah oh oon neepotay*

No, but I have a nephew.

Do you have any brothers and sisters? (formal)

Do you have any children? (informal)

I have two sisters.

This is my wife.

**1** **Warm up** (1 minute)

Say "See you soon".
(pp.8-9)

Say "I am married"
(pp.10-11) and "This is
my wife". (pp.12-13)

# ESSERE E AVERE
## To be and to have

There are some essential verbs that you can use to
make a range of useful expressions. The first of these
are **essere** (*to be*) and **avere** (*to have*). In Italian the
verb form varies according to the pronoun (*I, you, he,
she*, and so on). The pronoun itself is often omitted,
as it is implied by the verb.

**2** **Essere: to be** (5 minutes)

Familiarize yourself with the different forms of **essere**
(*to be*) and, when you are confident, practise the
sentences below. Note that descriptive words can have
different endings depending on what is being described.

| | |
|---|---|
| **(io) sono**<br>*(ee-oh) sonoh* | I am |
| **(tu) sei**<br>*(too) say* | you are<br>(informal singular) |
| **(Lei) è**<br>*(lay) ay* | you are<br>(formal singular) |
| **(lui/lei) è**<br>*(loo-ee/lay) ay* | he/she/it is |
| **(noi) siamo**<br>*(noy) see-ahmoh* | we are |
| **(voi) siete**<br>*(voy) see-aytay* | you are<br>(plural) |
| **(loro) sono**<br>*(loroh) sonoh* | they are |

**Sono inglese.**
*sonoh eenglesay*
I'm English.

| | |
|---|---|
| **Di dov'è?/Di dove sei?**<br>*dee dovay/dee dovay say* | Where are you from?<br>(formal/informal) |

| | |
|---|---|
| **È contenta?**<br>*ay kontayntah* | Is she happy? |

| | |
|---|---|
| **Siamo italiani.**<br>*see-ahmoh eetahleeahnee* | We're Italian. |

## 3 Avere: to have (5 minutes)

Practise **avere** (to have) and the sample sentences, then test yourself.

| | |
|---|---|
| I have | **(io) ho** <br> *(eeoh) oh* |
| you have <br> (informal singular) | **(tu) hai** <br> *(too) ahee* |
| you have <br> (formal singular) | **(Lei) ha** <br> *(lay) ah* |
| he/she/it has | **(lui/lei) ha** <br> *(loo-ee/lay) ah* |
| we have | **(noi) abbiamo** <br> *(noy) abbeeahmoh* |
| you have (plural) | **(voi) avete** <br> *(voy) avetay* |
| they have | **(loro) hanno** <br> *(loroh) annoh* |

**Ha dei broccoli?**
*ah day brokkolee*
Do you have any broccoli?

| | |
|---|---|
| Marco has a meeting. | **Marco ha una riunione.** <br> *markoh ah oonah* <br> *reeooneeonay* |
| Do you have a <br> mobile phone? | **Ha un cellulare?** <br> *ah oon chaylloolaray* |
| How many brothers and <br> sisters do you have? | **Quanti fratelli ha?** <br> *kwantee fratellee ah* |

## 4 Negatives (4 minutes)

**la bicicletta**
*lah beechee-klettah*
bicycle

It is easy to make sentences negative in Italian. Just put **non** in front of the verb: **non siamo inglesi** (we're not English), **non ho fratelli** (I don't have any brothers).

| | |
|---|---|
| He's not married. | **Non è sposato.** <br> *non ay spozatoh* |
| I'm not sure. | **Non sono sicuro/a.** <br> *non sonoh seekooroh/ah* |
| We don't have any <br> children. | **Non abbiamo figli.** <br> *non abbeeamoh feelyee* |

**Non ho l'auto.**
*non oh la-ootoh*
I don't have a car.

# RIPASSA E RIPETI
## Review and repeat

**Risposte**
*Answers* (Cover with flap)

### 1 How many?

**1** tre
*tray*

**2** nove
*novay*

**3** quattro
*kwattroh*

**4** due
*dooay*

**5** otto
*ottoh*

**6** dieci
*deeaychee*

**7** cinque
*cheenkway*

**8** sette
*settay*

**9** sei
*say*

### 1 How many? (2 minutes)

Hide the answers with the cover flap. Then say these Italian numbers aloud. Check you have remembered the Italian correctly.

3 **2** 9 **3** 4
**1**
2 **4** **5** 8 10 **6**
5 **7** 7 6 **9**
**8**

### 2 Hello

**1** Buonasera, mi chiamo...
*bwonasayrah, mee keeamoh...*

**2** Piacere.
*peeahcheray*

**3** Sì sono sposato/a, e ho due figli. E Lei?
*see sonoh spozatoh/ ah, ay oh dooay feelyee. ay lay*

**4** Arrivederci a domani.
*arreevederchee ah domanee*

### 2 Hello (4 minutes)

You meet someone in a formal situation. Join in the conversation, replying in Italian following the English prompts.

   **Buonasera, mi chiamo Suzi.**
**1** Answer the greeting and give your name.

   **Questo è mio marito, Piero.**
**2** Say "Pleased to meet you".

   **Lei è sposato/a?**
**3** Say "Yes, I'm married and I have two sons. And you?"

   **Noi abbiamo tre figlie.**
**4** Say "Goodbye. See you tomorrow."

## 3 To have or to be (5 minutes)

Fill in the blanks with the correct form of **avere** (*to have*) or **essere** (*to be*). Check you have remembered the Italian correctly.

❶ (io) _____ sposato/a.

❷ (noi) _____ quattro figli.

❸ (lei) _____ inglese.

❹ (Lei) _____ un fratello?

❺ (voi) _____ figli?

❻ (io) non _____ il cellulare.

❼ (tu) _____ sicuro.

❽ (noi) _____ italiani.

### 3 To have or be

❶ **sono**
*sonoh*

❷ **abbiamo**
*abbeeahmoh*

❸ **è**
*ay*

❹ **ha**
*ah*

❺ **avete**
*avetay*

❻ **ho**
*oh*

❼ **sei**
*say*

❽ **siamo**
*see-ahmoh*

## 4 Family (4 minutes)

Say the Italian for each of the numbered family members. Check you have remembered the Italian correctly.

grandfather ❷   ❸ father
sister ❶   ❹ brother
❺ grandmother   ❻ daughter   ❼ mother   ❽ son

### 4 Family

❶ **la sorella**
*lah sorellah*

❷ **il nonno**
*eel nonnoh*

❸ **il padre**
*eel padray*

❹ **il fratello**
*eel fratelloh*

❺ **la nonna**
*lah nonnah*

❻ **la figlia**
*lah feelyah*

❼ **la madre**
*lah madray*

❽ **il figlio**
*eel feelyoh*

**Warm up** (1 minute)

Count up to ten.
(pp.10-11)

Remind yourself how to
say "hello" and "goodbye".
(pp.8-9)

Ask "Do you have a mobile
phone?" (pp.14-15)

# AL BAR
## In the café

In a typical café-bar you can either stand at the counter
or sit at a table with waiter service, which can be more
expensive. You can have a variety of soft or alcoholic
drinks. The standard coffee is an **espresso**, a small,
black coffee. You can also order pastries, sandwiches,
and other snacks.

**Words to remember** (5 minutes)

Look at the words below and say them
out loud a few times. Conceal the Italian
with the cover flap and try to remember
each one in turn. Practise also the words
on the right.

**lo zucchero**
*loh tsookkeroh*
sugar

| | |
|---|---|
| **il caffè macchiato** *eel kaffay makeeatoh* | espresso with a little milk |
| **la tisana** *lah teezanah* | herbal tea |
| **il tè con latte** *eel tay kon lattay* | tea with milk |
| **il panino** *eel paneenoh* | sandwich |

**il caffè (espresso)**
*eel kaffay (espressoh)*
small, black coffee

**Cultural tip** Italians are not big tea drinkers and when
they do have tea they add some lemon rather than milk.
So if you want milk in your tea you may have to ask for a
little cold milk (**un po' di latte freddo**).

**In conversation** (4 minutes)

**Vorrei un cappuccino,
per favore.**
*vorray oon
kappoocheenoh, per
favoray*

I'd like a cappuccino,
please.

**Altro, signore?**
*altroh, seennyoray*

Anything else, sir?

**Ha delle brioche?**
*ah dellay breeosh*

Do you have
any croissants?

**la brioche**
*lah breeosh*
croissant

**la crema**
*lah kremah*
custard cream

**il cappuccino**
*eel kappoocheenoh*
coffee with frothy milk

### 4 Useful phrases (5 minutes)

Learn these phrases. Read the English under the pictures and say the phrase in Italian as shown on the right. Then cover up the answers on the right and test yourself.

A coffee, please.

**Un caffè, per favore.**
*oon kaffay, per favoray*

Anything else?

**Altro?**
*altroh*

A croissant, too, please.

**Anche una brioche, per favore.**
*ankay oonah breeosh, per favoray*

How much is that?

**Quant'è?**
*kwantay*

**Sì, certo.**
*see, chertoh*

Yes, certainly.

**Allora, prendo una brioche. Quant'è?**
*allorah, prendoh oonah breeosh. kwantay*

I'll have a croissant, then. How much is that?

**Quattro euro, per favore.**
*kwattroh ayooroh, per favoray*

Four euros, please.

# AL RISTORANTE
## In the restaurant

### ① Warm up (1 minute)

Say "I'd like". (pp.18–19)

Say "I don't have a brother". (pp.14–15)

Ask "Do you have any croissants?" (pp.18–19)

There are a variety of different types of eating places in Italy. In a bar you can find a few snacks. A **trattoria** is a traditional restaurant with fast service. In the more formal restaurants, it is often necessary to book. Pizzerias are a relaxed and cheap way of dining out, and are ideal for big groups.

### ② Words to remember (3 minutes)

Memorize these words. Conceal the Italian with the cover flap and test yourself.

| | |
|---|---|
| **il menù** *eel menoo* | menu |
| **la lista dei vini** *lah leesta day veenee* | wine list |
| **i primi piatti** *ee preemee peeattee* | starters |
| **i secondi piatti** *ee seekondee peeattee* | main courses |
| **i dessert** *ee dessert* | desserts |
| **la colazione** *lah kolatseeonay* | breakfast |
| **il pranzo** *eel pranzoh* | lunch |
| **la cena** *lah chenah* | dinner |

cup ❽

saucer ❼

❻ spoon

❹ knife

fork ❺

### ③ In conversation (4 minutes)

**Buongiorno, ha un tavolo per quattro?**
*bwonjornoh, ah oon tavoloh per kwattroh*

Hello, do you have a table for four?

**Ha la prenotazione?**
*ah lah prenotatseeonay*

Do you have a reservation?

**Sì, a nome Gatti.**
*see, anomay gattee*

Yes, in the name of Gatti.

### 4 Match and repeat (4 minutes)

Look at the numbered items in this table setting and match them with the Italian words on the right. Read the Italian words aloud. Now, conceal the Italian with the cover flap and test yourself.

glass **1**

**2** napkin

plate **3**

**1** il bicchiere
*eel beekkyayray*

**2** il tovagliolo
*eel tovallyohloh*

**3** il piatto
*eel peeattoh*

**4** il coltello
*eel koltelloh*

**5** la forchetta
*lah forkettah*

**6** il cucchiaio
*eel kookee-ayoh*

**7** il piattino
*eel peeahteenoh*

**8** la tazza
*lah tattsah*

### 5 Useful phrases (3 minutes)

Practise these phrases and then test yourself using the cover flap to conceal the Italian.

| | |
|---|---|
| What do you have for dessert? | **Cosa avete come dessert?** *kozah avaytay komay dessert* |
| The bill, please. | **Il conto, per favore.** *eel kontoh, per favoray* |

**Benissimo. Che tavolo vuole?**
*beneesseemoh. kay tavoloh vwolay*

Fine. Which table would you like?

**Vicino alla finestra, per favore.**
*veecheenoh allah feenestrah, per favoray*

Near the window, please.

**Certo. Ecco.**
*chertoh. ekkoh*

Very well. Here you are.

# VOLERE
## To want

In this section, you will learn the different forms of a verb that are essential to everyday conversation, **volere** (*to want*), including a useful polite form, **vorrei** (*I would like*). Remember to use this form when requesting something because **voglio** (*I want*) may sound too strong.

---

### 1 Warm up (1 minute)

What are "breakfast", "lunch", and "dinner" in Italian? (pp.20-1)

Say "I", "you" (informal), "he", "she", "we", "you" (plural), "they". (pp.14-15)

---

### 2 Volere: to want (6 minutes)

Say the different forms of **volere** (*to want*) aloud. Use the cover flap to test yourself and, when you are confident, practise the sample sentences below.

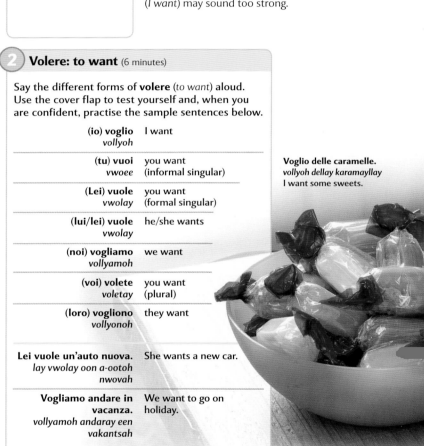

| | | |
|---|---|---|
| **(io) voglio** *vollyoh* | I want | |
| **(tu) vuoi** *vwoee* | you want (informal singular) | |
| **(Lei) vuole** *vwolay* | you want (formal singular) | |
| **(lui/lei) vuole** *vwolay* | he/she wants | |
| **(noi) vogliamo** *vollyamoh* | we want | |
| **(voi) volete** *voletay* | you want (plural) | |
| **(loro) vogliono** *vollyonoh* | they want | |

**Voglio delle caramelle.**
*vollyoh dellay karamayllay*
I want some sweets.

| | |
|---|---|
| **Lei vuole un'auto nuova.** *lay vwolay oon a-ootoh nwovah* | She wants a new car. |
| **Vogliamo andare in vacanza.** *vollyamoh andaray een vakantsah* | We want to go on holiday. |

---

**Conversational tip** In Italian **del** the word for *some* changes depending on what follows. For example, **Voglio del caffè** (*I want some coffee*, masculine singular), **Voglio della birra** (*I want some beer*, feminine singular), **Voglio dei limoni** (*I want some lemons*, masculine plural), and **Voglio delle caramelle** (*I want some sweets*, feminine plural). **Della** may be shortened to **dell'** before a vowel.

### 3 Polite requests (4 minutes)

There is a form of **volere** used for polite requests:
**(io) vorrei** (*I would like*), as in **Vorrei un caffè** (*I'd like
a coffee*). Practise the following sample sentences and
then test yourself using the cover flap.

I'd like a beer. **Vorrei una birra.**
*vorray oonah beerah*

I'd like a table
for tonight.
**Vorrei un tavolo
per stasera.**
*vorray oon tavoloh
per staserah*

I'd like the
menu, please.
**Vorrei il menù,
per favore.**
*vorray eel menoo,
per favoray*

### 4 Put into practice (4 minutes)

Join in this conversation. Read the Italian beside the
pictures on the left and then follow the instructions
to make your reply in Italian. Test yourself by hiding
the answers with the cover flap.

**Buonasera. Ha la
prenotazione?**
*bwonasayrah. ah lah
prenotatseeonay*

**No, ma vorrei
un tavolo per tre.**
*noh, mah vorray oon
tavoloh per tray*

Good evening. Do you
have a reservation?

Say: No, but I would
like a table for three.

**Benissimo. Che
tavolo vuole?**
*beneesseemoh. kay
tavoloh vwolay*

**Vicino alla finestra,
per favore.**
*veecheenoh allah
feenestrah, per favoray*

Fine. Which table
would you like?

Say: Near the
window please.

Say "I am married"
(pp.12-13) and "I'm
not sure". (pp.14-15)

Ask "Do you have any
brothers?" (pp.12-13)

Say "I'd like a sandwich".
(pp.18-19)

# LE PIETANZE
## Dishes

Italy is famous for its cuisine and the quality of its
restaurants. It also offers a wide variety of regional
dishes. Pasta is a typically Italian dish, prepared in
dozens of different ways. Although traditionally
Italian cuisine is meat-based, many restaurants
now offer a vegetarian menu.

**Cultural tip** In many restaurants you will be
able to choose a cheaper *set menu* **il menù fisso**
or **il menù turistico**. *Salad* (**l'insalata**) is generally
served as a *side dish* (**il contorno**).

**2** **Match and repeat** (4 minutes)

Look at the numbered items and match them to the
Italian words in the panel on the left.

**1** **la verdura**
*lah vairdoorah*

**2** **la frutta**
*lah froottah*

**3** **il formaggio**
*eel formajjoh*

**4** **la frutta secca**
*la froottah sekkah*

**5** **la minestra**
*lah meenestrah*

**6** **il pollo**
*eel polloh*

**7** **il pesce**
*eel peshay*

**8** **la pasta**
*lah pastah*

**9** **i frutti di mare**
*ee froottee dee maray*

**10** **la carne**
*lah karnay*

fruit **2**

vegetables **1**

cheese **3**

**5** soup

chicken **6**

**8** pasta

**9** seafood

## 3 Words to remember: cooking methods (3 minutes)

The ending may vary depending on the gender of item described.

| | |
|---|---|
| fried (m/f) | **fritto/a** |
| | *freettoh/ah* |
| grilled | **alla griglia** |
| | *allah greellyah* |
| roasted (m/f) | **arrosto** |
| | *arrostoh* |
| boiled (m/f) | **lesso/a** |
| | *layssoh/ah* |
| steamed | **al vapore** |
| | *al vaporay* |
| rare (meat) | **al sangue** |
| | *al sangway* |

**Vorrei una bistecca ben cotta.**
*vorray oona beestekkah ben kottah*
I'd like my steak well done.

## 6 Say it (2 minutes)

What is **al vapore**?

I'm allergic to seafood.

I'd like a beer.

## 4 Words to remember: drinks (3 minutes)

Familiarize yourself with these words.

| | |
|---|---|
| water | **l'acqua** (f) |
| | *lahkkwah* |
| fizzy water | **l'acqua gassata** (f) |
| | *lahkkwah gassatah* |
| still water | **l'acqua naturale** (f) |
| | *lahkkwah natooralay* |
| wine | **il vino** |
| | *eel veenoh* |
| beer | **la birra** |
| | *lah beerah* |
| fruit juice | **il succo di frutta** |
| | *eel sookkoh dee froottah* |

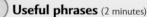
nuts 4

fish 7

## 5 Useful phrases (2 minutes)

Practise these phrases and then test yourself.

| | |
|---|---|
| I am a vegetarian. | **Sono vegetariano/a.** |
| | *sonoh vejetareeanoh/ah* |
| I am allergic to nuts. | **Sono allergico/a alla frutta secca.** |
| | *sonoh allerjeekoh/ah allah froottah sekkah* |
| What are "tagliatelle"? | **Cosa sono le tagliatelle?** |
| | *kozah sonoh lay tallyatellay* |

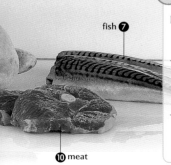
10 meat

# RIPASSA E RIPETI
## Review and repeat

### 1 What food?

❶ **lo zucchero**
*loh tsookkeroh*

❷ **la verdura**
*lah vairdoorah*

❸ **i frutti di mare**
*ee froottee dee maray*

❹ **la carne**
*lah karnay*

❺ **il bicchiere**
*eel beekkyayray*

### 1 What food? (4 minutes)

Name the numbered items.

❷ vegetables    sugar ❶

seafood ❸

meat ❹

glass ❺

### 2 This is my...

❶ **Questo è mio marito.**
*kwestoh ay meeoh mareetoh*

❷ **Questa è mia figlia.**
*kwestah ay meeah feellyah*

❸ **Queste sono le mie sorelle.**
*kwestay sonoh lay meeay sorellay*

### 2 This is my... (4 minutes)

Say these phrases in Italian. Use **mio**, **mia**, **miei**, or **mie**.

❶ This is my husband.

❷ This is my daughter.

❸ These are my sisters.

### 3 I'd like...

❶ **Vorrei un caffè.**
*vorray oon caffay*

❷ **Vorrei un cappuccino.**
*vorray oon kappoocheenoh*

❸ **Vorrei una brioche.**
*vorray oonah breeosh*

❹ **Vorrei lo zucchero.**
*vorray loh tsookkeroh*

### 3 I'd like... (3 minutes)

Say "I'd like" the following:

croissant ❸

❹ sugar    ❶ black coffee

cappuccino ❷

⑥ pasta

knife ⑦

⑧ cheese

beer ⑩

⑨ napkin

### ① What food?

⑥ **la pasta**
*lah pastah*

⑦ **il coltello**
*eel koltelloh*

⑧ **il formaggio**
*eel formajjoh*

⑨ **il tovagliolo**
*eel tovallyohloh*

⑩ **la birra**
*lah beerrah*

### ④ Restaurant (4 minutes)

You arrive at a restaurant. Join in the conversation, replying in Italian where you see the English prompts.

**Buonasera.**
① Ask "Do you have a table for one?"

**Ha la prenotazione?**
② Say "Yes, in the name of Gatti."

**Benissimo.**
③ Say "I'd like the menu, please".

**Vuole anche la lista dei vini?**
④ Say "No. Fizzy water, please".

**Ecco.**
⑤ Say "I don't have a glass".

### ④ Restaurant

① **Ha un tavolo per uno?**
*ah oon tavoloh per oonoh*

② **Non fumatori.**
*non foomatoree*

③ **Vorrei il menù, per favore.**
*vorray eel menoo, per favoray*

④ **No, acqua gassata, per favore.**
*noh, ahkkwah gassatah, per favoray*

⑤ **Non ho il bicchiere.**
*non oh eel beekkyeray*

## 1 Warm up (1 minute)

How do you say "he is" and "they are"? (pp.14–15)

Now say "he is not" and "they are not". (pp.14–15)

What is Italian for "my mother"? (pp.10–11)

# I GIORNI E I MESI
## Days and months

In Italian, *days of the week* (**i giorni della settimana**) and *months* (**i mesi**) do not have capital letters. Notice that with months you generally use **in**: **in ottobre** (*in October*); with days you use nothing: **lunedì** (*on Monday*), but when it means every Monday you use the article (**il/la**): **il lunedì** (*on Mondays*).

## 2 Words to remember: days of the week (5 minutes)

Familiarize yourself with these words and test yourself using the flap.

| | |
|---|---|
| **lunedì** *loonedee* | Monday |
| **martedì** *martedee* | Tuesday |
| **mercoledì** *merkoledee* | Wednesday |
| **giovedì** *jovedee* | Thursday |
| **venerdì** *venerdee* | Friday |
| **sabato** *sabatoh* | Saturday |
| **domenica** *domeneekah* | Sunday |
| **oggi** *ojjee* | today |
| **domani** *domanee* | tomorrow |
| **ieri** *yayree* | yesterday |

**Ci vediamo domani.**
*chee vedeeamoh domanee*
We meet tomorrow.

**Ho una prenotazione per oggi.**
*oh oonah prenotatseeonay per ojjee*
I have a reservation for today.

## 3 Useful phrases: days (2 minutes)

Learn these phrases and then test yourself using the cover flap.

| | |
|---|---|
| **La riunione non è martedì.** *lah reeooneeonay non ay martedee* | The meeting isn't on Tuesday. |
| **La domenica lavoro.** *lah domeneekah lavoroh* | I work on Sundays. |

## 4 Words to remember: months of the year (5 minutes)

Familiarize yourself with these words and test yourself using the flap.

**Il nostro anniversario è in luglio.**
*eel nostroh anneeversareeoh*
*ay een loollyoh*
Our anniversary is in July.

**Natale è in dicembre.**
*natalay ay een deechembray*
Christmas is in December.

| | | |
|---|---|---|
| January | **gennaio** | *jennaheeoh* |
| February | **febbraio** | *febbraheeoh* |
| March | **marzo** | *martsoh* |
| April | **aprile** | *apreelay* |
| May | **maggio** | *majjeeoh* |
| June | **giugno** | *jooneeoh* |
| July | **luglio** | *loollyoh* |
| August | **agosto** | *agostoh* |
| September | **settembre** | *settembray* |
| October | **ottobre** | *ottobray* |
| November | **novembre** | *novembray* |
| December | **dicembre** | *deechembray* |
| month | **mese** | *mezay* |
| year | **anno** | *annoh* |

## 5 Useful phrases: months (2 minutes)

Learn these phrases and then test yourself using the cover flap.

My children are on holiday in August.
**I miei bambini sono in vacanza in agosto.**
*ee mee-ayee bambeenee sonoh een vakantsah een agostoh*

My birthday is in June.
**Il mio compleanno è in giugno.**
*eel mee-oh kompleahnnoh ay een jooneeoh*

**1 Warm up** (1 minute)

Count in Italian from
1 to 10. (pp.10-11)

Say "I have a reservation".
(pp.20-1)

Say "The meeting is on
Wednesday". (pp.28-9)

# L'ORA E I NUMERI
## Time and numbers

On a day-to-day basis Italians use the 12-hour clock,
sometimes adding **di mattina** (*in the morning*), **di
pomeriggio** (*in the afternoon*), **di sera** (*in the evening*),
or **di notte** (*at night*). To say the time you say **Sono le**...,
as in **Sono le dieci** (*It's ten o'clock*), except for *It's one
o'clock*, which is **È l'una**.

**2 Words to remember: time** (4 minutes)

Memorize how to tell the time in Italian.

| | |
|---|---|
| **l'una** <br> *loonah* | one o'clock |
| **l'una e cinque** <br> *loonah ay cheenkway* | five past one |
| **l'una e un quarto** <br> *loonah ay oon kwartoh* | quarter past one |
| **l'una e venti** <br> *loonah ay ventee* | twenty past one |
| **l'una e mezzo** <br> *loonah ay metsoh* | half past one |
| **le due meno un quarto** <br> *lay dooay menoh oon kwartoh* | quarter to two |
| **le due meno dieci** <br> *lay dooay meno deeaychee* | ten to two |

**3 Useful phrases** (2 minutes)

Learn these phrases and then test yourself using
the cover flap.

| | |
|---|---|
| **Che ore sono?** <br> *kay oray sonoh* | What time is it? |
| **A che ora vuole <br> la colazione?** <br> *ah kay orah voo-olay <br> lah kolatseeonay* | What time do you <br> want breakfast? |
| **Ho una prenotazione <br> per le dodici.** <br> *oh oonah prenotatseeonay <br> per lay dodeechee* | I have a reservation <br> for twelve o'clock. |

## 4 Words to remember: higher numbers (6 minutes)

To say 21, 31, and so on, you say **ventuno**, **trentuno**, etc. After that just add the number as in **ventidue** (22), **ventitré** (23), **trentadue** (32), **trentatré** (33).

To say the date, you generally use the regular number: **Oggi è il 26 settembre** (Today is 26th September).

The exception is the first day of the month when you say *the first*, as in **Domani è il primo febbraio** (Tomorrow is the first of February).

**Sono ottantacinque euro.**
*sonoh ottantacheenkway ayooroh*
That's eighty-five euros.

| | | |
|---|---|---|
| eleven | **undici** | *oondeechee* |
| twelve | **dodici** | *dodeechee* |
| thirteen | **tredici** | *traydeechee* |
| fourteen | **quattordici** | *kwattordeechee* |
| fifteen | **quindici** | *kweendeechee* |
| sixteen | **sedici** | *sedeechee* |
| seventeen | **diciassette** | *deechassettay* |
| eighteen | **diciotto** | *deechottoh* |
| nineteen | **diciannove** | *deechannovay* |
| twenty | **venti** | *ventee* |
| thirty | **trenta** | *trentah* |
| forty | **quaranta** | *kwarantah* |
| fifty | **cinquanta** | *cheenkwantah* |
| sixty | **sessanta** | *sessantah* |
| seventy | **settanta** | *settantah* |
| eighty | **ottanta** | *ottantah* |
| ninety | **novanta** | *novantah* |
| hundred | **cento** | *chentoh* |
| three hundred | **trecento** | *traychentoh* |
| thousand | **mille** | *meellay* |
| ten thousand | **diecimila** | *deeaycheemeelah* |
| two hundred thousand | **duecentomila** | *dooaychentomeelah* |
| one million | **un milione** | *oon meeleeonay* |

## 5 Say it (2 minutes)

twenty-five

sixty-eight

eighty-four

ninety-one

It's five to ten.

It's half past eleven.

What time is lunch?

# GLI APPUNTAMENTI
## Appointments

### 1 Warm up (1 minute)

Say the days of the week.
(pp.28-9)

Say "It's three o'clock".
(pp.30-1)

What's the Italian for
"today", "tomorrow", and
"yesterday"? (pp.28-9)

Business in Italy is still generally conducted more
formally than in Britain or the United States; always
address business contacts as **Lei**. Italians also tend
to take a longer lunch break and, except in big cities,
people often go home for their midday meal.

**Benvenuto.**
*benvenootoh*
Welcome.

### 2 Useful phrases (5 minutes)

Learn these phrases and then test yourself.

| | |
|---|---|
| **Fissiamo un appuntamento per domani?** *feesseeamoh oon appoontamentoh per domanee* | Shall we meet tomorrow? |
| **Con chi?** *kon kee* | With whom? |
| **Quando è libero/a?** *kwandoh ay leeberoh/ah* | When are you free? |
| **Mi dispiace, sono impegnato/a.** *mee deespeeachay, sonoh eempennyatoh/ah* | I'm sorry, I am busy. |
| **Va bene giovedì?** *vah benay jovedee* | How about Thursday? |
| **Per me va bene.** *per may vah benay* | That's good for me. |

**la stretta
di mano**
*lah strettah
dee manoh*
handshake

### 3 In conversation (4 minutes)

**Buongiorno. Ho un
appuntamento.**
*bwonjornoh. oh oon
appoontamentoh*

Hello. I have
an appointment.

**Con chi?**
*kon kee*

With whom?

**Con il signor Baroni.**
*kon eel seennyor baronee*

With Mr Baroni.

**4** **Put into practice** (5 minutes)

Practise these phrases. Then cover up the text on the right and say the answering part of the dialogue in Italian. Check your answers and repeat if necessary.

**Fissiamo un appuntamento per giovedì?**
*feesseeamoh oon appoontamentoh per jovedee*

Shall we meet on Thursday?

Say: Sorry, I'm busy.

**Mi dispiace, giovedì sono impegnato.**
*mee deespeeachay, jovedee sonoh eempennyatoh*

---

**Quando è libero?**
*kwandoh ay liberoh*

When are you free?

Say: Tuesday afternoon.

**Martedì pomeriggio.**
*martedee pomereejjoh*

---

**Per me va bene.**
*per may vah benay*

That's good for me.

Ask: At what time?

**A che ora?**
*ah kay orah*

---

**Alle quattro, se per Lei va bene.**
*allay kwattroh, say per lay vah benay*

At four o'clock, if that's good for you.

Say: It's good for me.

**Per me va bene.**
*per may vah benay*

---

**Benissimo, a che ora?**
*beneesseemoh, ah kay orah*

Very good, at what time?

**Alle tre, ma sono un po' in ritardo.**
*allay tray, mah sonoh oon poh een reetardoh*

At three o'clock, but I'm a little late.

**Non si preoccupi. Prego, si accomodi.**
*non see prayokkoopee. pregoh, see akkomodee*

Don't worry. Take a seat, please.

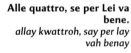

**1** **Warm up** (1 minute)

How do you say "I'm sorry"? (pp.32-3)

Ask "I'd like an appointment". (pp.32-3)

How do you say "with whom?" in Italian? (pp.32-3)

# AL TELEFONO
## On the telephone

In Italy you always dial the *full area code* (**il prefisso**) and the number.
The emergency number for *police* (**Carabinieri**), *ambulance* (**l'ambulanza**), or *fire services* (**i vigili del fuoco**) is 112.

**2** **Match and repeat** (4 minutes)

Match the numbered items to the Italian in the panel on the left and test yourself.

**1** **il caricabatterie**
*eel karikabatereeay*

**2** **il telefono**
*eel telayfonoh*

**3** **la segreteria telefonica**
*la segretereeah telayfoneekah*

**4** **gli auricolari**
*lly awreekolaree*

**5** **il cellulare**
*eel chelloolaray*

**6** **la carta SIM**
*la karta seem*

telephone **2**

charger **1**

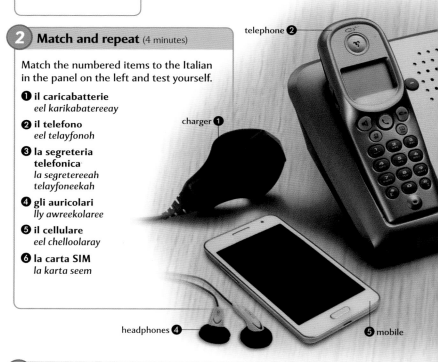

headphones **4**

**5** mobile

**3** **In conversation** (4 minutes)

**Pronto? Bonanni.**
*prontoh? bonannee*

Hello? Bonanni's.

**Buongiorno. Vorrei parlare con il dottor Pieri.**
*bwonjornoh. vorray parlaray kon eel dottor pyayree*

Hello. I'd like to speak to Dr Pieri.

**Chi parla?**
*kee parlah*

Who's speaking?

SIM card **6**

**Vorrei comprare una carta SIM.**
*vorray kompraray oonah karta SIM*
I'd like to buy a SIM card.

**3** answering machine

## 4 Useful phrases (4 minutes)

Practise these phrases. Then test yourself using the cover flap.

I'd like the number for Mario.

**Posso avere il numero di Mario?**
*possoh averay eel noomayroh dee mareeoh*

I'd like to speak to Federico Martini.

**Vorrei parlare con Federico Martini.**
*vorray parlaray kon fedayreekoh marteenee*

Can I leave a message?

**Posso lasciare un messaggio?**
*possoh lasharay oon messajjoh*

Sorry, I have the wrong number.

**Scusi, ho sbagliato numero.**
*skoozee, oh sballyatoh noomayroh*

## 5 Say it (2 minutes)

I'd like to speak to Mr Hachart.

Can I leave a message for Emma?

**Luciano Salvetti, della tipografia Bartoli.**
*loochanoh salvettee, della teepografeeah bartolee*

Luciano Salvetti of Bartoli Printers.

**Mi dispiace, la linea è occupata.**
*mee deespeeachay, lah leeneah ay okkoopatah*

I'm sorry. The line is busy.

**Può farmi richiamare, per favore?**
*puoh farmee reekeeamaray, per favoray*

Can he call me back, please?

# RIPASSA E RIPETI
## Review and repeat

### 1 Sums

❶ **sedici**
*sedeechee*

❷ **trentanove**
*trentanovay*

❸ **cinquantatré**
*cheenkwantatray*

❹ **settantaquattro**
*settantakwattroh*

❺ **novantanove**
*novantanovay*

❻ **quarantuno**
*kwarantoonoh*

### 1 Sums (4 minutes)

Say the answers
to these sums out
loud in Italian.
Then check you have
remembered correctly.

❶ 10 + 6 = ?
❷ 14 + 25 = ?
❸ 66 - 13 = ?
❹ 40 + 34 = ?
❺ 90 + 9 = ?
❻ 46 - 5 = ?

### 3 Telephones (3 minutes)

What are the numbered
items in Italian?

mobile ❶

❷ SIM card

### 2 To want

❶ **vuole**
*vwolay*

❷ **vogliamo**
*vollyamoh*

❸ **vogliono**
*vollyonoh*

❹ **vuoi**
*vwoee*

❺ **voglio**
*vollyoh*

❻ **volete**
*voletay*

### 2 To want (3 minutes)

Fill the gaps with
the correct form
of **volere** (to want).

❶ Signora, _____ un caffè?

❷ Io e Matteo _____ un
tavolo per due.

❸ (loro) _____ delle
caramelle.

❹ (tu) _____ una birra?

❺ (io) _____ una macchina
nuova.

❻ (voi) _____ dei bicchieri?

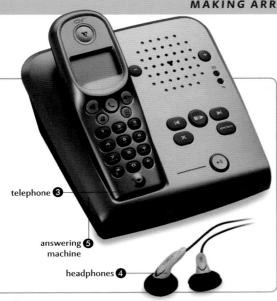

telephone **3**

answering **5** machine

headphones **4**

## 3 Telephones

**1** il cellulare
*eel chelloolaray*

**2** la carta SIM
*la karta seem*

**3** il telefono
*eel telayfonoh*

**4** gli auricolari
*lly awreekolaree*

**5** la segreteria
telefonica
*la segretereeah
telayfoneekah*

### 4 When? (2 minutes)

What do these sentences mean?

**1** La riunione è giovedì.

**2** Voglio andare in vacanza domani.

**3** Il mio compleanno è in agosto.

**4** Il nostro anniversario è in dicembre.

## 4 When?

**1** The meeting is
on Thursday.

**2** I want to go on
holiday tomorrow.

**3** My birthday is
in August.

**4** Our anniversary
is in December.

### 5 Time (3 minutes)

Say these times in Italian.

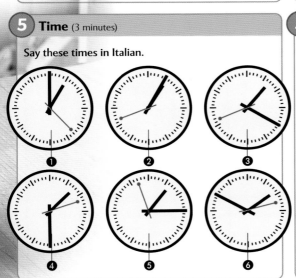

## 5 Time

**1** l'una
*loonah*

**2** l'una e cinque
*loonah ay cheenkway*

**3** l'una e venti
*loonah ay ventee*

**4** l'una e mezzo
*loonah ay metsoh*

**5** l'una e un quarto
*loonah ay
oon kwartoh*

**6** le due meno dieci
*lay dooay
menoh deeaychee*

**1** **Warm up** (1 minute)

Count to 100 in tens.
(pp.10-11 and pp.30-1)

Ask "At what time?"
(pp.30-1)

Say "half-past one".
(pp.30-1)

# ALLA BIGLIETTERIA
## At the ticket office

In Italy you must be sure to *validate* (**convalidare**) your ticket before getting on the train by stamping it in one of the special small yellow machines installed in every train station for this purpose. Fines are imposed on travellers who have forgotten to validate their tickets.

**2** **Words to remember** (3 minutes)

Learn these words and then test yourself.

| | |
|---|---|
| **la stazione** *lah statseeonay* | station |
| **il treno** *eel trenoh* | train |
| **la prenotazione** *la prenotatseeonay* | reservation |
| **il biglietto** *eel beellyettoh* | ticket |
| **sola andata** *solah andatah* | single |
| **andata e ritorno** *andatah ay reetornoh* | return |
| **prima/seconda classe** *preemah/sekondah klassay* | first/second class |
| **la coincidenza** *la koeencheedentsa* | connection |

**il passeggero**
*eel passejjayroh*
passenger

**il cartello**
*eel kartelloh*
sign

**La stazione è affollata.**
*lah statseeonay ay affollahtah*
The station is crowded.

**3** **In conversation** (4 minutes)

**Due biglietti per Roma, per favore.**
*dooay beellyettee per rohmah, per favoray*

Two tickets to Rome, please.

**Andata e ritorno?**
*andatah ay reetornoh*

Return?

**Sì. C'è la prenotazione obbligatoria?**
*see. chay lah prenotatseeonay obbleegatoryah*

Yes. Do I need to reserve seats?

### 4 Useful phrases (5 minutes)

**Il treno per Firenze è in ritardo.**
*eel trenoh per firentsay ay
een reetardoh*
The train to Florence is late.

**il binario**
*eel beenareeoh*
platform

Learn these phrases and then test yourself using the cover flap.

| | |
|---|---|
| How much is a ticket to Genoa? | **Quanto costa un biglietto per Genova?** *kwantoh kostah oon beellyettoh per jenovah* |
| Do you accept credit cards? | **Accettate la carta di credito?** *acchettatay lah kartah dee kredeetoh* |
| Do I have to change? | **Devo cambiare?** *devoh kambeearay* |
| Which platform does the train leave from? | **Da quale binario parte il treno?** *dah kwalay beenareeoh partay eel trenoh* |
| Are there discounts? | **Ci sono delle riduzioni?** *chee sonoh dellay reedootseeonee* |
| What time does the train to Naples leave? | **A che ora parte il treno per Napoli?** *ah kay orah partay eel trenoh per napolee* |

### 5 Say it (2 minutes)

Which platform does the train for Genoa leave from?

Three return tickets to Naples, please.

**Cultural tip** Most train stations have *automatic ticket machines* (**la biglietteria automatica**) that accept credit and debit cards as well as cash.

**No. Sono quaranta euro.**
*noh. sonoh kwarantah ayooroh*

No. It's forty euros.

**Accettate la carta di credito?**
*acchettatay lah kartah dee kredeetoh*

Do you accept credit cards?

**Certo. Il treno parte dal binario uno.**
*chertoh. eel trenoh partay dal beenareeoh oonoh*

Certainly. The train leaves from platform one.

How do you say "train"?
(pp.38-9)

What does "Da quale
binario parte il treno?"
mean? (pp.38-9)

Ask "When are you
free?" (pp.32-3)

# ANDARE E PRENDERE
## To go and to take

**Andare** (*to go*) and **prendere** (*to take*) are essential
verbs in Italian that you will need to use frequently in
everyday conversation as you find your way around.
You can also use **prendere** when you talk about food
and drink - for example, to say **prendo un caffè**
(*I'll have a coffee*).

**2** **Andare: to go** (6 minutes)

Say the different forms of **andare** (*to go*) aloud. Use the
cover flaps to test yourself and, when you are
confident, practise the sample sentences below.

| | |
|---|---|
| **(io) vado**<br>*(eeoh) vadoh* | I go |
| **(tu) vai**<br>*(too) vaee* | you go (informal singular) |
| **(Lei) va**<br>*(lay) vah* | you go (formal singular) |
| **(lui/lei) va**<br>*(looee/lay) vah* | he/she/it goes |
| **(noi) andiamo**<br>*(noy) andeeamoh* | we go |
| **(voi) andate**<br>*(voy) andatay* | you go (plural) |
| **(loro) vanno**<br>*(loroh) vannoh* | they go |
| **Dove va, signora?**<br>*dovay vah, seennyorah* | Where are you going, madam? |
| **Vorrei andare in treno.**<br>*vorray andaray een trenoh* | I'd like to go by train. |

**Vado a Pisa.**
*vadoh ah peesah*
I am going to Pisa.

**Conversational tip** In Italian the present tense
includes a sense of continuous action. You use the
same verb form to say *I go* and *I am going*.
**Vado a Roma** means both *I am going to Rome*
and *I go to Rome*. The same is true of other
verbs - for example, **prendo il taxi** means
*I am taking the taxi* and *I take the taxi*.

## 3 Prendere: to take (6 minutes)

**Prendo la metro tutti i giorni.**
*prendoh lah metroh toottee
ee jornee*
I take the metro every day.

Say the different forms of **prendere** *(to take)* aloud
and test yourself.

| | |
|---|---|
| **(io) prendo** <br> *(eeoh) prendoh* | I take |
| **(tu) prendi** <br> *(too) prendee* | you take (informal) |
| **(Lei) prende** <br> *(lay) prenday* | you take (formal) |
| **(lui/lei) prende** <br> *(looee/lay) prenday* | he/she/it takes |
| **(noi) prendiamo** <br> *(noy) prendeeamoh* | we take |
| **(voi) prendete** <br> *(voy) prendetay* | you take (plural) |
| **(loro) prendono** <br> *(loroh) prendonoh* | they take |

**Non voglio prendere
un taxi.**
*non vollyoh prenderay
oon taxee*

I don't want
to take a taxi.

**Prenda la prima a sinistra.**
*prenda lah preemah
ah seeneestrah*

Take the first
on the left.

**Lui prende il vitello.**
*looee prenday eel veetelloh*

He'll have the veal.

## 4 Put into practice (2 minutes)

Cover the text on the right and complete the dialogue
in Italian.

**Dove va?**    **Vado alla stazione.**
*dovay vah*    *vadoh allah statseeonay*

Where are you going?

Say: I'm going to
the station.

**Vuole prendere la metro?**    **No, voglio andare
in autobus.**
*vwolay prenderay lah metroh*    *noh, vollyoh andaray
een a-ootoboos*

Do you want to take
the metro?

Say: No, I want to go by bus.

## 1 Warm up (1 minute)

Say "I'd like to go to the station". (pp.40-1)

Ask "Where are you going?" (pp.40-1)

Say "fruit" and "cheese". (pp.24-5)

# TAXI, AUTOBUS E METRO
## Taxi, bus, and metro

In Italy you generally don't hail taxis, but go to a taxi rank. You can buy bus tickets at a newsagent's, which you then validate in he machine on the bus. You can use the same tickets both on the buses and on the metro.

## 2 Words to remember (4 minutes)

Familiarize yourself with these words.

| | |
|---|---|
| **l'autobus** (m) <br> *la-ootoboos* | bus |
| **il pullman** <br> *eel poolman* | coach |
| **la stazione dei pullman/ della metro** <br> *lah statseeonay day poolman/dellah metroh* | coach/metro station |
| **la fermata dell'autobus** <br> *lah fermatah della-ootoboos* | bus stop |
| **il biglietto** <br> *eel beellyettoh* | fare |
| **il posteggio dei taxi** <br> *eel postejjoh day taxee* | taxi rank |

**Passa di qui il quarantasei?**
*passah dee kwee eel kwarantasay*
Does the number 46 stop here?

## 3 In conversation: taxi (2 minutes)

**Al mercato di San Lorenzo, per favore.**
*al merkatoh dee san lorentsoh, per favoray*

To the San Lorenzo market, please.

**Benissimo, signore.**
*beneesseemoh, seennyoray*

Very well, sir.

**Mi lasci qui, per favore.**
*mee lashee kwee, per favoray*

Can you drop me here, please?

## 4 Useful phrases (4 minutes)

Learn these phrases and then test yourself using the cover flap.

| | |
|---|---|
| I'd like a taxi to go to the Colosseum. | **Vorrei un taxi per andare al Colosseo.** *vorray oon taxee per andaray al kolossayoh* |
| When is the next bus to the Capitol? | **Quando passa il prossimo autobus per il Campidoglio?** *kwandoh passah eel prosseemoh a-ootoboos per eel kampeedollyoh* |
| How do you get to the Vatican? | **Scusi, per andare al Vaticano?** *skoozee, per andaray al vateekahnoh* |
| Please wait for me. | **Mi aspetti, per favore.** *mee aspettee, per favoray* |

**Cultural tip** In Italy the metro exists only in Milan, Rome, and Naples. There are only a few lines and they are identified by numbers (M1, M2, M3 in Milan) or letters of the alphabet (MA, MB in Rome). Look for the relevant end station to find the direction you need.

## 6 Say it (2 minutes)

Do you go to the train station?

The Vatican, please.

When's the next coach to Rome?

## 5 In conversation: bus (2 minutes)

**Scusi, va al museo?**
*skoozee, vah al moozayoh*

Do you go to the museum?

**Sì. Non è lontano.**
*see. non ay lontanoh*

Yes. It's not very far.

**Può dirmi quando devo scendere?**
*pwoh deermee kwandoh devoh shenderay*

Can you tell me when to get off?

# IN AUTO
## On the road

**1** **Warm up** (1 minute)

How do you say "I have..."? (pp.14-15)

Say "my father", "my sister", and "my parents". (pp.12-13)

Say "I'm going to Rome". (pp.40-1)

Be sure to familiarize yourself with the Italian rules of the road before driving in Italy. Italian **autostrade** (*motorways*) are fast but expensive *toll* (**il pedaggio**) roads. You usually take a ticket as you join the motorway and pay according to the distance travelled as you leave it.

**2** **Match and repeat** (4 minutes)

Match the numbered items to the list on the left, then test yourself.

**1** **il bagagliaio**
*eel bagallyaeeoh*

**2** **il parabrezza**
*eel parabretsah*

**3** **il cofano**
*eel kofanoh*

**4** **la ruota**
*lah rwotah*

**5** **la gomma**
*lah gommah*

**6** **lo sportello**
*loh sportelloh*

**7** **il paraurti**
*eel parahoortee*

**8** **i fari**
*ee faree*

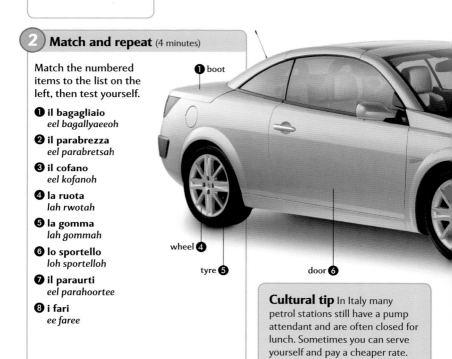

**1** boot

wheel **4**

tyre **5**

door **6**

**Cultural tip** In Italy many petrol stations still have a pump attendant and are often closed for lunch. Sometimes you can serve yourself and pay a cheaper rate.

**3** **Road signs** (2 minutes)

**Senso unico**
*senso uneekoh*

One way

**Rotatoria**
*rotatoreeah*

Roundabout

**Dare la precedenza**
*daray lah prechedentsah*

Give way

### 4 Useful phrases (4 minutes)

Learn these phrases and then test yourself using the cover flap.

My indicator doesn't work. **La freccia non funziona.**
*lah frechah non foontseeonah*

Fill it up, please. **Il pieno, per favore.**
*eel pyaynoh, per favoray*

**2** windscreen

**3** bonnet

headlights **8**   **7** bumper

### 5 Words to remember (3 minutes)

Familiarize yourself with these words then test yourself using the flap.

| | |
|---|---|
| driving licence | **la patente** *lah patentay* |
| petrol | **la benzina** *lah bendseenah* |
| diesel | **il gasolio** *eel gazolyoh* |
| oil | **l'olio** (m) *lohlyoh* |
| engine | **il motore** *eel motoray* |
| gearbox | **il cambio** *eel kambeeoh* |
| indicator | **la freccia** *lah frechah* |
| exhaust | **la marmitta** *lah marmeettah* |
| flat tyre | **la gomma a terra** *lah gommah ah terrah* |

### 6 Say it (1 minute)

My gearbox doesn't work.

I have a flat tyre.

**Diritto di precedenza**
*deereettoh dee prechedentsah*

Priority road

**Divieto di accesso**
*deevyaytoh dee acchessoh*

No entry

**Sosta vietata**
*sostah veeaytatah*

No parking

**Risposte**
**Answers** (Cover with flap)

# RIPASSA E RIPETI
## Review and repeat

### 1 Transport

❶ **l'autobus**
*la-ootoboos*

❷ **il taxi**
*eel taxee*

❸ **l'auto**
*la-ootoh*

❹ **la bicicletta**
*lah beecheeklettah*

❺ **la metro**
*lah metroh*

### 1 Transport (3 minutes)

Name these forms of transport in Italian.

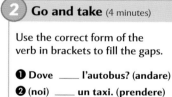

❶ bus

taxi ❷

### 2 Go and take

❶ **va**
*vah*

❷ **prendiamo**
*prendeeamoh*

❸ **vado**
*vadoh*

❹ **prende**
*prenday*

❺ **vanno**
*vannoh*

❻ **prendi**
*prendee*

### 2 Go and take (4 minutes)

Use the correct form of the verb in brackets to fill the gaps.

❶ Dove _____ l'autobus? (andare)

❷ (noi) _____ un taxi. (prendere)

❸ (io) _____ a Pisa. (andare)

❹ _____ un caffè, signor Gatti? (prendere)

❺ (loro) _____ in treno. (andare)

❻ (tu) _____ la seconda a sinistra. (prendere)

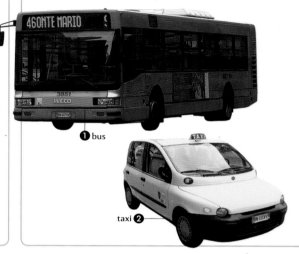

**3** car

**4** bicycle

metro **5**

### 3 Lei or tu?
(4 minutes)

Use the correct form of *you*.

**1** You are in a café. Ask "Do you have croissants?"

**2** You are with a friend. Ask "Do you want a beer?"

**3** You are talking to a business contact. Ask "Do you have an appointment?"

**4** You are on the bus. Ask "Do you go to the station?"

**5** Ask your friend where she's going tomorrow.

**6** Ask your (female) client "Are you free on Wednesday?"

### Risposte
*Answers* (Cover with flap)

### 3 Lei or tu?

**1** Ha delle brioche?
*ah dellay breeosh*

**2** Vuoi una birra?
*vwoee oonah beerah*

**3** Ha un appuntamento?
*ah oon appoontamentoh*

**4** Va alla stazione?
*vah allah statseeonay*

**5** Dove vai domani?
*dovay vaee domanee*

**6** È libera mercoledì?
*ay leeberah merkoledee*

### 4 Tickets (4 minutes)

You're buying tickets at a train station. Join in the conversation, replying in Italian following the numbered English prompts.

**Buongiorno.**
**1** I'd like two tickets to Ferrara.

**Solo andata o andata e ritorno?**
**2** Return, please.

**Sono trenta euro.**
**3** What time does the train leave?

**Alle quindici e dieci.**
**4** What platform does the train leave from?

**Dal binario sette.**
**5** Thank you.

### 4 Tickets

**1** Vorrei due biglietti per Ferrara.
*vorray dooay beellyettee per ferrarah*

**2** Andata e ritorno, per favore.
*andatah ay reetornoh, per favoray*

**3** A che ora parte il treno?
*ah kay orah partay eel trenoh*

**4** Da quale binario parte il treno?
*dah kwalay beenareeoh partay eel trenoh*

**5** Grazie.
*gratseeay*

# IN CITTÀ
## About town

**1** **Warm up** (1 minute)

Ask "How do you get to the museum?" (pp.42-3)

Say "I want to take the metro" and "I don't want to take a taxi". (pp.40-1)

Most Italian towns (**la città**) and larger villages (**il paese**) still have a market day for fresh produce and a thriving local community of small shops and businesses. There may be parking restrictions in the town centre. In Rome, parking in the central **zona tutelata** is prohibited on weekdays.

**2** **Match and repeat** (4 minutes)

Match the numbered locations to the words in the panel.

**1** **il municipio**
*eel mooneecheepeeoh*

**2** **la chiesa**
*lah keeayzah*

**3** **il ponte**
*eel pontay*

**4** **il centro città**
*eel chentroh cheettah*

**5** **il parcheggio**
*eel parkejjoh*

**6** **la piazza**
*lah peeatsah*

**7** **il museo**
*eel moozayoh*

church **2**

**3** **Words to remember** (4 minutes)

Familiarize yourself with these words and test yourself using the cover flap.

| | |
|---|---|
| **il benzinaio** <br> *eel bentseenaeeoh* | petrol station |
| **l'azienda turistica** (f) <br> *latsyayndah tooreesteekah* | tourist information |
| **la piscina** <br> *lah peesheenah* | swimming pool |
| **la biblioteca** <br> *lah beebleeotaykah* | library |

**1** town hall      town centre **4**

## 4 Useful phrases (4 minutes)

**Il duomo è in centro.**
*eel dwomoh ay een chentroh*
The cathedral is in
the centre.

Learn these phrases and then test yourself using
the cover flap.

| | |
|---|---|
| Is there an art gallery in town? | **C'è una pinacoteca in città?** *chay oonah peenacotekah een cheettah* |
| Is it far from here? | **È lontano da qui?** *ay lontanoh da kwee* |
| There is a swimming pool near the bridge. | **C'è una piscina vicino al ponte.** *chay oonah peesheenah veecheenoh al pontay* |
| There isn't a library. | **Non c'è una biblioteca.** *non chay oonah beebleeotaykah* |

## 5 Put into practice (2 minutes)

bridge ❸

car park ❺

square ❻

museum ❼

Join in this conversation. Read the Italian on the
left and follow the instructions to make your reply.
Then test yourself by concealing the answers with
the cover flap.

| | |
|---|---|
| **Dica?** *deekah* Can I help you? | **C'è una biblioteca in città?** *chay oonah beebleeotaykah een cheettah* |
| Ask: Is there a library in town? | |
| **No, ma c'è un museo.** *noh, mah chay oon moozayoh* No, but there's a museum. | **E per andare al museo?** *ay per andaray al moozayoh* |
| Ask: How do I get to the museum? | |
| **È nella piazza.** *ay nellah peeatsah* It's in the square. | **Grazie.** *gratseeay* |
| Say: Thank you. | |

# LE INDICAZIONI
## Finding your way

### 1 Warm up (1 minute)

How do you say "to the station"? (pp.40-1)

Say "Take the first on the left". (pp.40-1)

Ask "Where are you going?" (pp.40-1)

You'll often find a *town map* (**pianta della città**) situated around town, usually near the town hall or tourist office. In the older parts of Italian towns there are often narrow streets in which you will usually find a one-way system in operation. Parking is usually restricted.

### 2 Useful phrases (4 minutes)

Practise these phrases and then test yourself.

| | |
|---|---|
| **Giri a sinistra/destra.** *jeeree ah seeneestrah/destrah* | Turn left/right. |
| **A sinistra/destra.** *ah seeneestrah/destrah* | On the left/right. |
| **Sempre dritto.** *sempray dreettoh* | Straight on. |
| **Per andare alla piscina?** *per andaray allah peesheenah* | How do I get to the swimming pool? |
| **La prima a sinistra.** *ah preemah ah seeneestrah* | First on the left. |
| **La seconda a destra.** *lah sekondah ah destrah* | Second on the right. |

**il municipio**
*eel mooneecheepeeoh*
town hall

**la zona pedonale**
*lah tsonah pedonalay*
pedestrian zone

**Alla piazza giri a sinistra.**
*allah peeatsah jeeree ah seeneestrah*
At the square, turn left.

### 3 In conversation (4 minutes)

**C'è un ristorante in città?**
*chay oon reestorantay een cheettah*

Is there a restaurant in town?

**Sì, vicino alla stazione.**
*see, veecheenoh allah statseeonay*

Yes, near the station.

**E per andare alla stazione?**
*ay per andaray allah statseeonay*

How do I get to the station?

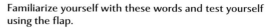

### 4 Words to remember (4 minutes)

**Mi sono persa.**
*mee sonoh persah*
I'm lost.

Familiarize yourself with these words and test yourself using the flap.

| | | |
|---|---|---|
| traffic lights | **il semaforo** *eel semaforoh* | |
| corner | **l'angolo** (m) *langoloh* | |
| street/road | **la strada** *lah stradah* | |
| junction | **l'incrocio** (m) *leenkrochoh* | |
| map | **la pianta** *lah peeantah* | |
| flyover | **il cavalcavia** *eel kavalkaveeah* | |
| opposite | **davanti a** *davantee ah* | |
| at the end of the street | **in fondo alla strada** *een fondoh allah stradah* | |

**il monumento**
*eel monoomentoh*
monument

**Dove siamo?**
*dovay seeahmoh*
Where are we?

### 5 Say it (2 minutes)

Turn right at the end of the street.

It's opposite the town hall.

It's ten minutes by bus.

**Al semaforo giri a sinistra.**
*al semaforoh jeeree ah seeneestrah*

Turn left at the traffic lights.

**È lontano?**
*ay lontanoh*

Is it far?

**No, cinque minuti a piedi.**
*noh, cheenkway meenootee ah peeaydee*

No, it's five minutes on foot.

## 1 Warm up (1 minute)

Say the days of the week in Italian. (pp.28-9)

How do you say "At six o'clock"? (pp.30-1)

Ask "What time is it?" (pp.30-1)

# IL TURISMO
## Sightseeing

Most national museums close on Mondays; a few are open on some public holidays. Many shops close for lunch, especially in small towns, and public buildings and banks are generally closed in the afternoon. Stores often close on Sundays, except in some tourist areas.

## 2 Words to remember (4 minutes)

Familiarize yourself with these words and test yourself using the flap.

| | |
|---|---|
| **la guida**<br>*lah gweedah* | guidebook |
| **la tariffa ridotta**<br>*lah tareefah reedottah* | concessionary rate |
| **l'orario di apertura** (m)<br>*lorareeoh dee apertoorah* | opening times |
| **il giorno festivo**<br>*eel jornoh festeevoh* | public holiday |
| **l'entrata libera**<br>*lentratah leebayrah* | free entrance |

**la visita guidata**
*lah veeseetah gweedatah*
guided tour

**Cultural tip** You will be asked to pay an entrance fee in most museums, historic buildings, and even in some churches. *Children* (**bambini**), *students* (**studenti**), or *pensioners* (**pensionati**) can ask for the concessionary rate, which is sometimes available.

## 3 In conversation (3 minutes)

**È aperto oggi pomeriggio?**
*ay apertoh ojjee pomereejjoh*

Do you open this afternoon?

**Sì, ma chiudiamo alle sei.**
*see, mah kyoodeeamoh allay say*

Yes, but we close at six o'clock.

**C'è l'accesso per i disabili?**
*chay lacchayssoh per ee deezabeelee*

Do you have disabled access?

## 4 Useful phrases (3 minutes)

Learn these phrases and then test yourself using the cover flap.

| | |
|---|---|
| What time do you open/close? | **A che ora aprite/chiudete?** *ah kay orah apreetay/ keeoodetay* |
| Where are the toilets? | **Dov'è la toilette?** *dovay lah toyeeletay* |
| Is there disabled access? | **C'è l'accesso per i disabili?** *chay lacchayssoh per ee deezabeelee* |

## 5 Put into practice (4 minutes)

Cover the text on the right and complete the dialogue in Italian.

**Spiacente. Il museo è chiuso.** *speeachentay. eel moozayoh ay keeoozoh*

Sorry. The museum is closed.

Ask: Do you open on Mondays?

**È aperto il lunedì?** *ay apertoh eel loonedee*

**Sì, ma chiude presto.** *see, mah keeooday prestoh*

Yes, but we close early.

Ask: At what time?

**A che ora?** *ah kay orah*

---

**Sì, là c'è l'ascensore.** *see, lah chay lashaynsoray*

Yes, there's a lift over there.

**Grazie. Vorrei quattro biglietti.** *gratseeay. vorray kwattroh beellyetTee*

Thank you. I'd like four entrance tickets.

**Ecco a Lei. La guida è gratuita.** *ekkoh ah lay. lah gweedah ay gratweetah*

Here you are. The guidebook is free.

## 1 Warm up (1 minute)

Say "You're on time".
(pp.14-15)

What's the Italian for
"ticket"? (pp.38-9)

Say "I am going to New
York". (pp.40-1)

# ALL'AEROPORTO
## At the airport

Although the airport environment is largely
universal, it is sometimes useful to be able to
understand key words and phrases in Italian.
It's a good idea to make sure you have a few
one-euro coins when you arrive at the airport;
you may need to pay for a baggage trolley.

## 2 Words to remember (4 minutes)

| | |
|---|---|
| **il check-in**<br>*eel chekeen* | check-in |
| **le partenze**<br>**lay partentsay** | departures |
| **gli arrivi**<br>*lly arreevee* | arrivals |
| **la dogana**<br>*lah doganah* | customs |
| **il controllo passaporti**<br>*eel kontrolloh passaportee* | passport control |
| **il terminale**<br>*eel termeenal* | terminal |
| **l'uscita**<br>*loosheetah* | gate |
| **il numero del volo**<br>*eel noomeroh del voloh* | flight number |

Familiarize yourself with these
words and test yourself using
the flap.

**Qual è l'uscita del volo per Roma?**
*kwalay loosheetah del voloh per rohmah*
What gate does the flight for Rome
leave from?

## 3 Useful phrases (3 minutes)

Learn these phrases and then test yourself
using the cover flap.

| | |
|---|---|
| **Il volo da Alghero è**<br>**in orario?**<br>*eel voloh dah algayroh ay*<br>*een orareeoh* | Is the flight from<br>Alghero on time? |

| | |
|---|---|
| **Non trovo i miei bagagli.**<br>*non trovoh ee*<br>*mee-ayee bagallyee* | I can't find<br>my baggage. |

| | |
|---|---|
| **Il volo per Londra è in**<br>**ritardo.**<br>*eel voloh per londrah ay*<br>*een reetardoh* | The flight<br>to London<br>is delayed. |

## 4 Put into practice (3 minutes)

Join in this conversation. Read the Italian on the left and follow the instructions to make your reply. Then test yourself by concealing the answers with the cover flap.

**Buonasera. Dica?**
*bwonasayrah. dikah*

Hello. Can I help you?

Ask: Is the flight to Milan on time?

**Il volo per Milano è in orario?**
*eel voloh per meelanoh ay een orareeoh*

---

**Sì, signore.**
*see, seennyoray*

Yes, sir.

Ask: What gate does it leave from?

**Qual è l'uscita del volo?**
*kwalay loosheetah del voloh*

## 5 Match and repeat (4 minutes)

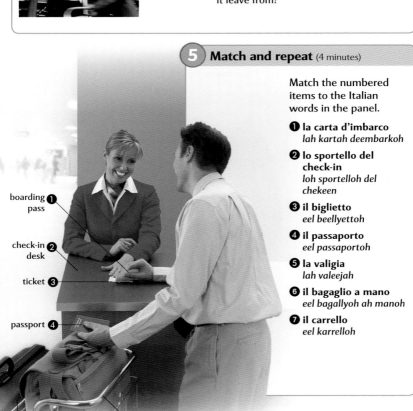

Match the numbered items to the Italian words in the panel.

❶ **la carta d'imbarco**
*lah kartah deembarkoh*

❷ **lo sportello del check-in**
*loh sportelloh del chekeen*

❸ **il biglietto**
*eel beellyettoh*

❹ **il passaporto**
*eel passaportoh*

❺ **la valigia**
*lah valeejah*

❻ **il bagaglio a mano**
*eel bagallyoh ah manoh*

❼ **il carrello**
*eel karrelloh*

boarding pass ❶

check-in desk ❷

ticket ❸

passport ❹

❼ trolley

❺ suitcase  ❻ hand luggage

# RIPASSA E RIPETI
## Review and repeat

### 1 Places

❶ **il museo**
*eel moozayoh*

❷ **il municipio**
*eel mooneecheepeeoh*

❸ **il ponte**
*eel pontay*

❹ **la piazza**
*lah peeatsah*

❺ **il parcheggio**
*eel parkejjoh*

❻ **il duomo**
*eel dwomoh*

❼ **il centro città**
*eel chentroh cheettah*

### 1 Places (4 minutes)

Name the numbered places in Italian.

❶ museum　　❷ town hall　　❸ bridge

❹ square　　❺ car park　　❻ cathedral

❼ town centre

### 2 Car parts

❶ **il parabrezza**
*eel parabretsah*

❷ **la freccia**
*lah frechah*

❸ **la gomma**
*lah gommah*

❹ **lo sportello**
*loh sportelloh*

❺ **il paraurti**
*eel parahoortee*

### 2 Car parts (3 minutes)

Name these car parts in Italian.

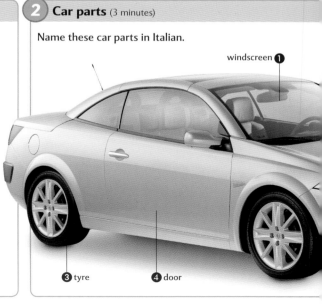

windscreen ❶

❸ tyre　　❹ door

## **3** Questions (4 minutes)

Ask the questions in Italian that match the following answers:

**1** Il pullman parte alle otto.

**2** Sono tre euro e venti.

**3** No grazie, non voglio vino.

**4** Il treno parte dal binario sette.

**5** Vado a Roma.

**6** Sì, il diciotto passa di qui.

**7** Il museo è in centro.

## **3** Questions

**1** A che ora parte il pullman?
*ah kay orah partay eel poolman*

**2** Quant'è?
*kwantay*

**3** Vuole del vino?
*vwolay del veenoh*

**4** Da quale binario parte il treno?
*dah kwalay beenareeoh partay eel trenoh*

**5** Dove va?
*dovay vah*

**6** Passa di qui il diciotto?
*passah dee kwee eel deechottoh*

**7** Dov'è il museo?
*dovay eel moozayoh*

## **4** Verbs (4 minutes)

Fill in the blanks with the right form of the verb in brackets.

**1** (io) ____ scozzese. (essere)

**2** (noi) ____ l'autobus. (prendere)

**3** Il treno ____ a Verona. (andare)

**4** (loro) ____ tre bambine. (avere)

**5** (tu) ____ un tè? (volere)

**6** Quanti figli ____ signora? (avere)

## **4** Verbs

**1** sono
*sonoh*

**2** prendiamo
*prendeeamoh*

**3** va
*vah*

**4** hanno
*annoh*

**5** vuoi
*vwoee*

**6** ha
*ah*

**2** indicator

**5** bumper

## 1 Warm up (1 minute)

Ask "How much is that?" (pp.18-19) and "Do you accept credit cards?" (pp.38-9)

Ask "Do you have children?" (pp.12-13)

# PRENOTARE UNA CAMERA
## Booking a room

In Italy you can stay in a standard hotel or *inn* (**l'albergo**). There is also the small, *family-run hotel* (**la pensione**), which is usually cheaper. Another option is a self-catering *holiday apartment* (**l'appartamento per le vacanze**).

## 2 Useful phrases (3 minutes)

Practise these phrases and then test yourself by concealing the Italian on the left with the cover flap.

| | |
|---|---|
| **La colazione è compresa?**<br>*lah kolatseeonay ay komprezah* | Is breakfast included? |

| | |
|---|---|
| **Accettate animali domestici?**<br>*acchayttatay aneemalee domesteechee* | Do you accept pets? |

| | |
|---|---|
| **C'è il servizio in camera?**<br>*chay eel sayrveetsyoh een kamayrah* | Is there room service? |

| | |
|---|---|
| **A che ora devo lasciare la camera?**<br>*ah kay orah devoh lasharay lah kamayrah* | What time do I have to vacate the room? |

## 3 In conversation (5 minutes)

**Avete una camera?**
*avetay oonah kamayrah*

Do you have any rooms?

**Sì, abbiamo una matrimoniale.**
*see, abbeeamoh oonah matreemoneealay*

Yes, we have a double room.

**È possibile avere anche un lettino?**
*ay posseebeelay averay ankay oon letteenoh*

Is it possible to have a cot as well?

## 4 **Words to remember** (4 minutes)

Familiarize yourself with these words and test yourself by concealing the Italian on the right with the cover flap.

**La camera ha la vista sul parco?**
*lah kamayrah ah lah veestah sool parkoh*
Does the room have a view over the park?

| | |
|---|---|
| room | **la camera**<br>*lah kamayrah* |
| single room | **la camera singola**<br>*lah kamayrah seengolah* |
| double room | **la camera matrimoniale**<br>*lah kamayrah matreemoneealay* |
| twin room | **la camera a due letti**<br>*lah kamayrah ah dooay layttee* |
| bathroom | **il bagno**<br>*eel bannyoh* |
| shower | **la doccia**<br>*lah docchah* |
| breakfast | **la colazione**<br>*lah kolatseeonay* |
| key | **la chiave**<br>*lah keeavay* |
| balcony | **il balcone**<br>*eel balkonay* |

## 5 **Say it** (2 minutes)

Do you have a single room, please?

For six nights.

Does the room have a balcony?

**Cultural tip** Generally in a hotel you have to pay extra if you want breakfast, but in a **pensione** it is included in the price. It usually consists of a choice of coffee or tea, pastries and/or bread with jam and butter, cereal, and juice.

**Non c'è problema.
Per quante notti?**
*non chay problemah. per kwantay nottee*

No problem. How many nights?

**Per tre notti.**
*per tray nottee*

For three nights.

**Benissimo. Ecco a Lei la chiave.**
*beneesseemoh. ekkoh ah lay lah keeavay*

Very good. Here's the key.

# IN ALBERGO
## In the hotel

**1** **Warm up** (1 minute)

How do you say "Is there...?" and "There isn't..."? (pp.48-9)

What does "Dica?" mean? (pp.48-9)

Although the larger hotels almost always have bathrooms en suite, there are still some **pensioni** where you will have to share the facilities. This can also be the case in some *youth hostels* (**ostelli della gioventù**), where a whole family can stay the night for a very reasonable cost.

**2** **Match and repeat** (6 minutes)

Match the numbered items in this hotel bedroom with the Italian text in the panel and test yourself using the cover flap.

**1** **il comodino**
*eel komodeenoh*

**2** **la lampada**
*lah lampadah*

**3** **il mini bar**
*eel meenee bar*

**4** **le tende**
*lay tenday*

**5** **il divano**
*eel deevanoh*

**6** **il guanciale**
*eel gwanchalay*

**7** **il cuscino**
*eel kusheenoh*

**8** **il letto**
*eel lettoh*

**9** **il copriletto**
*eel kopreelettoh*

**10** **la coperta**
*lah kopertah*

**1** bedside table

**2** lamp

**3** minibar

**4** curtains

**5** sofa

**6** pillow

**7** cushion

**8** bed

**9** bedspread

**10** blanket

**Cultural tip** You'll find that the price of rooms varies according to the season, especially in tourist resorts. The highest prices are charged during *the high season* (**l'alta stagione**). Accommodation is generally much cheaper in *the low season* (**la bassa stagione**). It's a good idea to check before you book.

## 3 Useful phrases (5 minutes)

Learn these phrases and then test yourself using the cover flap.

| | |
|---|---|
| The room is too cold/hot. | **In camera fa troppo freddo/caldo.** *een kamayrah fah troppoh freddoh/kaldoh* |

| | |
|---|---|
| There are no towels. | **Non ci sono gli asciugamani.** *non chee sonoh lly ashugamanee* |

| | |
|---|---|
| I'd like some soap. | **Vorrei del sapone.** *vorray del saponay* |

| | |
|---|---|
| The shower doesn't work very well. | **La doccia non funziona bene.** *lah docchah non funtseeonah benay* |

| | |
|---|---|
| The lift is not working. | **L'ascensore non funziona.** *lashensoray non funtseeonah* |

## 4 Put into practice (3 minutes)

Cover the text on the right and then complete the dialogue in Italian.

| | |
|---|---|
| **Buonasera. Dica?** *bwonasayrah. deekah* | **Vorrei dei guanciali.** *vorray day gwanchalee* |
| Hello. Can I help you? | |
| Say: I'd like some pillows. | |

| | |
|---|---|
| **La cameriera glieli porta subito.** *lah kamereeayrah llyaylee portah soobeetoh* | **E la televisione non funziona.** *ay lah televeezeeonay non foontseeonah* |
| The maid will bring you some right away. | |
| Say: And the television doesn't work. | |

# IN CAMPEGGIO
## At the campsite

**1** **Warm up** (1 minute)

Ask "Can I?" (pp.34-5)

What is Italian for
"the shower"? (pp.60-1)

Say "I'd like some
towels". (pp.60-1)

Camping is quite popular in Italy among Italians and visitors. Campsites are numerous and well organized. The local tourist office can usually provide a list of official campsites in the area where you plan to stay. Respect any signs announcing **campeggio vietato** (*camping forbidden*).

**2** **Useful phrases** (3 minutes)

Learn these phrases and then test yourself by concealing the Italian with the cover flap.

**Il campeggio è tranquillo.**
*eel kampayjjoh ay trankweelloh*
The campsite is quiet.

**la direzione del campeggio**
*lah deeraytseeonay del kampayjjoh*
campsite office

**i rifiuti**
*ee reefeeootee*
litter bin

| | |
|---|---|
| **È possibile noleggiare una bicicletta?** *ay posseebeelay nolayjjaray oonah beecheeklettah* | Can I rent a bicycle? |
| **L'acqua è potabile?** *lahkkwah ay potabeelay* | Is this drinking water? |
| **È permesso accendere i falò?** *ay permessoh acchenderay ee faloh* | Are campfires allowed? |
| **È proibito giocare a pallone.** *ay proeebeetoh jokaray ah pallonay* | Ball games are forbidden. |

**il telo protettivo**
*eel teloh protetteevoh*
fly sheet

**3** **In conversation** (5 minutes)

**Vorremmo una piazzola per tre notti.**
*vorremmoh oonah peeatsolah per tray nottee*

I need a pitch for three nights.

**Ce n'è una vicino alla piscina.**
*chay nay oonah veecheenoh allah peesheenah*

There's one near the swimming pool.

**Quant'è?**
*kwantay*

How much is it?

## 5 **Say it** (2 minutes)

I need a pitch for four nights.

Can I rent a tent?

Where's the electrical hook-up?

**i bagni**
*ee banyee*
toilets

**la presa di corrente**
*lah praysah dee korrentay*
electrical hook-up

**la corda**
*lah kordah*
guy rope

**il picchetto**
*eel peekettoh*
peg

## 4 **Words to remember** (4 minutes)

Familiarize yourself with these words and test yourself using the flap.

| | |
|---|---|
| tent | **la tenda** *lah tendah* |
| caravan | **la roulotte** *lah roolott* |
| camper van | **il camper** *eel kamper* |
| air mattress | **il materassino gonfiabile** *eel matayraseenoh gonfeeyabeelay* |
| sleeping bag | **il sacco a pelo** *eel sakkoh ah peloh* |
| pitch | **la piazzola** *lah peeatsolah* |
| campfire | **il falò** *eel faloh* |
| drinking water | **l'acqua potabile** (f) *lahkkwah potabeelay* |
| rubbish | **l'immondizia** (f) *leemmondeetseeah* |
| showers | **le docce** *lay docchay* |
| torch | **la torcia** *lah torchah* |
| backpack | **lo zaino** *loh tsa-eenoh* |
| camping gas | **il gas da campeggio** *eel gas dah kampayjjoh* |

**Cinquanta euro, una notte anticipata.**
*cheenkwantah ehooroh, oonah nottay anteecheepatah*

Fifty euros, one night in advance.

**È possibile affittare un barbecue?**
*ay posseebeelay affeettaray oon barbeku*

Can I rent a barbecue?

**Sì, ma deve versare una cauzione.**
*see, mah devay versaray oonah kaootseeonay*

Yes, but you must pay a deposit.

**1 Warm up** (1 minute)

How do you say "hot" and "cold"? (pp.60-1)

What is the Italian for "bedroom", "bed", and "pillow"? (pp.60-1)

# DESCRIZIONE
## Descriptions

Adjectives are words used to describe people, things, and places. In Italian you generally put the adjective after the thing it describes – for example, **una camera singola** (*a single room*), but you will sometimes see them placed before – for example, **una bella donna** (*a beautiful woman*).

**2 Words to remember** (7 minutes)

Adjectives usually change depending on whether the thing described is masculine, feminine, masculine plural, or feminine plural. In most cases, adjectives end in **-o** for masculine singular words and **-a** for the feminine. Plural endings are **-i** for masculine and **-e** for feminine. Some adjectives end in **-e** for the masculine and the feminine, changing to **-i** in the plural. Others never change.

**Le montagne sono alte.**
*lay montanyay sonoh altay*
The mountains are high.

| | |
|---|---|
| **grande** *granday* | big, large |
| **piccolo/piccola** *peekkoloh/peekkolah* | small |
| **alto/alta** *altoh/altah* | high, tall |
| **basso/bassa** *bassoh/bassah* | short |
| **caldo/calda** *kaldoh/kaldah* | hot |
| **freddo/fredda** *freddoh/freddah* | cold |
| **buono/buona** *bwonoh/bwonah* | good |
| **cattivo/cattiva** *katteevoh/katteevah* | bad |
| **lento/lenta** *lentoh/lentah* | slow |
| **veloce** *velochay* | fast |
| **duro/dura** *dooroh/doorah* | hard |
| **morbido/morbida** *morbeedoh/morbeedah* | soft |
| **bello/bella** *belloh/bellah* | beautiful |
| **brutto/brutta** *broottoh/broottah* | ugly |

**La chiesa è vecchia.**
*lah keeayzah eh vekkeeah*
The church is old.

**La casa è piccola.**
*lah kasah ay peekkolah*
The house is small.

**Il paese è molto bello.**
*eel pahesay ay moltoh belloh*
The village is very beautiful.

## 3 Useful phrases (4 minutes)

You can emphasize a description by using **molto** (*very*), **troppo** (*too*), or **più** (*more*) before the adjective.

| | |
|---|---|
| The coffee is cold. | **Il caffè è freddo.** *eel kaffay ay freddoh* |
| My room is very noisy. | **La mia camera è molto rumorosa.** *lah mee-ah kamayrah ay moltoh roomorosah* |
| The car is too small. | **L'auto è troppo piccola.** *la-ootoh ay troppoh peekkolah* |
| I'd like a softer bed. | **Vorrei un letto più morbido.** *vorray oon lettoh peeoo morbeedoh* |

## 4 Put into practice (3 minutes)

Join in this conversation. Cover up the text on the right and complete the dialogue in Italian. Check and repeat if necessary.

| | |
|---|---|
| **Ecco la camera.** *ekkoh lah kamayrah* Here is the bedroom. Say: The view is very beautiful. | **La vista è molto bella.** *lah veestah ay moltoh bellah* |
| **Il bagno è là.** *eel bannyoh ay lah* The bathroom is over there. Say: It is too small. | **È troppo piccolo.** *ay troppoh peekkoloh* |
| **Non abbiamo altre camere.** *non abbeeamoh altray kamayray* We don't have any other rooms. Say: We'll take it. | **La prendiamo.** *lah prendeeamoh* |

**Risposte**
*Answers* (Cover with flap)

# RIPASSA E RIPETI
## Review and repeat

## 1 Adjectives

❶ **piccola**
*peekkolah*

❷ **morbido**
*morbeedoh*

❸ **buono**
*bwonoh*

❹ **freddo**
*freddoh*

❺ **grande**
*granday*

## 1 Adjectives (3 minutes)

Put the word in brackets into Italian using the correct masculine or feminine form.

❶ La camera è troppo _____ . (small)
❷ Vorrei un guanciale più _____ . (soft)
❸ Il caffè è molto _____ . (good)
❹ In questo bagno fa _____ . (cold)
❺ Vorrei un letto più _____ . (big)

## 2 Campsite

❶ **la presa di corrente**
*lah praysah dee korrentay*

❷ **la tenda**
*lah tendah*

❸ **i rifiuti**
*ee reefeeootee*

❹ **la corda**
*lah kordah*

❺ **i bagni**
*ee banyee*

❻ **la roulotte**
*lah roolott*

## 2 Campsite (3 minutes)

Name these items you might find in a campsite.

tent ❷

guy rope ❹

electrical ❶
hook-up

litter bin ❸

### 3 At the hotel (4 minutes)

You are booking a room in a hotel. Follow the conversation, replying in Italian following the English prompts.

**Buongiorno.**
❶ Do you have a double room?

**Sì. Per quante notti?**
❷ Three nights. Do you accept pets?

**Certo.**
❸ Is breakfast included?

**No. Sono cinque euro.**
❹ That's fine. We'll take it.

### 3 At the hotel

❶ **Avete una camera matrimoniale?**
*avetay oonah kamerah matreemonyalay*

❷ **Tre notti. Accettate animali domestici?**
*tray nottee. acchayttatay aneemalee domesteechee*

❸ **La colazione è compresa?**
*lah kolatseeonay ay komprezah*

❹ **Va bene. La prendiamo.**
*vah benay. lah prendeeamoh*

### 4 Negatives (5 minutes)

Make these sentences negative using the correct form of the verb in brackets.

❶ (io) _____ figli. (avere)

❷ (Lei) _____ a Genova domani. (andare)

❸ (lui) _____ vino. (volere)

❹ (io) _____ lo zucchero nel caffè. (volere)

❺ La camera _____ molto bella. (essere)

### 4 Negatives

❶ **non ho**
*non oh*

❷ **non va**
*non vah*

❸ **non vuole**
*non vwolay*

❹ **non voglio**
*non vollyoh*

❺ **non è**
*non ay*

❺ toilets

❻ caravan

# I NEGOZI
## Shops

**1** **Warm up** (1 minute)

Ask "How do I get to the station?" (pp.50-1)

Say "Turn left at the traffic lights", and "The station is opposite the café". (pp.50-1)

Small, traditional specialized shops are still very common in Italy. But you can also find big supermarkets and shopping malls on the outskirts of cities. Local markets selling fresh, local produce can be found everywhere. You can find out the market day at the tourist office.

**2** **Match and repeat** (5 minutes)

Match the shops numbered 1-9 below and right to the Italian in the panel. Then test yourself using the cover flap.

**❶ la panetteria**
*lah panettayreeah*

**❷ la pasticceria**
*lah pastee-chayreeah*

**❸ gli alimentari**
*lly aleementaree*

**❹ la salumeria**
*lah saloomay-reeah*

**❺ il tabaccaio**
*eel tabakkaeeoh*

**❻ la libreria**
*lah leebrayreeah*

**❼ la pescheria**
*lah payskayreeah*

**❽ la macelleria**
*lah machayllay-reeah*

**❾ la banca**
*lah bankah*

❶ baker

❷ cake shop

❹ delicatessen

❺ tobacconist

❼ fishmonger

❽ butcher

**Cultural tip** Although most Italian pharmacies also sell cosmetics and toiletries, the best shop in which to buy these items is **la profumeria**. Some are very upmarket and offer a wider range of brands. **Il tabaccaio** (*tobacconist*) is the only licensed outlet for cigarettes and stamps (except the post office in the case of stamps). Sometimes you will find a tobacconist counter within the premises of a bar.

**Dov'è il fioraio?**
*dovay eel feeoraeeoh*
Where is the florist?

**3** **Words to remember** (4 minutes)

Familiarize yourself with these words and then test yourself.

| | |
|---|---|
| dairy | **la latteria** <br> *lah lattereeah* |
| wine shop | **l'enoteca** (f) <br> *laynotekah* |
| antique shop | **l'antiquario** (m) <br> *lanteekwareeoh* |
| hairdresser | **il parrucchiere** <br> *eel parrookyayray* |
| jeweller | **la gioielleria** <br> *la joyayllereeah* |
| post office | **le poste** <br> *lay postay* |
| leather goods shop | **la pelletteria** <br> *lah pellettereeah* |
| travel agent | **l'agenzia di viaggi** <br> *lajentseeah dee veeajjee* |
| shoe repairer | **il calzolaio** <br> *eel kaltsolaeeoh* |

**3** grocer

**6** bookshop

**9** bank

**5** **Say it** (2 minutes)

Where is the bank?

Do you sell cheese?

Where do I pay?

**4** **Useful phrases** (3 minutes)

Familiarize yourself with these phrases.

| | |
|---|---|
| Where is the hairdresser? | **Dov'è il parrucchiere?** <br> *dovay eel parrookyayray* |
| Where do I pay? | **Dove pago?** <br> *dovay pagoh* |
| I'm just looking, thank you. | **Do solo un'occhiata, grazie.** <br> *doh soloh oonokyatah, gratseeay* |
| Do you sell SIM cards? | **Avete carte SIM?** <br> *avetay kartay seem* |
| Can I exchange this? | **Posso cambiare questo?** <br> *possoh kambeearay kwestoh* |
| Can you give me the receipt? | **Mi dà lo scontrino?** <br> *mee dah loh skontreenoh* |
| I'd like to place an order. | **Vorrei fare un'ordinazione.** <br> *vorray faray oonordeenatseeonay* |

# AL MERCATO
## At the market

**1 Warm up** (1 minute)

What are 40, 56, 77, 82, and 94 in Italian? (pp. 30-1)

Say "big" and "small" in Italian. (pp.64-5)

Italy uses the metric system of weights and measures. You need to ask for produce in *kilograms* - **chili**, for short - or grams. Some larger items tend to be priced individually, **l'uno** (each). In many Italian markets you will find foodstuffs and also stalls selling clothing and household goods.

## 2 Match and repeat (4 minutes)

Match the numbered items in this scene with the text in the panel.

❶ **il finocchio**
*eel feenokeeoh*

❷ **il cavolfiore**
*eel kavolfeeoray*

❸ **la lattuga**
*lah lattoogah*

❹ **i peperoni**
*ee paypaironee*

❺ **le patate**
*lay patatay*

❻ **l'aglio** (m)
*lalyoh*

❼ **i pomodori**
*ee pomodoree*

❽ **gli asparagi**
*lly asparajee*

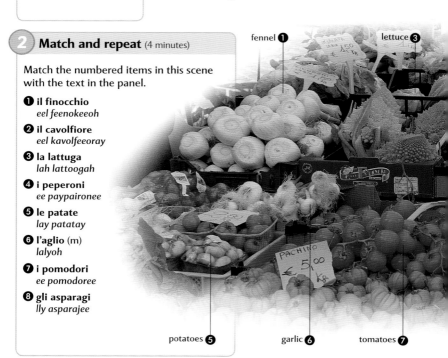

fennel ❶    lettuce ❸

potatoes ❺    garlic ❻    tomatoes ❼

## 3 In conversation (3 minutes)

**Vorrei dei pomodori.**
*vorray day pomodoree*

I'd like some tomatoes.

**Quanti chili?**
*kwantee keelee*

How many kilos?

**Due chili, per favore.**
*dooay keelee, per favoray*

Two kilos, please.

**Cultural tip** Italy uses the European currency, the euro. This is divided into 100 cents, which the Italians call **centesimi**. You will usually hear the price given as: **dieci euro e venti** (€10.20), **sei euro e novantanove** (€6,99), etc. Italians use a comma for the decimal point.

asparagus **8**   **2** cauliflower

peppers **4**

## 4 Useful phrases (5 minutes)

Learn these phrases. Then conceal the answers on the right using the cover flap. Read the English under the pictures and say the phrase in Italian as shown on the right.

**Quel formaggio è troppo caro.**
*kwel formajjoh ay troppoh karoh*

That cheese is too expensive.

**Quanto costa quello lì?**
*kwantoh kostah kwelloh lee*

How much is that one?

## 5 Say it (2 minutes)

Three kilos of potatoes, please.

The peppers are too expensive.

How much is the lettuce?

**Basta così.**
*bastah kosee*

That'll be all.

**Altro, signore?**
*altroh, seennyoray*

Anything else, sir?

**Basta così, grazie. Quant'è?**
*bastah kozee, gratseeay. kwantay*

That'll be all, thank you. How much?

**Due euro e cinquanta.**
*dooay ayooroh ay cheenkwantah*

Two euros fifty.

# AL SUPERMERCATO
## At the supermarket

**1** **Warm up** (1 minute)

What are these items, which you could buy in a supermarket? (pp.24-5)

la carne
il pesce
il formaggio
il succo di frutta
il vino
l'acqua

Prices in supermarkets are usually lower than in smaller shops. They offer all kinds of products, with the larger out-of-town **ipermercati** (*hypermarkets*) extending to clothes, household goods, garden furniture, and DIY products. They may also stock regional products.

**2** **Match and repeat** (5 minutes)

Look at the numbered items and match them to the Italian words in the panel on the left.

**1** gli articoli per la casa
*lly arteekolee per lah kazah*

**2** la frutta
*lah froottah*

**3** le bibite
*lay beebeetay*

**4** i piatti pronti
*ee pyattee prontee*

**5** i cosmetici
*ee kosmeteechee*

**6** i latticini
*ee latteecheenee*

**7** la verdura
*lah verdoorah*

**8** i surgelati
*ee soorjelatee*

household **1** products

fruit **2**

drinks **3**

ready meals **4**

vegetables **7**

frozen foods **8**

**Cultural tip** It is not usually possible to take unweighed fruit and vegetables sold by the kilo directly to the supermarket check-out. There is usually a self-service weighing machine.

## 3 Useful phrases (3 minutes)

Learn these phrases and then test yourself using the cover flap.

| | |
|---|---|
| May I have a bag please? | **Posso avere un sacchetto, per favore?** <br> *possoh avayray oon sakkayttoh, per favoray* |
| Where is the drinks aisle? | **Qual è la fila delle bibite?** <br> *kwalay lah feelah dellay beebeetay* |
| Where is the check-out, please? | **Dov'è la cassa?** <br> *dovay lah kassah* |
| Please key in your PIN. | **Può battere il pin.** <br> *pwoh battayray eel pin* |

**⑤ beauty products**

**⑥ dairy products**

## 4 Words to remember (4 minutes)

Learn these words and then test yourself using the cover flap.

| | |
|---|---|
| bread | **il pane** <br> *eel panay* |
| milk | **il latte** <br> *eel lattay* |
| butter | **il burro** <br> *eel boorroh* |
| ham | **il prosciutto** <br> *eel proshoottoh* |
| salt | **il sale** <br> *eel salay* |
| pepper | **il pepe** <br> *eel paypay* |
| toilet paper | **la carta igienica** <br> *lah kartah eejeneekah* |
| nappies | **i pannolini** <br> *ee pannoleenee* |
| washing-up liquid | **il detersivo per i piatti** <br> *eel deterseevoh per ee pyattee* |

## 5 Say it (2 minutes)

Where's the dairy products aisle?

May I have some ham, please?

Where are the frozen foods?

# SCARPE E ABBIGLIAMENTO
## Clothes and shoes

**1** **Warm up** (1 minute)

Say "I'd like…". (pp.22-3)

Ask "Do you have…?" (pp.14-5)

Say "38", "42", and "46". (pp.30-1)

Say "big" and "small". (pp.64-5)

Clothes and shoes are measured in metric sizes. Even allowing for conversion of sizes, Italian clothes tend to be cut very small. Note that clothes size is **la taglia** but shoe size is **il numero**.

**2** **Match and repeat** (3 minutes)

Match the numbered items of clothing to the Italian words in the panel on the left. Test yourself using the cover flap.

**1** **la camicia**
*lah kameechah*

**2** **la cravatta**
*lah kravattah*

**3** **la giacca**
*lah jakkah*

**4** **la tasca**
*lah taskah*

**5** **la manica**
*lah maneekah*

**6** **i pantaloni**
*ee pantalonee*

**7** **la gonna**
*lah gonnah*

**8** **i collant**
*ee kollant*

**9** **le scarpe**
*lay skarpay*

shirt **1**

tie **2**

jacket **3**

pocket **4**

sleeve **5**

trousers **6**

**Cultural tip** Like most of Europe, Italy uses the continental system of sizes. Italian dress sizes usually range from 36 (UK 8, US 6) through to 48 (UK 18, US 14) and shoe sizes from 37 (UK 4, US 5 ½) to 46 (UK 11, US 12). For men's shirts, a size 41 is a 16-inch collar, 43 is a 17-inch collar, and 45 is an 18-inch collar.

## 3 Useful phrases (5 minutes)

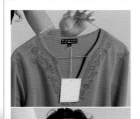

Learn these phrases and then test yourself using the cover flap.

Do you have a larger size?
**Ha la taglia più grande?**
*ah lah tallyah peeoo granday*

It's not what I want.
**Non è quello che cerco.**
*non ay kwelloh kay cherkoh*

I'll take the pink one.
**Prendo quella rosa.**
*prendoh kwellah rozah*

## 4 Words to remember (4 minutes)

Colours are adjectives (see p.64) and in most cases have a masculine and a feminine form. The latter is usually formed by changing the final **o** to an **a**.

| | |
|---|---|
| red | **rosso/rossa** *rossoh/rossah* |
| white | **bianco/bianca** *blankoh/blankah* |
| blue | **azzurro/azzurra** *adzoorroh/adzoorrah* |
| yellow | **giallo/gialla** *jalloh/jallah* |
| green | **verde** *verday* |
| black | **negro/negra** *negroh/negrah* |

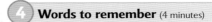

**7** skirt

**8** tights

**9** shoes

## 5 Say it (2 minutes)

What shoe size?

I'll take the black one.

I'd like a 38.

Do you have a smaller size?

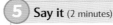

# RIPASSA E RIPETI
## Review and repeat

### 1 Market

❶ il finocchio
*eel feenokkeeoh*

❷ l'aglio
*lalyoh*

❸ i pomodori
*ee pomodoree*

❹ la lattuga
*lah lattoogah*

❺ il cavolfiore
*eel kavolfeeoray*

❻ gli asparagi
*lly asparajee*

### 1 Market (3 minutes)

Name the numbered vegetables in Italian.

❶ fennel
❷ garlic
❸ tomatoes
❹ lettuce
❺ cauliflower
❻ asparagus

### 2 Description

❶ These shoes are too expensive.
❷ My room is very small.
❸ I'd like a bigger size.

### 2 Description (2 minutes)

What do these sentences mean?

❶ Queste scarpe sono troppo care.
❷ La mia camera è molto piccola.
❸ Vorrei una taglia più grande.

### 3 Shops

❶ la panetteria
*lah panettayreeah*

❷ gli alimentari
*lly aleementaree*

❸ la libreria
*lah leebrayreeah*

❹ la pescheria
*lah payskayreeah*

❺ la pasticceria
*lah pasteechayreeah*

❻ la macelleria
*lah machayllayreeah*

### 3 Shops (3 minutes)

Name the numbered shops in Italian.
Then check your answers.

❶ baker

❷ grocer

❸ bookshop

❹ fishmonger

❺ cake shop

❻ butcher

## 4 Supermarket (3 minutes)

What is the Italian for the numbered product categories?

**1** household products

**2** beauty products

**3** drinks

**4** dairy products

**5** frozen foods

## 4 Supermarket

**1** gli articoli per la casa
*lly arteekolee per lah kazah*

**2** i cosmetici
*ee kosmeteechee*

**3** le bibite
*lay beebeetay*

**4** i latticini
*ee latteecheenee*

**5** i surgelati
*ee soorjelatee*

## 5 Museum (4 minutes)

Follow this conversation replying in Italian following the English prompts.

**Buongiorno, dica?**
**1** I'd like five tickets.

**Sono settanta euro.**
**2** That's very expensive! Two are children.

**Non ci sono riduzioni per bambini.**
**3** How much is a guide?

**Quindici euro.**
**4** Five tickets then, and a guide.

**Ottantacinque euro.**
**5** Here you are. Where are the toilets?

**Là, a destra.**
**6** Thank you.

## 5 Museum

**1** Vorrei cinque biglietti.
*vorray cheenkway beellyettee*

**2** È molto caro! Due sono bambini.
*ay moltoh karoh. dooay sonoh bambeenee*

**3** Quanto costa la guida?
*kwantoh kostah lah gweedah*

**4** Allora cinque biglietti e una guida.
*allorah cheenkway beellyettee ay oonah gweedah*

**5** Ecco a lei. Dove sono le toilette?
*ekkoh ah lay. dovay sonoh lay twaletay*

**6** Grazie.
*gratseeay*

## 1 Warm up (1 minute)

Ask "which platform?"
(pp.38-9)

What is the Italian for the
following family
members: sister, brother,
mother, father, son, and
daughter? (pp.10-11)

# IL LAVORO
## Jobs

Some occupations have commonly used feminine
forms, for example, **l'infermiere** (*male nurse*) and
**l'infermiera** (*female nurse*). Others stay the same:
**il/la giornalista** (*male/female journalist*). To describe
your job, you don't always use **un** (*a*); you say, for
example, **sono medico** (*I'm a doctor*).

## 2 Words to remember: jobs (7 minutes)

Familiarize yourself with these words and test yourself
using the flap. The feminine alternative is shown.

| | |
|---|---|
| **medico** <br> *medeekoh* | doctor |
| **dentista** <br> *denteestah* | dentist |
| **infermiere/a** <br> *eenfermyeray/ah* | nurse |
| **insegnante** <br> *eensennyantay* | teacher |
| **ragioniere/a** <br> *rajonyeray/ah* | accountant |
| **avvocato** <br> *avvokatoh* | lawyer |
| **grafico/a** <br> *grafeekoh/ah* | designer |
| **consulente finanziario** <br> *konsoolentay* <br> *feenantseearyoh* | financial consultant |
| **segretario/a** <br> *segretaryoh/ah* | secretary |
| **commerciante** <br> *kommerchantay* | shopkeeper |
| **elettricista** <br> *elettreecheestah* | electrician |
| **idraulico** <br> *eedraooleekoh* | plumber |
| **cuoco/a** <br> *kwokoh/ah* | cook/chef |
| **libero/a professionista** <br> *leeberoh/ah* <br> *professyoneestah* | self-employed |

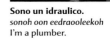

**Sono un idraulico.**
*sonoh oon eedraooleekoh*
I'm a plumber.

**È studentessa.**
*ay stoodentessah*
She is a student.

## 3 Put into practice (4 minutes)

Join in this conversation. Use the cover flap to conceal the text on the right and complete the dialogue in Italian.

**Che lavoro fa?**
*kay lavoroh fah*

What do you do?

Say: I am a financial consultant.

**Sono consulente finanziario.**
*sonoh konsoolentay feenantseearyoh*

---

**Per quale azienda lavora?**
*per kwalay adzyendah lavorah*

What company do you work for?

Say: I'm self-employed.

**Sono libero professionista.**
*sonoh leeberoh professyoneestah*

---

**Interessante!**
*eenteressantay*

How interesting!

Ask: What is your profession?

**E Lei che lavoro fa?**
*ay lay kay lavoroh fah*

---

**Sono dentista.**
*sonoh denteestah*

I'm a dentist.

Say: My sister is a dentist, too.

**Anche mia sorella è dentista.**
*ankay mee-ah sorellah ay denteestah*

## 4 Words to remember: workplace (3 minutes)

Familiarize yourself with these words and test yourself.

| | |
|---|---|
| head office | **la sede centrale** *lah seday chentralay* |
| branch | **la filiale** *lah feelyalay* |
| department | **il reparto** *eel repartoh* |
| office worker | **l'impiegato/a** *leempyegatoh/ah* |
| manager | **il direttore/la direttrice** *eel deerettoray/lah deerettreechay* |

**La sede centrale è a Napoli.**
*lah seday chentralay ay ah napolee*
Head office is in Naples.

# L'UFFICIO
## The office

An office environment or business situation has its own vocabulary in any language, but there are many items for which the terminology is virtually universal. Be aware that Italian computer keyboards may have a different layout to the standard English QWERTY convention.

### 1 Warm up (1 minute)

Practise different ways of introducing yourself in different situations (pp.8-9). Mention your name, occupation, and any other information you'd like to volunteer (pp.12-3, pp.14-5).

### 2 Words to remember (5 minutes)

Familiarize yourself with these words. Read them aloud several times and try to memorize them. Conceal the Italian with the cover flap and test yourself.

| | |
|---|---|
| **il computer** <br> *eel komputer* | computer |
| **il mouse** <br> *eel maoos* | mouse |
| **l'email** (f) <br> *leemayl* | e-mail |
| **internet** (f) <br> *eenternet* | internet |
| **la password** <br> *lah password* | password |
| **la segreteria telefonica** <br> *lah segretereeah telayfoneekah* | voicemail |
| **la password del wifi** <br> *lah password dell weefee* | Wi-Fi code |
| **la fotocopiatrice** <br> *lah fotokopyatreechay* | photocopier |
| **l'agenda** (f) <br> *lajendah* | diary |
| **il biglietto da visita** <br> *eel beellyettoh dah veeseetah* | business card |
| **la riunione** <br> *lah reeoonyonay* | meeting |
| **la conferenza** <br> *lah konferentsah* | conference |
| **l'ordine del giorno** (m) <br> *lordeenay del jornoh* | agenda |

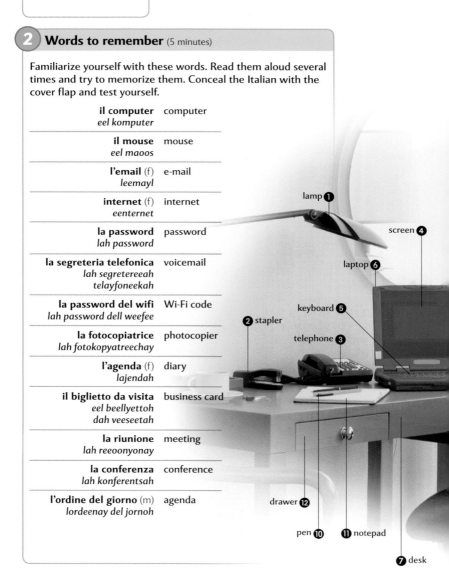

lamp ❶

screen ❹

laptop ❻

keyboard ❺

❷ stapler

telephone ❸

pen ❿   ⓫ notepad

drawer ⓬

❼ desk

### 3 Useful phrases (2 minutes)

Learn these phrases and then test yourself using the cover flap.

| I need to make some photocopies. | **Ho bisogno di fare delle fotocopie.**<br>*oh beezonnyoh dee faray dellay fotokopyay* |
| I'd like to arrange an appointment. | **Vorrei fissare un appuntamento.**<br>*vorray feessaray oon appoontamentoh* |
| I want to send an e-mail. | **Voglio mandare un'email.**<br>*vollyoh mandaray oon eemayl* |

### 4 Match and repeat (5 minutes)

Match the numbered items to the Italian words on the right.

### 5 Say it (2 minutes)

I'd like to arrange a meeting.

Do you have a business card?

I have a laptop.

clock **8**

printer **9**

**13** swivel chair

❶ **la lampada**
*lah lampadah*

❷ **la spillatrice**
*lah speellatreechay*

❸ **il telefono**
*eel telayfonoh*

❹ **lo schermo**
*loh skayrmoh*

❺ **la tastiera**
*lah tastyerah*

❻ **il computer portatile**
*eel komputer portateelay*

❼ **la scrivania**
*lah skreevaneeah*

❽ **l'orologio** (m)
*lorolojoh*

❾ **la stampante**
*lah stampantay*

❿ **la penna**
*lah pennah*

⓫ **il bloc-notes**
*eel bloknotays*

⓬ **il cassetto**
*eel kassettoh*

⓭ **la sedia girevole**
*lah sedya jeerayvolay*

## 1 Warm up (1 minute)

Say "How interesting!" (pp.78-9), "library" (pp.48-9), and "appointment". (pp.32-3)

Ask "What is your profession?" and answer "I'm an accountant". (pp.78-9)

# IL MONDO ACCADEMICO
## Academic world

Italian students may take a short degree course, **la laurea breve**. There is also a longer course, **la laurea**, which is equivalent to a masters degree. The title **dottore** or **dottoressa** is used by all graduates and most professionals.

## 2 Useful phrases (3 minutes)

Learn these phrases and then test yourself using the cover flap.

| | |
|---|---|
| **Di cosa si occupa?** <br> *dee kozah see okkoopah* | What is your field? |
| **Mi occupo di ricerca scientifica.** <br> *mee okkoopoh dee reecherkah shenteefeekah* | I am doing scientific research. |
| **Sono laureato in legge.** <br> *sonoh laooreatoh een lejjay* | I have a degree in law. |
| **Tengo una conferenza sull'architettura moderna.** <br> *tayngoh oonah konferentsah soollarkeetettoorah modernah* | I am giving a lecture on modern architecture. |

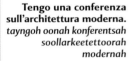

## 3 In conversation (5 minutes)

**Buongiorno, sono la professoressa Lanzi.**
*bwonjornoh, sonoh lah professoressah lantsee*

Hello, I'm Professor Lanzi.

**Dove insegna?**
*dovay eensennyah*

Where do you teach?

**Insegno all'università di Pisa.**
*eensennyoh allooneeverseetah dee pisah*

I teach at the University of Pisa.

## 4 Words to remember (4 minutes)

Familiarize yourself with these words and then test yourself.

**Abbiamo uno stand alla fiera commerciale.**
*abbyamoh oonoh stend allah fyerah kommerchalay*
We have a stand at the trade fair.

| | |
|---|---|
| conference/ lecture | **la conferenza** *lah konferentsah* |
| seminar | **il seminario** *eel semeenaryoh* |
| conference room | **la sala conferenze** *lah salah konferentsay* |
| lecture theatre | **l'aula delle lezioni** (f) *laoolah dellay letseeonee* |
| exhibition | **la mostra** *lah mostrah* |
| university lecturer | **il professore universitario/ la professoressa universitaria** *eel professoray ooneeverseetareeoh/ lah professoressah ooneeverseetaryah* |
| medicine | **la medicina** *lah medeecheenah* |
| science | **la scienza** *lah schentsah* |
| literature | **la letteratura** *lah letteratoorah* |
| engineering | **l'ingegneria** (f) *leenjennyereeah* |
| information technology | **l'informatica** (f) *leenformateekah* |

## 5 Say it (2 minutes)

I'm doing research in medicine.

I have a degree in literature.

She's the professor.

**Di cosa si occupa?**
*dee kozah see okkoopah*

What's your field?

**Di fisica. Mi occupo di ricerca.**
*dee feeseekah. mee okkoopoh dee reecherkah*

Physics. I'm doing research.

**Interessante!**
*eenteressantay*

How interesting!

**1** **Warm up** (1 minute)

Ask "Can I...?" (pp.34–5)

Say "I want to send an e-mail". (pp.80–1)

Ask "I'd like to arrange an appointment". (pp.80–1)

# I CONTATTI COMMERCIALI
## In business

You will make a good impression if you make the effort to begin a meeting with a few words in Italian, even if your vocabulary is limited. After that all parties will probably be happy to continue in English.

**2** **Words to remember** (6 minutes)

Familiarize yourself with these words and then test yourself by concealing the Italian with the cover flap.

il cliente
*eel klyentay*
client

la relazione
*lah relatseeyonay*
report

| | |
|---|---|
| **l'ordinativo** (m) *lordeenateevoh* | order |
| **la consegna** *lah konsennyah* | delivery |
| **il pagamento** *eel pagamentoh* | payment |
| **il budget** *eel bajjet* | budget |
| **il prezzo** *eel pretsoh* | price |
| **i documenti** *ee dokoomentee* | documents |
| **la fattura** *lah fattoorah* | invoice |
| **il preventivo** *eel preventeevoh* | estimate |
| **i profitti** *ee profeettee* | profits |
| **le vendite** *lay vendeetay* | sales |
| **le cifre** *lay cheefray* | figures |

**Cultural tip** In general, business dealings are formal, but a long lunch with wine is still a feature of doing business in Italy. As a client, you can expect to be taken out to a restaurant, and as a supplier you should consider entertaining your customers.

## 3 Useful phrases (6 minutes)

Practise these phrases. Notice the use of the word **può** (*can you*) as a preface to polite requests.

**Firmiamo il contratto?**
*feermyamoh eel kontrattoh*
Shall we sign the contract?

**il dirigente**
*eel deereejentay*
executive

**Può mandarmi il contratto, per favore?**
*pwoh mandarmee eel kontrattoh, per favoray*

Can you send me the contract, please?

**Abbiamo fissato il prezzo?**
*abbeeamoh feessatoh eel pretsoh*

Have we agreed a price?

**il contratto**
*eel kontrattoh*
contract

**Quando può effettuare la consegna?**
*kwandoh pwoh effettwaray lah konsennyah*

When can you make the delivery?

**Quant'è il budget?**
*kwantay eel bajjet*

What's the budget?

### 4 Say it (2 minutes)

Can you send me the estimate?

Have we agreed a budget?

When can you send me the contract?

**Può mandarmi la fattura?**
*pwoh mandarmee lah fattoorah*

Can you send me the invoice?

# *RIPASSA E RIPETI*
## Review and repeat

### 1 At the office

**❶ la spillatrice**
*lah speellatreechay*

**❷ la lampada**
*lah lampadah*

**❸ il computer portatile**
*eel komputer portateelay*

**❹ la penna**
*lah pennah*

**❺ la scrivania**
*lah skreevaneeah*

**❻ il bloc-notes**
*eel bloknotays*

**❼ l'orologio** (m)
*lorolojoh*

### 1 At the office (4 minutes)

Name these items in Italian.

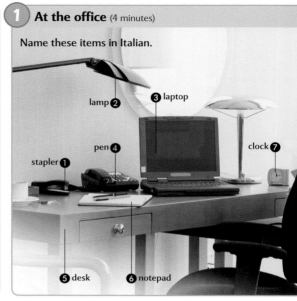

lamp ❷   ❸ laptop

pen ❹   clock ❼

stapler ❶

❺ desk   ❻ notepad

### 2 Jobs

**❶ medico**
*medeekoh*

**❷ idraulico**
*eedraooleekoh*

**❸ commerciante**
*kommerchantay*

**❹ ragioniere/a**
*rajonyeray/ah*

**❺ studente/essa**
*stoodentay/essah*

**❻ avvocato**
*avvokatoh*

### 2 Jobs (3 minutes)

What are these jobs in Italian?

❶ doctor

❷ plumber

❸ shopkeeper

❹ accountant

❺ student

❻ lawyer

## 3 Work (4 minutes)

Answer these questions following the English prompts.

**Per quale azienda lavora?**
❶ Say "I work for myself".

**Dove insegna?**
❷ Say "I teach at the University of Pisa".

**Di cosa si occupa?**
❸ Say "I'm doing scientific research".

**Quando può mandare il preventivo?**
❹ Say "I can send the estimate tomorrow".

## 3 Work

❶ **Sono libero professionista.**
*sonoh leeberoh professyoneestah*

❷ **Insegno all'università di Pisa.**
*eensennyoh allooneeverseetah dee pisah*

❸ **Mi occupo di ricerca scientifica.**
*mee okkoopoh dee reecherkah sheenteefeekah*

❹ **Posso mandare il preventivo domani.**
*possoh mandaray eel preventeevoh domanee*

## 4 How much? (4 minutes)

Answer the question with the price shown in brackets.

❶ **Quant'è un caffè?** (€1,80)

❷ **Quanto costa la camera?** (€47)

❸ **Quanto costa un chilo di pomodori?** (€1,25)

❹ **Quanto costa una piazzola per tre giorni?** (€50)

## 4 How much?

❶ **Un euro e ottanta**
*oon ayooroh ay ottantah*

❷ **Quarantasette euro**
*kwarantasettay ayooroh*

❸ **Un euro e venticinque**
*oon ayooroh ay venteecheenkway*

❹ **Cinquanta euro**
*cheenkwantah ayooroh*

# IN FARMACIA
## At the chemist

**Waric up** (1 minute)

Say "I'm allergic to nuts".
(pp.24-5)

Say the verb "avere" (to
have) in all its forms (io,
tu, Lei, lui/lei, noi, voi,
loro) (pp.14-5).

Italian pharmacists study for over four years
before qualifying and they can give advice about
minor health problems and are permitted to
dispense a wide variety of medicines, even giving
injections, if necessary. There is a *duty pharmacist*
(**farmacia di turno**) in most towns.

## 2 Match and repeat (3 minutes)

Match the numbered items to the Italian
words in the panel on the left and test
yourself using the cover flap.

❶ **la fascia**
  *lah fasheeah*

❷ **lo sciroppo**
  *loh sheeroppoh*

❸ **le gocce**
  *lay gocchay*

❹ **il cerotto**
  *eel chayrottoh*

❺ **l'iniezione** (f)
  *leenyetsyonay*

❻ **la pomata**
  *lah pomatah*

❼ **la supposta**
  *lah sooppostah*

❽ **la compressa**
  *lah kompressah*

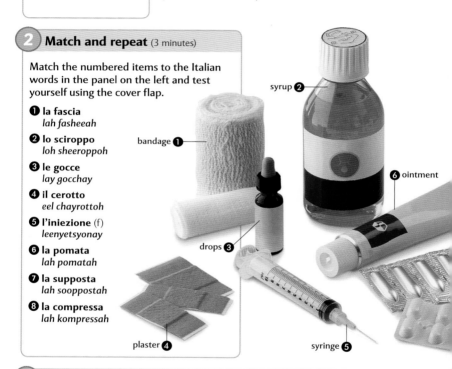

syrup ❷

bandage ❶

❻ ointment

drops ❸

plaster ❹

syringe ❺

## 3 In conversation (3 minutes)

**Buongiorno. Dica?**
*bwonjornoh. deekah*

Hello. What would
you like?

**Ho mal di pancia.**
*oh mal dee panchah*

I have a stomach ache.

**Ha anche la diarrea?**
*ah ankay lah deearreah*

Do you also have diarrhoea?

## 4 **Words to remember** (2 minutes)

Familiarize yourself with these words and test yourself using the flap.

**Ho mal di testa.**
*oh mal dee testah*

I have a headache.

| | |
|---|---|
| headache | **mal di testa**<br>*mal dee testah* |
| stomach ache | **mal di pancia**<br>*mal dee panchah* |
| diarrhoea | **la diarrea**<br>*lah deearreah* |
| cold | **il raffreddore**<br>*eel raffreddoray* |
| cough | **la tosse**<br>*lah tossay* |
| sunburn | **l'eritema solare** (m)<br>*lereetemah solaray* |
| toothache | **mal di denti**<br>*mal dee dentee* |

## 6 **Say it** (2 minutes)

I have a cold.

Do you have that as an ointment?

Do you have a cough?

**7** suppository

**8** tablet

## 5 **Useful phrases** (4 minutes)

Learn these phrases and then test yourself using the cover flap.

| | |
|---|---|
| I have sunburn. | **Ho l'eritema solare.**<br>*oh lereetemah solaray* |
| Do you have that as a syrup? | **Lo ha in sciroppo?**<br>*loh ah een sheeroppoh* |
| I'm allergic to penicillin. | **Sono allergico/a alla penicillina.**<br>*sonoh allerjeekoh/ ah allah peneecheelleenah* |

**No, ma ho mal di testa.**
*noh, mah oh mal dee testah*

No, but I have a headache.

**Prenda questo.**
*prendah kwestoh*

Take this.

**Lo ha in compresse?**
*loh ah een kompressay*

Do you have that as tablets?

# IL CORPO
## The body

**Warm up** (1 minute)

Say " I have a toothache"
and "I have sunburn".
(pp.88-9)

Say the Italian for "red",
"green", "black", and
"yellow". (pp.74-5)

A common phrase for talking about aches and pains
is **mi fa male il/la...** (*my ... hurts*). Another useful
expression is **ho un dolore a...** (*I have a pain in...*).
Note that **a** joins with the definite article (*the*) to
produce these combinations: **il** (**al**), **lo** (**allo**),
**la** (**alla**), **gli** (**agli**), **i** (**ai**), and **le** (**alle**).

## 2 Match and repeat: body (6 minutes)

Match the numbered parts of the body
with the list on the left. Test yourself by
using the cover flap.

1 **la mano**
*lah manoh*

2 **la testa**
*lah testah*

3 **la spalla**
*la spallah*

4 **il gomito**
*eel gomeetoh*

5 **i capelli**
*ee kapellee*

6 **il braccio**
*eel brachoh*

7 **il collo**
*eel kolloh*

8 **il petto**
*eel pettoh*

9 **lo stomaco**
*loh stomakoh*

10 **la gamba**
*lah gambah*

11 **il ginocchio**
*eel jeenokkyoh*

12 **il piede**
*eel pyeday*

1 hand
4 elbow
5 hair
2 head
6 arm
shoulder 3
7 neck
chest 8
stomach 9
leg 10
knee 11
12 foot

### 3 Match and repeat: face (3 minutes)

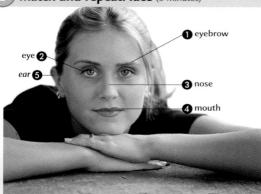

❶ eyebrow
eye ❷
ear ❺
❸ nose
❹ mouth

Match the numbered facial features with the list on the right.

❶ **il sopracciglio**
*eel sopracheelyoh*

❷ **l'occhio** (m)
*lokkeeoh*

❸ **il naso**
*eel nasoh*

❹ **la bocca**
*lah bokkah*

❺ **l'orecchio** (m)
*lorekkyoh*

### 4 Useful phrases (3 minutes)

Learn these phrases and then test yourself using the cover flap.

My back hurts. **Mi fa male la schiena.**
*mee fah malay lah skyenah*

I have a rash on my arm. **Ho un arrossamento sul braccio.**
*oh oon arrossamentoh sool brachoh*

I don't feel well. **Non mi sento bene.**
*non mee sentoh benay*

### 5 Put into practice (2 minutes)

Join in this conversation and test yourself using the cover flap.

**Cosa c'è?**
*kozah chay*
What's the matter?
Say: I don't feel well.

**Non mi sento bene.**
*non mee sentoh benay*

**Dove ti fa male?**
*dovay ti fah malay*
Where does it hurt?
Say: I have a pain in my shoulder.

**Ho un dolore alla spalla.**
*oh oon doloray allah spallah*

# DAL MEDICO
## At the doctor's

**1** **Warm up** (1 minute)

Say "I have a headache". (pp.88-9)

Now, say "He needs some ointment". (pp.88-9)

What is the Italian for "I don't have a son". (pp.10-15)

Unless it's an emergency, you'll have to book an appointment with the doctor and pay when you leave. You can usually reclaim the cost if you have medical insurance. Find the names and addresses of local doctors from **il municipio** (*town hall*) or a local pharmacy may be able to advise.

**2** **Useful phrases you may hear** (3 minutes)

Learn these phrases and then test yourself using the cover flap to conceal the Italian on the left.

| | |
|---|---|
| **Non è grave.** *non ay gravay* | It's not serious. |
| **Deve fare dei controlli.** *devay faray day kontrollee* | You need to have tests. |
| **Ha una frattura.** *ah oonah frattoorah* | You have a fracture. |
| **Deve andare all'ospedale.** *devay andaray allospedalay* | You need to go to hospital. |

**Fa qualche cura?**
*fah kwalkay koorah*
Are you taking any medication?

**3** **In conversation** (5 minutes)

**Cosa c'è?**
*kozah chay*

What's the matter?

**Ho un dolore al petto.**
*oh oon doloray al pettoh*

I have a pain in my chest.

**Ora la visito.**
*orah lah veezeetoh*

Now I will examine you.

## 4 Useful phrases you may need to say (4 minutes)

**Sono incinta.**
*sonoh eencheentah*
I am pregnant.

Learn these phrases and then test yourself using the cover flap.

| | |
|---|---|
| I am diabetic. | **Sono diabetico/a.** <br> *sonoh deeabeteekoh/ah* |
| I am epileptic. | **Sono epilettico/a.** <br> *sonoh epeeletteekoh/ah* |
| I'm asthmatic. | **Sono asmatico/a.** <br> *sonoh asmateekoh/ah* |
| I have a heart condition. | **Ho disturbi cardiaci.** <br> *oh deestoorbee kardeeachee* |
| I have a fever. | **Ho la febbre.** <br> *oh lah febbray* |
| It's urgent. | **È urgente.** <br> *ay oorjentay* |
| I feel breathless. | **Faccio fatica a respirare.** <br> *facchyoh fatikah ah respeeraray* |

### Cultural tip
If you are an EU national, you are entitled to free emergency medical treatment in Italy on production of a European Health Insurance Card or E111 form. For an ambulance call 112.

## 5 Say it (2 minutes)

My son needs to go to hospital.

It's not urgent.

**È grave?**
*ay gravay*

Is it serious?

**No, è solo un'indigestione.**
*noh, ay soloh oon eendeejestyonay*

No, you only have indigestion.

**Che sollievo!**
*kay soleeayvoh*

What a relief!

## 1 Warm up (1 minute)

Say "There's a lift over there". (pp.52-3)

Ask "Do I need...?" (pp.92-3)

What is the Italian for "mouth" and "head"? (pp.90-1)

# ALL'OSPEDALE
## At the hospital

It is useful to know a few basic phrases relating to hospitals for use in an emergency or in case you need to visit a friend or colleague in hospital. Emergency departments will treat all urgent cases free of charge, but citizens of non-EU countries need to sign a payment declaration.

## 2 Useful phrases (5 minutes)

Familiarize yourself with these phrases. Conceal the Italian with the cover flap and test yourself.

| | |
|---|---|
| **Qual è l'orario di visita?** *kwalay lorareeoh dee veezeetah* | What are the visiting hours? |
| **Quanto ci vuole?** *kwantoh chee vwolay* | How long does it take? |
| **Farà male?** *farah malay* | Will it hurt? |
| **Si sdrai sul lettino.** *see zdraee sool letteenoh* | Please lie down on the bed. |
| **Non deve mangiare.** *non devay manjaray* | You must not eat. |
| **Non muova la testa.** *non mwovah lah testah* | Don't move your head. |
| **Apra la bocca.** *aprah lah bokkah* | Open your mouth. |
| **Deve fare le analisi del sangue.** *devay faray lay analeezee del sangway* | You need a blood test. |

**Dov'è la sala d'aspetto?**
*dovay lah salah daspettoh*
Where is the waiting room?

**la flebo**
*lah flayboh*
intravenous drip

**Si sente meglio?**
*see sentay mellyoh*
Are you feeling better?

## 3 **Words to remember** (4 minutes)

**La radiografia è normale.**
*lah radeeografeeah*
*ay normalay*
The X-ray is normal.

Memorize these words and test yourself using the cover flap.

| | |
|---|---|
| emergency department | **il pronto soccorso** *eel prontoh sokkorsoh* |
| children's ward | **il reparto di pediatria** *eel repartoh dee pedyatryah* |
| operating theatre | **la sala operatoria** *lah salah operatoreeah* |
| waiting room | **la sala d'aspetto** *lah salah daspettoh* |
| corridor | **il corridoio** *eel korreedoyoh* |
| stairs | **le scale** *lay skalay* |
| lift | **l'ascensore** (m) *lashensoray* |

## 4 **Put into practice** (3 minutes)

Join in this conversation. Read the Italian on the left and follow the instructions to make your reply. Then test yourself by hiding the answers with the cover flap.

**Forse c'è un'infezione.**
*forsay chay ooneenfetsyonay*

You may have an infection.

Ask: Do I need tests?

**Devo fare dei controlli?**
*devoh faray day kontrollee*

**Prima di tutto deve fare le analisi del sangue.**
*preemah dee toottoh devay faray lay analeezee del sangway*

First you will need a blood test.

Ask: Will it hurt?

**Farà male?**
*farah malay*

## 5 **Say it** (2 minutes)

Does he need a blood test?

Where is the children's ward?

Do I need an X-ray?

**No, non si preoccupi.**
*noh, non see prayokkoopee*

No, don't worry.

Ask: How long does it take?

**Quanto ci vuole?**
*kwantoh chee vwolay*

# *RIPASSA E RIPETI*
## Review and repeat

### 1 The body

**1** la testa
*lah testah*

**2** il braccio
*eel brachoh*

**3** il petto
*eel pettoh*

**4** lo stomaco
*loh stomakoh*

**5** la gamba
*lah gambah*

**6** il ginocchio
*eel jeenokkyoh*

**7** il piede
*eel pyeday*

### 1 The body (4 minutes)

Name the numbered body parts in Italian.

- **1** head
- **2** arm
- chest **3**
- stomach **4**
- leg **5**
- knee **6**
- **7** foot

### 2 On the phone

**1** Vorrei parlare con il signor Salvetti.
*vorray parlaray kon eel seennyor salvettee*

**2** Sono il dottor Pieri della Bonanni.
*sonoh eel dottor pyayree dellah bonannee*

**3** Posso lasciare un messaggio?
*possoh lasharay oon messajjoh?*

**4** L'appuntamento è lunedì alle undici.
*lappoontamentoh ay lunedee allay oondeechee*

**5** Grazie, arrivederci.
*gratseeay, arreevederchee*

### 2 On the phone (4 minutes)

You are arranging an appointment. Follow the conversation, replying in Italian following the English prompts.

**Pronto? Tipografia Bartoli.**
**1** I'd like to speak to Mr Salvetti.

**Chi parla, scusi?**
**2** It's Dr Pieri of Bonanni.

**Mi dispiace, il signor Salvetti è in riunione.**
**3** Can I leave a message?

**Certo.**
**4** The appointment is on Monday at 11am.

**Benissimo.**
**5** Thank you, goodbye.

### 3 Clothing (3 minutes)

Say the Italian words for the numbered items of clothing.

tie ❶

❷ jacket

❹ skirt

trousers ❸

❻ tights

shoes ❺

### 3 Clothing

❶ **la cravatta**
*lah kravattah*

❷ **la giacca**
*lah jakkah*

❸ **i pantaloni**
*ee pantalonee*

❹ **la gonna**
*lah gonnah*

❺ **le scarpe**
*lay skarpay*

❻ **i collant**
*ee kollant*

### 4 At the doctor's (4 minutes)

Say these phrases in Italian.

❶ I don't feel well.
❷ Do I need tests?
❸ I have a heart condition.
❹ Do I need to go to hospital?
❺ I am pregnant.

### 4 At the doctor's

❶ **Non mi sento bene.**
*non mee sentoh benay*

❷ **Devo fare dei controlli?**
*devoh faray day kontrollee*

❸ **Ho disturbi cardiaci.**
*oh deestoorbee kardeeachee*

❹ **Devo andare all'ospedale?**
*devoh andaray allospedalay*

❺ **Sono incinta.**
*sonoh eencheentah*

# GLI ALLOGGI
## At home

**Warm up** (1 minute)

Say the months of the year in Italian. (pp.28–9)

Ask "Is there an art gallery?" (pp.48–9) and "How many brothers do you have?" (pp.14–5)

The *apartment block* (**il palazzo**) is the most common form of urban housing in Italy. A *detached house* (**la villetta**) is more usual in rural areas. To find out the total number of rooms, you will need to ask "**Quante stanze?**". If you want to know how many bedrooms, ask "**Quante camere?**".

**Match and repeat** (5 minutes)

Match the numbered items to the list and test yourself using the flap.

❶ **la finestra**
　*lah feenestrah*

❷ **il muro**
　*eel mooroh*

❸ **il comignolo**
　*eel comeennyoloh*

❹ **il tetto**
　*eel tettoh*

❺ **la grondaia**
　*lah grondayah*

❻ **il viale**
　*eel veealay*

❼ **la porta**
　*lah portah*

❽ **le persiane**
　*lay persyanay*

chimney ❸

window ❶　　❷ wall

driveway ❻

door ❼

**Cultural tip** You almost never see an Italian home without shutters or roller blinds at every window. These are closed at night and in the heat of the day. Curtains tend to be more for decoration. Most apartment blocks have at least one *balcony* (**il balcone**) for each apartment. These are often filled with plants to make up for the lack of a garden.

## 3 Words to remember (4 minutes)

**Quant'è l'affitto al mese?**
*kwantay laffeettoh al mezay*
What is the rent per month?

Familiarize yourself with these words and test yourself using the flap.

| | | |
|---|---|---|
| room | **la stanza** | *lah stantsah* |
| floor | **il pavimento** | *eel paveementoh* |
| ceiling | **il soffitto** | *eel soffeettoh* |
| bedroom | **la camera** | *lah kamayrah* |
| bathroom | **il bagno** | *eel bannyoh* |
| kitchen | **la cucina** | *lah koocheenah* |
| dining room | **la sala da pranzo** | *lah salah dah pranzoh* |
| living room | **il soggiorno** | *eel sojjornoh* |
| cellar | **la cantina** | *lah kanteenah* |
| attic | **la soffitta** | *lah soffeettah* |

roof ❹    gutter ❺

shutters ❽

## 4 Useful phrases (3 minutes)

Learn these phrases and test yourself.

Is there a garage?

**C'è il garage?**
*chay eel garadj*

Is it available soon?

**È libera subito?**
*ay leeberah soobeetoh*

Is the flat furnished?

**L'appartamento è ammobiliato?**
*appartamayntoh ay ammobeelyatoh*

## 5 Say it (2 minutes)

Is there a dining room?

Is it large?

Is it available in July?

# IN CASA
## In the house

What is the Italian for "table" (pp.20-1), "desk" (pp.80-1)," bed" (pp.60-1), and "toilet(s)"? (pp.52-3)

How do you say "soft", "beautiful", and "big"? (pp.64-5)

If you are renting accommodation in Italy, it is usual to be asked to pay for services such as electricity and heating on top of the basic rent; for short lets of holiday flats or villas they might well be included in the rent. You may be asked to *pay a deposit* (**versare una caparra** or **cauzione**) in case of damage.

**2** **Match and repeat** (3 minutes)

Match the numbered items to the list in the panel on the left. Then test yourself by concealing the Italian with the cover flap.

**1** **il piano di lavoro**
*eel peeanoh dee lavoroh*

**2** **il lavello**
*eel lavelloh*

**3** **il forno a microonde**
*eel fornoh ah meekrohonday*

**4** **il forno**
*eel fornoh*

**5** **il fornello**
*eel fornaylloh*

**6** **il frigorifero**
*eel freegoreeferoh*

**7** **la sedia**
*lah sedyah*

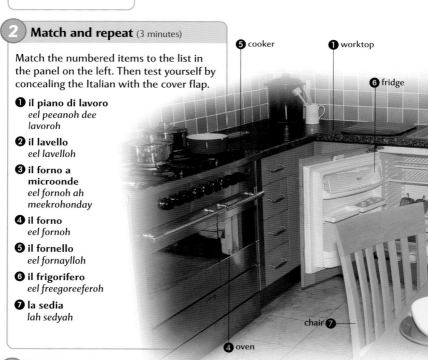

**5** cooker    **1** worktop

**6** fridge

chair **7**

**4** oven

**3** **In conversation** (3 minutes)

**Questo è il forno.**
*kwestoh ay eel fornoh*

This is the oven.

**C'è anche la lavastoviglie?**
*chay ankay lah lavastoveellyay*

Is there a dishwasher as well?

**Sì, e il congelatore è grande.**
*see, ay eel konjelatoray ay granday*

Yes, and there's a big freezer.

## 4 Words to remember (2 minutes)

Familiarize yourself with these words and test yourself using the flap.

**Il divano è nuovo.**
*eel deevanoh ay nwovoh*
The sofa is new.

❷ sink     microwave ❸

| | |
|---|---|
| wardrobe | **l'armadio** (m) *larmadeeoh* |
| armchair | **la poltrona** *lah poltronah* |
| fireplace | **il caminetto** *eel kameenettoh* |
| rug | **il tappeto** *eel tappaytoh* |
| bath | **la vasca** *lah vaskah* |
| toilet | **il bagno** *eel banyoh* |
| wash basin | **il lavandino** *eel lavandeenoh* |
| curtains | **le tende** *lay tenday* |

## 5 Useful phrases (4 minutes)

Learn these phrases and then test yourself using the cover flap to conceal the Italian.

| | |
|---|---|
| The fridge is broken. | **Il frigorifero è rotto.** *eel freegoreeferoh ay rottoh* |
| The curtains are ugly. | **Le tende sono brutte.** *lay tenday sonoh broottay* |
| Is electricity included? | **La luce è inclusa?** *lah loochay ay eenkloosah* |

## 6 Say it (2 minutes)

Is there a microwave?

I like the fireplace.

What a soft sofa!

**Il lavello è nuovo.**
*eel lavelloh ay nwovoh*

The sink is new.

**E qui c'è la lavatrice.**
*ay kwee chay lah lavatreechay*

And here's the washing machine.

**Che belle piastrelle!**
*kay bellay piastrellay*

What beautiful tiles!

# IL GIARDINO
## The garden

What is the Italian for "day" and "month"? (pp.28-9)

Say the days of the week. (pp.28-9)

The garden of a house or villa may be communal, or at least partly shared. Check with the estate agent or rental agent. Not a traditional pastime among Italians, gardening for pleasure has become more popular in recent years. Garden nurseries stock a wide range of plants.

**2** **Words to remember** (3 minutes)

Familiarize yourself with these words and test yourself using the flap.

| | |
|---|---|
| **il tosaerba** *eel tozaerbah* | lawnmower |
| **le cesoie** *lay chezoyay* | shears |
| **la vanga** *lah vangah* | spade |
| **il rastrello** *eel rastrelloh* | rake |
| **il vivaio** *eel veevayoh* | garden nursery |

terrace **1**

tree **2**

flowers **7**

soil **3**

**8** weeds

path **9**

**3** **Useful phrases** (4 minutes)

Learn these phrases and then test yourself using the cover flap.

| | |
|---|---|
| The gardener comes once a week. | **Il giardiniere viene una volta alla settimana.** *eel jardeenyeray vyenay oonah voltah allah setteemanah* |
| Can you mow the lawn? | **Può tagliare l'erba?** *pwoh tallyaray lerbah* |
| Is the garden private? | **Il giardino è privato?** *eel jardeenoh ay preevatoh* |
| The garden needs watering. | **Bisogna annaffiare il giardino.** *beezonnyah annaffyaray eel jardeenoh* |

**5** hedge

**4** lawn

**4** **Match and repeat** (5 minutes)

Match the numbered items to the words in the panel on the right.

**1** **il patio**
*eel pateeoh*

**2** **l'albero** (m)
*lalberoh*

**3** **la terra**
*lah terrah*

**4** **il prato**
*eel pratoh*

**5** **la siepe**
*lah syepay*

**6** **le piante**
*lay peeantay*

**7** **i fiori**
*ee feeoree*

**8** **le erbacce**
*lay erbacchay*

**9** **il vialetto**
*eel vyalettoh*

**10** **l'aiuola** (f)
*laywolah*

**6** plants

**10** flowerbed

**5** **Say it** (2 minutes)

The lawn needs water.

Are there any trees?

The gardener comes on Fridays.

# GLI ANIMALI
## Pets

If you want to take your dog or other pet to Italy, make sure you have the right documentation. Italy requires an Export Health Certificate. Pet passports are becoming more common and very useful. Consult your vet for details of how to obtain the necessary vaccinations and paperwork.

**1** **Warm up** (1 minute)

Say "My name is John".
(pp.8–9)

Say "Don't worry".
(pp.94–5)

What's "your" in Italian?
(pp.12–3)

**2** **Match and repeat** (3 minutes)

Match the numbered animals to the Italian words in the panel on the left. Then test yourself using the cover flap.

**1** **il gatto**
*eel gattoh*

**2** **il coniglio**
*eel koneellyoh*

**3** **l'uccello** (m)
*loocchelloh*

**4** **il pesce**
*eel peshay*

**5** **il cane**
*eel kanay*

**6** **il criceto**
*eel kreechetoh*

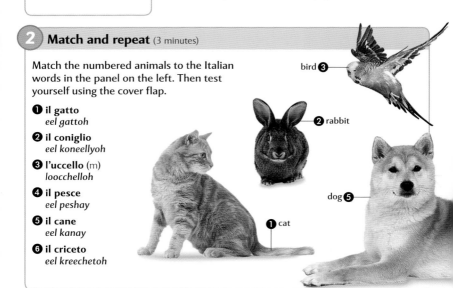

bird **3**

**2** rabbit

dog **5**

**1** cat

**3** **Useful phrases** (4 minutes)

Learn these phrases and then test yourself using the cover flap.

| | |
|---|---|
| **Questo cane è buono?** *kwestoh kanay ay bwonoh* | Is this dog friendly? |
| **Posso portare il cane?** *possoh portaray eel kanay* | Can I bring my dog? |
| **Ho paura dei gatti.** *oh paoorah day gattee* | I'm frightened of cats |
| **Il mio cane non morde.** *eel mee-oh kanay non morday* | My dog doesn't bite. |

**Questo gatto ha le pulci.**
*kwestoh gattoh ah lay poolchee*
This cat has fleas.

**Cultural tip** Many dogs in Italy are working dogs and you may encounter them tethered or roaming free. Approach farms and rural houses with particular care, and keep away from the dog's territory. Look out for warning notices such as **Attenti al cane** (*Beware of the dog*).

ATTENTI AL CANE

**4** **Words to remember** (4 minutes)

Familiarize yourself with these words and test yourself using the flap.

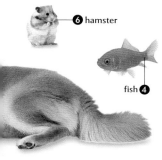

**Il mio cane non sta bene.**
*eel mee-oh kanay non stah benay*
My dog is not well.

**6** hamster

fish **4**

| | |
|---|---|
| vet | **il veterinario** *eel vetereenareeoh* |
| vaccination | **la vaccinazione** *lah vaccheenatsyonay* |
| pet passport | **il pet passport** *eel pet passport* |
| dog basket | **la cuccia** *lah koocchah* |
| cage | **la gabbia** *lah gabbyah* |
| dog bowl | **la ciotola del cane** *lah chotolah del kanay* |
| collar | **il collare** *eel kollaray* |
| lead | **il guinzaglio** *eel gweentsallyoh* |
| fleas | **le pulci** *lay poolchee* |

**5** **Put into practice** (3 minutes)

Join in this conversation. Read the Italian on the left and follow the instructions to make your reply. Then test yourself by concealing the answers with the cover flap.

**È suo il cane?**
*ay soo-oh eel kanay*

Is this your dog?

Say: Yes, he's called Sandy.

**Sì, si chiama Sandy.**
*see, see keeamah sendee*

---

**Ho paura dei cani.**
*oh paoorah day kanee*

I'm frightened of dogs.

Say: Don't worry.
He's friendly.

**Non si preoccupi.**
**È buono.**
*non see preokkoopee.*
*ay bwonoh*

# RIPASSA E RIPETI
## Review and repeat

**Risposte**
*Answers* (Cover with flap)

### 1 Colours

**1** nero
*neroh*

**2** azzurra
*azzoorrah*

**3** rosso
*rossoh*

**4** verde
*verday*

**5** gialli
*jallee*

### 1 Colours (4 minutes)

Complete the sentences with the Italian for the colour in brackets.

**1** Questa giacca c'è in _____? (black)

**2** Prendo la gonna _____. (blue)

**3** Ha questa camicia in _____? (red)

**4** No, ma c'è in _____ . (green)

**5** Ha pantaloni _____? (yellow)

### 2 Kitchen

**1** il fornello
*eel fornaylloh*

**2** il frigorifero
*eel freegoreeferoh*

**3** il lavello
*eel lavelloh*

**4** il forno a microonde
*eel fornoh ah
meekrohonday*

**5** il forno
*eel fornoh*

**6** la sedia
*lah sedyah*

### 2 Kitchen (4 minutes)

Say the Italian words for the numbered items.

cooker **1**    fridge **2**

**5** oven    chair **6**

## 3 House (4 minutes)

You are visiting a house in Italy. Join in the conversation, replying in Italian where you see the English prompts.

**Questo è il soggiorno.**
❶ What a lovely balcony!

**E la cucina è molto bella.**
❷ How many bedrooms?

**Ci sono tre camere.**
❸ Is there a garage?

**No, ma c'è un giardino molto grande.**
❹ Is the house available soon?

**La casa è libera da luglio.**
❺ What is the rent a month?

## 3 House

❶ **Che bel balcone!**
*kay bel balkonay*

❷ **Quante camere ci sono?**
*kwantay kameray chee sonoh*

❸ **C'è il garage?**
*chay eel garadj*

❹ **La casa è libera subito?**
*lah kazah ay leeberah soobeetoh*

❺ **Quant'è l'affitto al mese?**
*kwantay laffeettoh al mezay*

## 4 At home (3 minutes)

microwave ❹

❸ sink

Say the Italian for the following items.

❶ washing machine
❷ sofa
❸ cellar
❹ dining room
❺ tree
❻ garden

## 4 At home

❶ **la lavatrice**
*lah lavatreechay*

❷ **il divano**
*eel deevanoh*

❸ **la cantina**
*lah kanteenah*

❹ **la sala da pranzo**
*lah salah dah pranzoh*

❺ **l'albero**
*lalberoh*

❻ **il giardino**
*eel jardeenoh*

# LE POSTE E LA BANCA
## Post office and bank

Cashpoints/ATMs are plentiful in Italy. In tourist resorts there are also bureaux de change (**il cambio**). Stamps are available from tobacconists (**il tabaccaio**) as well as post offices.

### 2 Words to remember: post (3 minutes)

| | |
|---|---|
| **la busta** *lah boostah* | envelope |
| **il pacco** *eel pakkoh* | parcel |
| **via aerea** *veeah a-ayreah* | by air mail |
| **raccomandata** *rakkomandatah* | registered post |
| **i francobolli** *ee frankobollee* | stamps |
| **il postino** *eel posteenoh* | postman |
| **la cassetta delle lettere** *lah kassettah dellay letteray* | post box |

Familiarize yourself with these words and test yourself using the cover flap to conceal the Italian on the left.

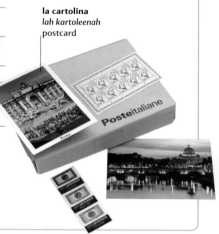

**la cartolina**
*lah kartoleenah*
postcard

### 3 In conversation (3 minutes)

**Vorrei prelevare dei soldi.**
*vorray prelevaray day soldee*

I'd like to withdraw some money.

**Ha un documento d'identità?**
*ah oon dokoomentoh deedenteetah*

Do you have any identification?

**Sì, ecco il mio passaporto.**
*see, ekkoh eel mee-oh passaportoh*

Yes, here's my passport.

### 4 Words to remember: bank (2 minutes)

Familiarize yourself with these words and test yourself using the cover flap to conceal the Italian on the right.

**Come posso pagare?**
*komay possoh pagaray*
How can I pay?

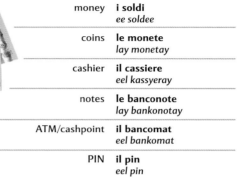

**la carta di credito**
*lah kartah dee kredeetoh*
credit card

| | |
|---|---|
| money | **i soldi** *ee soldee* |
| coins | **le monete** *lay monetay* |
| cashier | **il cassiere** *eel kassyeray* |
| notes | **le banconote** *lay bankonotay* |
| ATM/cashpoint | **il bancomat** *eel bankomat* |
| PIN | **il pin** *eel pin* |

### 5 Useful phrases (4 minutes)

Learn these phrases and then test yourself using the cover flap.

| | |
|---|---|
| I'd like to change some money. | **Vorrei cambiare dei soldi.** *vorray kambyaray day soldee* |
| What is the exchange rate? | **Quant'è il cambio?** *kwantay eel kambyoh* |
| I'd like to withdraw some money. | **Vorrei prelevare dei soldi.** *vorray prelevaray day soldee* |

### 6 Say it (2 minutes)

Can I pay by credit card?

Do I need my PIN?

I'd like some stamps.

**Può battere il pin.**
*pwoh battayray eel pin*

Please key in your PIN.

**Devo anche firmare?**
*devoh ankay feermaray*

Do I need to sign as well?

**No, non è necessario.**
*noh, non ay nechessaryoh*

No, that's not necessary.

# RIPARAZIONI
## Repairs

**1 Warm up** (1 minute)

What is the Italian for "doesn't work"? (pp.60-1)

What's the Italian for "today" and "tomorrow"? (pp.28-9)

You can combine the Italian words on these pages with the vocabulary you learned in week 10 to help you explain basic problems and cope with arranging most repairs. When organizing building work or a repair, it's a good idea to agree the price and method of payment in advance.

## 2 Words to remember (4 minutes)

Familiarize yourself with these words and test yourself using the flap.

| | |
|---|---|
| **l'idraulico** *leedraooleekoh* | plumber |
| **l'elettricista** *lelettreecheestah* | electrician |
| **il meccanico** *eel mekkaneekoh* | mechanic |
| **il muratore** *eel mooratoray* | builder |
| **l'imbianchino** *leembyankeenoh* | decorator |
| **il falegname** *eel falennyamay* | carpenter |
| **il tecnico** *eel tayneekoh* | technician |
| **la donna delle pulizie** *lah donnah dellay pooleetsyay* | cleaner |

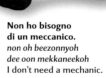

**la chiave**
*lah keeavay*
wheel brace

**Non ho bisogno di un meccanico.**
*non oh beezonnyoh dee oon mekkaneekoh*
I don't need a mechanic.

## 3 In conversation (3 minutes)

**La lavatrice non funziona.**
*lah lavatreechay non foontsyonah*

The washing machine is not working.

**Sì, il tubo è rotto.**
*see, eel tooboh ay rottoh*

Yes, the hose is broken.

**Può ripararlo?**
*pwoh reepararloh*

Can you repair it?

## 4 Useful phrases (3 minutes)

Learn these phrases and then test yourself using the cover flap.

| | |
|---|---|
| Please clean the bathroom. | **Può pulire il bagno?** *pwoh pooleeray eel bannyoh* |
| Can you repair the boiler? | **Può riparare la caldaia?** *pwoh reepararay lah kaldayah* |
| Do you know a good electrician? | **Conosce un bravo elettricista?** *konoshay oon bravoh elettreecheestah* |

**Dove posso farlo riparare?**
*dovay possoh farloh reepararay*
Where can I get this repaired?

## 5 Put into practice (4 minutes)

**Posso cominciare domani.**
*possoh komeencharay domanee*
I can start tomorrow.

**le piante**
*lay peeantay*
plans

Cover up the text on the right and complete the dialogue in Italian.

**Il suo muretto è rotto.**
*eel soo-oh mooray-ttoh ay rottoh*
Your wall is broken.

Ask: Do you know a good builder?

**Conosce un bravo muratore?**
*konoshay oon bravoh mooratoray*

**Sì, ce n'è uno in paese.**
*see, chenay oonoh een paesay*
Yes, there is one in the village.

Ask: Do you have his phone number?

**Ha il suo numero di telefono?**
*ah eel soo-oh noomeroh dee telayfonoh*

**No, deve cambiarlo.**
*noh, devay kambeearloh*

No, you need to change it.

**Può farlo oggi?**
*pwoh farloh ojjee*

Can you do it today?

**No, torno domani.**
*noh, tornoh domanee*

No, I'll come back tomorrow.

## 1 Warm up (1 minute)

Say the days of the week in Italian. (pp.28-9)

How do you say "cleaner"? (pp.110-11)

Say "It's 9.30", "10.45", "12.00". (pp.30-1)

# VENIRE
## To come

The verb **venire** (*to come*) is a very common verb, which can be used to make a variety of useful idiomatic expressions. Remember that in Italian the sense of continuing action is implied in the simple present tense, for example, **vengo** can mean both *I come* and *I am coming*.

## 2 Venire: to come (6 minutes)

Say the different forms of **venire** (*to come*) aloud. Use the cover flap to test yourself and, when you are confident, practise the sample sentences below.

| | |
|---|---|
| **(io) vengo** <br> *(ee-oh) vengoh* | I come |
| **(tu) vieni** <br> *(too) vyenee* | you come <br> (informal singular) |
| **(Lei) viene** <br> *(lay) vyenay* | you come <br> (formal singular) |
| **(lui/lei) viene** <br> *(loo-ee/lay) vyenay* | he/she/it comes |
| **(noi) veniamo** <br> *(noy) veneeamoh* | we come |
| **(voi) venite** <br> *(voy) veneetay* | you come <br> (plural) |
| **(loro) vengono** <br> *(loroh) vengonoh* | they come |
| **Veniamo tutte le estati.** <br> *veneeamoh toottay lay estatee* | We come every summer. |
| **Vengo anch'io.** <br> *vengoh ankeeoh* | I am coming too. |
| **Vengono in treno.** <br> *vengonoh een trenoh* | They are coming by train. |

**Lei viene dalla Nigeria.**
*lay vyenay dallah neejayreeah*
She comes from Nigeria.

**Conversational tip** Note that when in English you say *come and see* in Italian this translates as **vieni a vedere** (*come to see*). In the same way *Shall I come and pick you up?* translated in Italian is **Vengo a prenderti?**.

## 3 Useful phrases (4 minutes)

Learn these phrases and then test yourself using the cover flap.

| | |
|---|---|
| When can I come? | **Quando posso venire?** *kwandoh possoh veneeray* |
| Come and see. | **Vieni a vedere.** *vyenee ah vederay* |
| The cleaner comes every Monday. | **La donna delle pulizie viene il lunedì.** *lah donnah dellay pooleetsyay vyenay eel loonedee* |
| Come with me. (informal/formal) | **Vieni/venga con me.** *vyenee/vengah kon may* |

**Venite alla mia festa?**
*veneetay allah mee-ah festah*
Are you coming to my party?

## 4 Put into practice (4 minutes)

Join in this conversation. Read the Italian on the left and follow the instructions to make your reply. Then test yourself by concealing the answers with the cover flap.

**Buongiorno. Parrucchiere Leo.**
*bwonjornoh. parrookkyeray layo*

Hello, this is Leo's hair salon.

Say: I'd like an appointment.

**Vorrei un appuntamento.**
*vorray oon appoontamentoh*

**Quando vuol venire?**
*kwando vwol veneeray*

When do you want to come?

Say: Can I come today?

**Posso venire oggi?**
*possoh veneeray ojjee*

**Sì certo, a che ora?**
*see chertoh, a kay orah*

Yes of course, what time?

Say: At 10.30.

**Alle dieci e mezzo.**
*allay deeaychee ay metsoh*

**Warm up** (1 minute)

What's the Italian for "big/tall" and "small/short"? (pp.64-5)

Say "The room is big" and "The bed is small". (pp.64-5)

# LA POLIZIA E IL CRIMINE
## Police and crime

In an emergency, you can contact the police by dialling 112. You may have to explain your problem in Italian, so some basic vocabulary is useful. In the event of a burglary, the police will usually come to the house.

## Words to remember: crime (4 minutes)

Familiarize yourself with these words.

**Voglio un avvocato.**
*vollyoh oonavvokatoh*
I want a lawyer.

| | |
|---|---|
| **il furto** *eel foortoh* | burglary |
| **il rapporto di polizia** *eel rapportoh dee poleetseeah* | police report |
| **il ladro** *eel ladroh* | thief |
| **la denuncia** *lah denoonchah* | statement |
| **il/la testimone** *eel/lah testeemonay* | witness |
| **l'avvocato** *lavvokatoh* | lawyer |

## Useful phrases (3 minutes)

Learn these phrases and then test yourself using the cover flap.

| | |
|---|---|
| **Sono stato/a derubato/a.** *sonoh statoh/ah deroobatoh/ah* | I've been robbed. |
| **Cosa hanno rubato?** *kozah annoh roobatoh* | What was stolen? |
| **Ha visto chi è stato?** *ah veestoh kee ay statoh* | Did you see who did it? |
| **Quando è successo?** *kwandoh ay succhessoh* | When did it happen? |

**gli oggetti di valore**
*lly ojjayttee dee valoray*
valuables

## 4 Words to remember: appearance (5 minutes)

Learn these words. Remember some adjectives have a feminine form.

**Ha i capelli scuri
e i baffi.**
*ah ee kapellee
skooree ay
ee baffee*
He has dark hair
and a moustache.

**Ha i capelli
neri corti.**
*ah ee kapellee
neree kortee*
He has short,
black hair.

| man/men | **l'uomo/gli uomini** |
| | *lwomoh/lly womeenee* |
| woman/women | **la donna/le donne** |
| | *lah donnah/lay donnay* |
| tall | **alto/alta** |
| | *altoh/altah* |
| short | **basso/bassa** |
| | *bassoh/bassah* |
| young | **giovane** |
| | *jovanay* |
| old | **vecchio/vecchia** |
| | *vekkyoh/vekkyah* |
| fat | **grasso/grassa** |
| | *grassoh/grassah* |
| thin | **magro/magra** |
| | *magroh/magrah* |
| beard | **la barba** |
| | *lah barbah* |
| glasses | **gli occhiali** |
| | *lly okkyalee* |
| long/short hair | **i capelli lunghi/corti** |
| | *ee kapellee loongee/kortee* |

**Cultural tip** If you are affected by a crime or other emergency in Italy, you can go to the **Carabinieri**, a force that is part of the army and operates even in small towns. Call them by dialling 112.

## 5 Put into practice (2 minutes)

Practise these phrases. Then use the cover flap to conceal the text on the right and follow the instructions to make your reply in Italian.

**Lo può descrivere?** **Basso e grasso.**
*loh pwoh deskreeveray* *bassoh ay grassoh*

Can you describe him?

Say: Short and fat.

**E i capelli?** **Capelli lunghi e barba.**
*ay ee kapellee* *kapellee loongee ay barbah*

And the hair?

Say: Long hair and a beard.

**Risposte**
**Answers** (Cover with flap)

# RIPASSA E RIPETI
## Review and repeat

### 1 To come

❶ **vengo**
*vengoh*

❷ **viene**
*vyenay*

❸ **veniamo**
*veneeamoh*

❹ **venite**
*veneetay*

❺ **vengono**
*vengonoh*

### 1 To come (3 minutes)

Put the correct form of **venire** (*to come*) into the gaps.

❶ (io) _____ alle quattro.

❷ Il giardiniere _____ una volta alla settimana.

❸ (noi) _____ in treno.

❹ (voi) _____ con noi?

❺ I miei genitori _____ lunedì.

### 2 Bank and post

❶ **la carta di credito**
*lah cartah dee kredeetoh*

❷ **le banconote**
*lay bankonotay*

❸ **il pacco**
*eel pakkoh*

❹ **i francobolli**
*ee frankobollee*

❺ **la cartolina**
*lah kartoleenah*

### 2 Bank and post office (4 minutes)

Name the numbered items in Italian.

parcel ❸

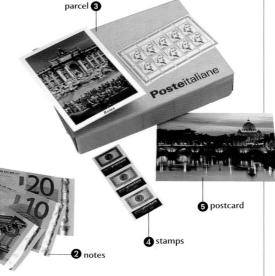

❺ postcard

❹ stamps

credit card ❶

❷ notes

### 3 Appearance (4 minutes)

What do these descriptions mean?

❶ Un uomo alto e magro.

❷ Una donna con i capelli corti e gli occhiali.

❸ Sono bassa e ho i capelli lunghi.

❹ È vecchia e grassa.

❺ Lui ha gli occhi azzurri e la barba.

### 3 Appearance

❶ A tall, thin man.

❷ A woman with short hair and glasses.

❸ I'm short and I have long hair.

❹ She is old and fat.

❺ He has blue eyes and a beard.

### 4 The pharmacy (4 minutes)

You are asking a pharmacist for advice. Join in the conversation, replying in Italian where you see the English prompts.

**Buongiorno, dica?**
❶ I have a cough.

**Ha anche il raffreddore?**
❷ No, but I have a headache.

**Prenda queste pastiglie.**
❸ Do you have that as a syrup?

**Certo. Ecco lo sciroppo.**
❹ Thank you. How much is that?

**Nove euro.**
❺ Here you are. Goodbye.

### 4 The pharmacy

❶ **Ho la tosse.**
*oh lah tossay*

❷ **No, ma ho mal di testa.**
*noh, mah oh mal dee testah*

❸ **Le ha in sciroppo?**
*lay ah een sheeroppoh*

❹ **Grazie. Quant'è?**
*gratseeay. kwantay*

❺ **Ecco. Arrivederci.**
*ekkoh. arreevederchee*

# IL TEMPO LIBERO
## Leisure time

Italy, with its long history and rich culture, provides numerous opportunities for cultural pursuits, as well as modern leisure activities. Many Italians are interested in the arts and spend the weekends in *historic cities* (**città d'arte**) or, when the weather's warm, at the seaside.

### 1 **Warm up** (1 minute)

What is the Italian for "museum" and "art gallery"? (pp.48–9)

Say "What beautiful curtains!" (pp.100–1)

Ask "Do you want...?' informally. (p.22–3)

### 2 **Words to remember** (4 minutes)

Familiarize yourself with these words and test yourself using the cover flap to conceal the Italian on the left.

|  |  |
|---|---|
| **il teatro** *eel tayatroh* | theatre |
| **il cinema** *eel cheenemah* | cinema |
| **la discoteca** *lah diskotekah* | discotheque |
| **la musica** *lah moozeekah* | music |
| **l'arte** (f) *lartay* | art |
| **lo sport** *loh sport* | sport |
| **viaggiare** *veeajjaray* | travelling |
| **i videogiochi** *ee veedayohjokkee* | video games |

**Amo l'opera.**
*amoh lopayrah*
I love opera.

**gli spettatori**
*lly spettatoree*
audience

### 3 **In conversation** (4 minutes)

**Vuoi giocare a tennis?**
*vwoee jokaray ah tennees*

Do you want to play tennis?

**No, lo sport non mi piace.**
*noh. loh sport non mee peeachay*

No, I don't like sport.

**Cosa fai nel tempo libero?**
*kozah faee nel tempoh leeberoh*

What do you do in your free time?

**Detesto i videogiochi.**
*detestoh ee veedayohjokkee*
I hate video games.

la galleria
*lah galereeah*
circle

la platea
*lah platayah*
stalls

## 4 Useful phrases (4 minutes)

Learn these phrases and then test yourself using the cover flap.

| | |
|---|---|
| What do you do (formal/informal) in your spare time? | **Cosa fa/fai nel tempo libero?** *kozah fah/faee nel tempoh leeberoh* |
| I like the theatre. | **Mi piace il teatro.** *mee peeachay eel teatroh* |
| I prefer the cinema. | **Io preferisco il cinema.** *ee-oh preferisko eel cheenemah* |
| I'm interested in art. | **Mi interessa l'arte.** *mee eenteressah lartay* |
| That's boring! | **Che noia!** *kay noeeah* |

## 5 Say it (2 minutes)

I'm interested in music.

I prefer sport.

I don't like opera.

**Mi piace lo shopping.**
*mee peeachay loh shoppeen*

I like shopping.

**Detesto lo shopping.**
*Detestoh loh shoppeen*

I hate shopping.

**Non c'è problema, vado da sola.**
*non chay problemah, vadoh dah solah*
No problem, I'll go on my own.

# LO SPORT E GLI HOBBY
## Sport and hobbies

**1** **Warm up** (1 minute)

Ask "Do you (formal) want to play tennis?" (pp.22-3, pp.118-19)

Say "I like the theatre" and "I prefer travelling". (pp.118-19)

Say "That doesn't interest me". (pp.118-19)

The verb **fare** (*to do*) is useful for talking about hobbies. With sports you can also use **giocare** (*to play*), for example, **gioco a tennis** (*I play tennis*). **Fare** is also used to describe the weather, as in **fa freddo** (*it's cold*).

**2** **Words to remember** (3 minutes)

Memorize these words and then test yourself.

|  |  |
|---|---|
| **il calcio**<br>*eel kalchoh* | football |
| **il rugby**<br>*eel regbee* | rugby |
| **il tennis**<br>*eel tennees* | tennis |
| **il nuoto**<br>*eel nwotoh* | swimming |
| **la vela**<br>*lah velah* | sailing |
| **la pesca**<br>*lah peskah* | fishing |
| **la pittura**<br>*lah peettoorah* | painting |
| **la palestra**<br>*lah palestrah* | gymnastics |

**il bunker**
*eel bunker*
bunker

**il golfista**
*eel golfeestah*
golfer

**Gioco a golf tutti i giorni.**
*jokoh ah golf toottee ee jornee*
I play golf every day.

**3** **Useful phrases** (4 minutes)

Familiarize yourself with these phrases.

| | |
|---|---|
| **Gioco a rugby.**<br>*jokoh ah regbee* | I play rugby. |
| **Gioca a tennis.**<br>*jokah ah tennees* | He plays tennis. |
| **Fa un corso di pittura.**<br>*fah oon korsoh dee peettoorah* | She is on a painting course. |

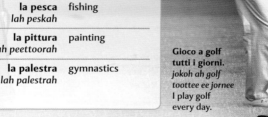

## 4 Fare: to do or to make (4 minutes)

The verb **fare** (to do or to make) is also used to describe the weather. Learn its different forms and practise the sample sentences below.

| | |
|---|---|
| I do | **(io) faccio**<br>(ee-oh) facchoh |
| you do<br>(informal singular) | **(tu) fai**<br>(too) faee |
| you do<br>(formal singular) | **(Lei) fa**<br>(lay) fah |
| he/she/it does | **(lui/lei) fa**<br>(loo-ee/lay) fah |
| we do | **(noi) facciamo**<br>(noy) facchamoh |
| you do (plural) | **(voi) fate**<br>(voy) fatay |
| they do | **(loro) fanno**<br>(loroh) fannoh |
| What do you do?<br>(formal/informal) | **Cosa fai/fate?**<br>kozah faee/fatay |
| I go hiking. | **Faccio escursionismo.**<br>facchoh ayskursyoneesmoh |

**Fa caldo oggi.**
fah kaldoh ojjee
It's hot today.

**la bandierina**
lah bandeeayreenah
flag

**il campo da golf**
eel kampoh
dah golf
golf course

## 5 Put into practice (3 minutes)

Learn these phrases. Then cover up the text on the right and complete the dialogue in Italian. Check your answers.

**Cosa ti piace fare?**
kozah tee peeachay faray

What do you like doing?

Say: I like playing tennis.

**Mi piace giocare
a tennis.**
mee peeachay jokaray
ah tennees

**Giochi anche a calcio?**
jokee anchay ah kalchoh

Do you play football as well?

Say: No. I play rugby.

**No. Gioco a rugby.**
noh. jokoh ah regbee

**Quando giochi?**
kwandoh jokee

When do you play?

Say: I play every week.

**Gioco tutte le settimane.**
jokoh toottay lay
setteemanay

# RAPPORTI SOCIALI
## *Socializing*

The Italian dinner table is the centre of their social world; you can expect to do a lot of socializing while enjoying food and wine. It is best to use the more polite **Lei** form at first to talk to people you meet socially; when they start to call you **tu**, you can reciprocate.

**2** **Useful phrases** (3 minutes)

Learn these phrases and then test yourself.

| | |
|---|---|
| **Vuol venire a cena con me?**<br>*vwol veneeray ah chenah con may* | Would you like to come to dinner with me? |
| **È libero/a mercoledì prossimo?**<br>*ay leeberoh/ah merkoledee prosseemoh* | Are you free next Wednesday? |
| **Magari un'altra volta.**<br>*magaree oonaltrah voltah* | Perhaps another time. |

l'ospite
*lospeetay*
guest

**Cultural tip** When you go to someone's house for the first time, it is usual to bring flowers, chocolate, or a bottle of good wine. If you are invited again, having seen your host's house, you can bring something a little more personal.

**3** **In conversation** (3 minutes)

**Vuol venire a cena da me martedì?**
*vwol veneeray ah chenah dah may martedee*

Would you like to come to dinner on Tuesday?

**Mi dispiace, martedì non posso.**
*mee deespeeachay, martedee non possoh*

I'm sorry, I can't on Tuesday.

**Facciamo giovedì?**
*facchamoh jovedee*

What about Thursday?

**la padrona di casa**
*lah padronah dee kazah*
hostess

## 4 Words to remember (3 minutes)

Familiarize yourself with these words and test
yourself using the flap.

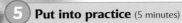

| | |
|---|---|
| party | **la festa**<br>*lah festah* |
| dinner party | **la cena**<br>*lah chenah* |
| invitation | **l'invito** (m)<br>*leenveetoh* |
| reception | **il rinfresco**<br>*eel reenfreskoh* |
| gift | **il regalo**<br>*eel regaloh* |

## 5 Put into practice (5 minutes)

Join in this conversation.

**Facciamo una festa
sabato. Siete liberi?**
*facchamoh oonah festah
sabatoh. seeaytay leeberee*

We are having a party on
Saturday. Are you free?

Say: Yes, how nice!

**Sì, che bello!**
*see, kay belloh*

---

**Benissimo.**
*beneesseemoh*

That's great.

Ask: What time does
it start?

**A che ora comincia?**
*ah kay orah komeenchah*

**Grazie dell'invito.**
*gratseeay delleenveetoh*
Thank you for inviting us.

---

**Benissimo.**
*beneesseemoh*

That's great.

**Porti suo marito.**
*portee soo-oh mareetoh*

Please bring your husband.

**Grazie. A che ora?**
*gratseeay. ah kay orah*

Thank you. At what time?

# RIPASSA E RIPETI
## Review and repeat

**Risposte**
*Answers* (Cover with flap)

### 1 Animals

❶ **il pesce**
*eel peshay*

❷ **l'uccello**
*loocchelloh*

❸ **il coniglio**
*eel koneellyoh*

❹ **il gatto**
*eel gattoh*

❺ **il criceto**
*eel kreechetoh*

❻ **il cane**
*eel kanay*

### 1 Animals (3 minutes)

Name the numbered animals in Italian.

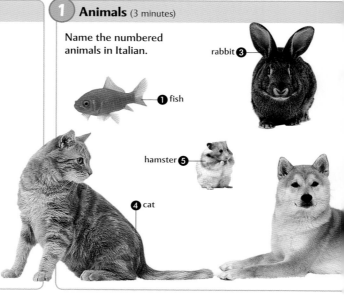

rabbit ❸

❶ fish

hamster ❺

❹ cat

### 2 I like...

❶ **Mi piace il rugby.**
*mee peeachay eel regbee*

❷ **Non mi piace il golf.**
*non mee peeachay eel golf*

❸ **Mi piace la pittura.**
*mee peeachay lah peettoorah*

### 2 I like... (4 minutes)

Say the following in Italian:

❶ I like rugby.
❷ I don't like golf.
❸ I like to paint.

bird **②**

**⑥** dog

### **3** To do (4 minutes)

Use the correct form of the verb **fare** (*to do*) in these sentences.

**❶** Tu _____ vela?

**❷** Lei _____ un corso di pittura.

**❸** Cosa le piace _____ ?

**❹** _____ freddo oggi.

**❺** Voi _____ palestra?

**❻** Io _____ nuoto.

### **3** To do

**❶** fai
*faee*

**❷** fa
*fah*

**❸** fare
*faray*

**❹** fa
*fah*

**❺** fate
*fatay*

**❻** faccio
*facchoh*

### **4** An invitation (4 minutes)

You are invited for lunch. Join in the conversation, replying in Italian following the English prompts.

**Vuol venire a pranzo da me sabato?**
**❶** I am sorry, I can't on Saturday.

**Facciamo domenica?**
**❷** Great. I am free on Sunday.

**Porti i bambini.**
**❸** Thank you. What time?

**All'una.**
**❹** See you on Sunday.

### **4** An invitation

**❶** Mi dispiace, sabato non posso.
*mee deespeeachay, sabatoh non possoh*

**❷** Benissimo. Sono libera domenica.
*beneesseemoh. sonoh leeberah domeneekah*

**❸** Grazie. A che ora?
*gratseeay. ah kay orah*

**❹** Arrivederci a domenica.
*arreevederchee ah domeneekah*

# Reinforce and progress

Regular practice is the key to maintaining and advancing your language skills. In this section you will find a variety of suggestions for reinforcing and extending your knowledge of Italian. Many involve returning to exercises in the book and using the dictionaries to extend their scope. Go back through the lessons in a different order, mix and match activities to make up your own 15-minute daily programme, or focus on topics that are of particular relevance to your current needs.

**1** **Warm up** (1 minute)

How do you say "he is" and "they are"? (pp.14-15)

Now say "he is not" and "they are not". (pp.14-15)

What is Italian for "my mother"? (pp.10-11)

**Keep warmed up**
Re-visit the Warm Up boxes to remind yourself of key words and phrases. Make sure you work your way through all of them on a regular basis.

**3** **I'd like...** (3 minutes)

Say "I'd like" the following:

croissant **3**

**4** sugar    **1** black coffee

cappuccino **2**

**Review and repeat again**
Work through a Review and Repeat lesson as a way of reinforcing words and phrases presented in the course. Return to the main lesson for any topic on which you are no longer confident.

**3** **In conversation: taxi** (2 minutes)

**Carry on conversing**
Re-read the In Conversation panels. Say both parts of the conversation, paying attention to the pronunciation. Where possible, try incorporating new words from the dictionary.

**Al mercato di San Lorenzo, per favore.**
al merkatoh dee san lorentsoh, per favoray

**Benissimo, signore.**
beneesseemoh, seennyoray

Very well, sir.

**Mi lasci qui, per favore.**
mee lashee kwee, per favoray

Can you drop me here, please?

**3** **Useful phrases** (5 minutes)

Learn these phrases and then test yourself using the cover flap.

| | |
|---|---|
| The room is too cold/hot. | **In camera fa troppo freddo/caldo.** *een kamayrah fah troppoh freddoh/ kaldoh* |
| There are no towels. | **Non ci sono gli asciugamani.** *non chee sonoh lly ashugamanee* |
| I'd like some soap. | **Vorrei del sapone.** *vorray del saponay* |
| The shower doesn't work very well. | **La doccia non funziona bene.** *lah docchah non funtseeonah benay* |

**Practise phrases**
Return to the Useful Phrases and Put into Practice exercises. Test yourself using the cover flap. When you are confident, devise your own versions of the phrases, using new words from the dictionary.

**Match, repeat, and extend**

Remind yourself of words related to specific topics by returning to the Match and Repeat and Words to Remember exercises. Test yourself using the cover flap. Discover new words in that area by referring to the dictionary and menu guide.

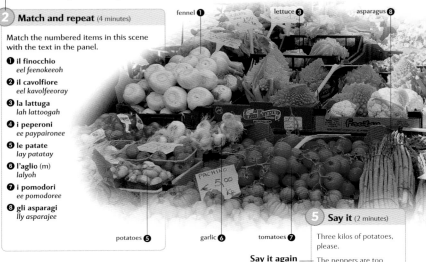

**2  Match and repeat** (4 minutes)

Match the numbered items in this scene with the text in the panel.

fennel ❶    lettuce ❸    asparagus ❽

❶ **il finocchio**
*eel feenokeeoh*

❷ **il cavolfiore**
*eel kavolfeeooray*

❸ **la lattuga**
*lah lattoogah*

❹ **i peperoni**
*ee paypaironee*

❺ **le patate**
*lay patatay*

❻ **l'aglio** (m)
*lalyoh*

❼ **i pomodori**
*ee pomodoree*

❽ **gli asparagi**
*lly asparajee*

potatoes ❺    garlic ❻    tomatoes ❼

**Say it again**
The Say It exercises are a useful instant reminder for each lesson. Practise these, using your own vocabulary variations from the dictionary or elsewhere in the lesson.

**5  Say it** (2 minutes)

Three kilos of potatoes, please.

The peppers are too expensive.

How much is the lettuce?

---

## Using other resources

In addition to working with this book, try the following language extension ideas:

**Visit Italy** and try out your new skills with native speakers. Find out if there is an Italian community near you. There may be shops, cafés, restaurants, and clubs. Try to visit some of these and use your Italian to order food and drink and strike up conversations. Most native speakers will be happy to speak Italian to you.

**Join a language class or club.** There are usually evening and day classes available at a variety of different levels. Or you could start a club yourself if you have friends who are also interested in keeping up their Italian.

**Look at Italian magazines** and newspapers. The pictures will help you to understand the text. Advertisements are also a useful way of expanding your vocabulary.

**Use the Internet,** where you can find all kinds of websites for learning languages, some of which offer free online help and activities. You can also find Italian websites for anything from renting a house to shampooing your pet. You can even access Italian radio and TV stations online. Start by going to an Italian search engine, such as *iltrovatore.it*, and keying a hobby or sport that interests you, or set yourself a challenge, such as finding a two-bedroom apartment for rent in Florence.

# MENU GUIDE

This guide lists the most common terms you may encounter on Italian menus or when shopping for food. If you can't find an exact phrase, try looking up its component parts.

## A

**abbacchio alla romana** *Roman-style spring lamb*
**acciughe sott'olio** *anchovies in oil*
**aceto** *vinegar*
**acqua** *water*
**acqua minerale gassata** *sparkling mineral water*
**acqua minerale non gassata** *still mineral water*
**acqua naturale** *still mineral water, tap water*
**affettato misto** *variety of cold, sliced meats*
**affogato al caffè** *hot espresso on ice cream*
**aglio** *garlic*
**agnello** *lamb*
**albicocche** *apricots*
**al forno** *roast*
**amatriciana** *chopped bacon and tomato sauce*
**ananas** *pineapple*
**anatra** *duck*
**anatra all'arancia** *duck in orange sauce*
**anguilla in umido** *stewed eel*
**anguria** *watermelon*
**antipasti** *starters*
**antipasti misti** *mixed starters*
**aperitivo** *aperitif*
**aragosta** *lobster*
**arancia** *orange*
**aranciata** *orangeade*
**aringa** *herring*
**arista di maiale al forno** *roast chine of pork*
**arrosto** *roast*
**arrosto di tacchino** *roast turkey*
**asparagi** *asparagus*
**avocado all'agro** *avocado with dressing*

## B

**baccalà** *dried cod*
**baccalà alla vicentina** *Vicentine-style dried cod*
**bagnacauda** *vegetables (often raw) in a sauce of oil, garlic, and anchovy*

**Barbaresco** *dry red wine from Piedmont*
**Barbera** *dry red wine from Piedmont*
**Bardolino** *dry red wine from the Veneto region*
**Barolo** *dark, dry red wine from Piedmont*
**basilico** *basil*
**bavarese** *ice-cream cake with cream*
**bel paese** *soft, white cheese*
**besciamella** *white sauce*
**bignè** *cream puff*
**birra** *beer*
**birra chiara** *light beer, lager*
**birra grande** *large beer*
**birra piccola** *small beer*
**birra scura** *dark beer*
**bistecca ai ferri** *grilled steak*
**bistecca (di manzo)** *steak*
**bolognese** *mince and tomato sauce*
**braciola di maiale** *pork steak*
**branzino al forno** *baked sea bass*
**brasato** *braised beef with herbs*
**bresaola** *dried, salted beef eaten with oil and lemon*
**brioche** *type of croissant*
**brodo** *clear broth*
**brodo di pollo** *chicken broth*
**brodo vegetale** *clear vegetable broth*
**budino** *pudding*
**burro** *butter*
**burro di acciughe** *anchovy butter*

## C

**caciotta** *tender, white cheese from Central Italy*
**caffè** *coffee*
**caffè corretto** *espresso with a dash of liqueur*
**caffè latte** *half coffee, half hot milk*
**caffè lungo** *weak espresso*
**caffè macchiato** *espresso with a dash of milk*
**caffè ristretto** *strong espresso*

**calamari in umido** *stewed squid*
**calamaro** *squid*
**calzone** *folded pizza with tomato and cheese*
**camomilla** *camomile tea*
**cannella** *cinnamon*
**cannelloni al forno** *baked egg pasta rolls stuffed with meat*
**cappuccino** *espresso with foaming milk sprinkled with cocoa powder*
**capretto al forno** *roast kid*
**carbonara** *sauce of egg, bacon, and cheese*
**carciofi** *artichokes*
**carciofini sott'olio** *baby artichokes in oil*
**carne** *meat*
**carote** *carrots*
**carpaccio** *finely sliced beef fillets with oil, lemon, and parmesan*
**carré di maiale al forno** *roast pork loin*
**cassata siciliana** *ice-cream cake with chocolate, glacé fruit, and ricotta*
**castagne** *chestnuts*
**cavoletti di Bruxelles** *Brussels sprouts*
**cavolfiore** *cauliflower*
**cavolo** *cabbage*
**cefalo** *mullet*
**cernia** *grouper (fish)*
**charlotte** *ice-cream cake with cream, biscuits, and fruit*
**Chianti** *dark red Tuscan wine*
**cicoria** *chicory*
**cicorino** *small chicory plants*
**ciliege** *cherries*
**cime di rapa** *sprouting broccoli*
**cioccolata** *chocolate*
**cioccolata calda** *hot chocolate*
**cipolle** *onions*
**cocktail di gamberetti** *shrimp cocktail*
**conchiglie alla marchigiana** *pasta shells in tomato sauce with ham, celery, carrot, and parsley*
**coniglio** *rabbit*

**coniglio in umido** *stewed rabbit*
**consommé** *clear meat or chicken broth*
**contorni** *vegetables*
**coperto** *cover charge*
**coppa** *cured neck of pork*
**costata alla fiorentina** *T-bone veal steak*
**costata di manzo** *T-bone beef steak*
**cotechino** *spiced pork sausage for boiling*
**cotoletta** *veal, pork, or lamb chop*
**cotoletta ai ferri** *grilled veal or pork chop*
**cotoletta alla milanese** *veal chop in breadcrumbs*
**cotoletta alla valdostana** *veal chop with ham and cheese, in breadcrumbs*
**cotolette di agnello** *lamb chops*
**cotolette di maiale** *pork chops*
**cozze** *mussels*
**cozze alla marinara** *mussels in white wine*
**crema** *custard dessert made with eggs and milk*
**crema al caffè** *coffee custard dessert*
**crema al cioccolato** *chocolate custard dessert*
**crema di funghi** *cream of mushroom soup*
**crema di piselli** *cream of pea soup*
**crema pasticciera** *confectioner's custard*
**crêpes Suzette** *pancakes flambéed with orange sauce*
**crescente** *fried bread made with flour, lard, and eggs*
**crespelle** *savoury pancake*
**crostata di frutta** *fruit tart*

## D, E

**dadi** *bouillon cubes*
**datteri** *dates*
**degustazione** *tasting*
**degustazione di vini** *wine tasting*
**dentice al forno** *baked dentex (type of sea bream)*
**digestivo** *digestive liqueur*
**dolci** *sweets, desserts, cakes*
**endivia belga** *white chicory*
**entrecôte (di manzo)** *beef entrecote*
**espresso** *strong, black coffee*

## F

**fagiano** *pheasant*
**fagioli** *beans*
**fagioli borlotti in umido** *borlotti (kidney beans) in sauce of tomato, vegetables, and herbs*
**fagiolini** *long, green beans*
**faraona** *guinea fowl*
**fegato** *liver*
**fegato alla veneta** *liver in butter with onions*
**fegato con salvia e burro** *liver in butter and sage*
**fettuccine** *ribbon-shaped pasta*
**fichi** *figs*
**filetti di pesce persico** *fillets of perch*
**filetti di sogliola** *fillets of sole*
**filetto ai ferri** *grilled fillet of beef*
**filetto al cognac** *fillet of beef flambé*
**filetto al pepe verde** *fillet of beef with green peppercorns*
**filetto al sangue** *rare fillet of beef*
**filetto ben cotto** *well-done fillet of beef*
**filetto (di manzo)** *fillet of beef*
**filetto medio** *medium-cooked fillet of beef*
**finocchi gratinati** *fennel au gratin*
**finocchio** *fennel*
**fonduta** *cheese fondue*
**formaggi misti** *variety of cheeses*
**fragole** *strawberries*
**fragole con gelato/panna** *strawberries and ice cream/ cream*
**frappé** *fruit or milk shake with crushed ice*
**Frascati** *dry white wine from area around Rome*
**frittata** *type of omelette*
**frittata alle erbe** *herb omelette*
**fritto misto** *mixed seafood in batter*
**frittura di pesce** *variety of fried fish*
**frutta** *fruit*
**frutta alla fiamma** *fruit flambé*
**frutta secca** *dried nuts and raisins*
**frutti di bosco** *mixture of strawberries, raspberries, mulberries, etc*
**frutti di mare** *seafood*
**funghi** *mushrooms*
**funghi trifolati** *mushrooms fried in garlic and parsley*

## G

**gamberetti** *shrimps*
**gamberi** *prawns*
**gamberoni** *king prawns*
**gazzosa** *clear lemonade*
**gelatina** *jelly*
**gelato** *ice cream*
**gelato di crema** *vanilla-flavoured ice cream*
**gelato di frutta** *fruit-flavoured ice cream*
**gnocchetti verdi agli spinaci e al gorgonzola** *small flour, potato, and spinach dumplings with melted gorgonzola*
**gnocchi** *small flour and potato dumplings*
**gnocchi alla romana** *small milk and semolina dumplings with butter*
**Gorgonzola** *strong blue cheese from Lombardy*
**grancevola** *spiny spider crab*
**granchio** *crab*
**granita** *crushed ice drink*
**grigliata di pesce** *grilled fish*
**grigliata mista** *mixed grill (meat or fish)*
**grissini** *thin, crisp breadsticks*
**gruviera** *Gruyère cheese*

## I

**indivia** *endive*
**insalata** *salad*
**insalata caprese** *salad of tomatoes and mozzarella*
**insalata di funghi porcini** *boletus mushroom salad*
**insalata di mare** *seafood salad*
**insalata di nervetti** *boiled beef or veal served cold with beans and pickles*
**insalata di pomodori** *tomato salad*
**insalata di riso** *rice salad*
**insalata mista** *mixed salad*
**insalata russa** *Russian salad*
**insalata verde** *green salad*
**involtini** *meat rolls stuffed with ham and herbs*

## L

**lamponi** *raspberries*
**lasagne al forno** *layers of pasta baked in meat sauce with cheese*
**latte** *milk*
**latte macchiato con cioccolato** *hot milk sprinkled with cocoa*
**lattuga** *lettuce*
**leggero** *light*

**legumi** *legumes or pulses*
**lemonsoda** *sparkling lemon drink*
**lenticchie** *lentils*
**lepre** *hare*
**limonata** *lemon-flavoured fizzy drink*
**limone** *lemon*
**lingua** *tongue*

# M

**macedonia di frutta** *fruit salad*
**maiale** *pork*
**maionese** *mayonnaise*
**mandarino** *mandarin*
**mandorla** *almond*
**manzo** *beef*
**marroni** *chestnuts*
**Marsala** *fortified wine*
**marzapane** *marzipan*
**mascarpone** *soft, mild cheese*
**medaglioni di vitello** *veal medallions*
**mela** *apple*
**melanzane** *aubergine*
**melone** *melon*
**menta** *mint*
**meringata** *meringue pie*
**merluzzo** *cod*
**merluzzo alla pizzaiola** *cod in tomato sauce with anchovies and capers*
**merluzzo in bianco** *cod with oil and lemon*
**messicani in gelatina** *rolls of veal in jelly*
**millefoglie** *pastry layered with custard*
**minestra in brodo** *noodle soup*
**minestrone** *vegetable soup with rice or pasta*
**mirtilli** *bilberries*
**more** *mulberries or blackberries*
**moscato** *sweet wine*
**mousse al cioccolato** *chocolate mousse*
**mozzarella** *buffalo cheese*
**mozzarella in carrozza** *fried slices of bread and mozzarella*

# N, O

**nasello** *hake*
**nocciole** *hazelnuts*
**noce moscata** *nutmeg*
**noci** *walnuts*
**nodino** *veal chop*
**olio** *oil*
**origano** *oregano*
**ossobuco** *stewed shin of veal*
**ostriche** *oysters*

# P

**paglia e fieno** *mixed plain and green tagliatelle*
**paillard di manzo** *slices of grilled beef*
**paillard di vitello** *slices of grilled veal*
**pane** *bread*
**panino** *filled roll*
**panna** *cream*
**parmigiana di melanzane** *aubergines baked with cheese*
**pasta al forno** *pasta baked in white sauce and grated cheese*
**pasta e fagioli** *thick soup with puréed borlotti beans and pasta rings*
**pasta e piselli** *pasta with peas*
**pasticcio di fegato d'oca** *baked pasta dish with goose liver*
**pasticcio di lepre** *baked pasta dish with hare*
**pasticcio di maccheroni** *baked macaroni*
**pastina in brodo** *noodle soup*
**patate** *potatoes*
**patate al forno/arrosto** *roast potatoes*
**patate fritte** *chips*
**patate in insalata** *potato salad*
**pecorino** *strong, hard sheep's milk cheese*
**penne** *pasta quills*
**penne ai quattro formaggi** *pasta with four cheeses sauce*
**penne all'arrabbiata** *pasta with tomato and chilli pepper sauce*
**penne panna e prosciutto** *pasta with cream and ham sauce*
**pepe** *pepper (spice)*
**peperoncino** *crushed chilli pepper*
**peperoni** *peppers*
**peperoni ripieni** *stuffed peppers*
**peperoni sott'olio** *peppers in oil*
**pera** *pear*
**pesca** *peach*
**pesce** *fish*
**pesce al cartoccio** *fish baked in foil with herbs*
**pesce in carpione** *marinaded fish*
**pesto** *sauce of basil, pine nuts, Parmesan, garlic, and oil*
**pinot** *dry white wine from the Veneto region*
**pinzimonio** *raw vegetables with oil and vinegar*
**piselli** *peas*

**piselli al prosciutto** *broth with peas, ham, and basil*
**pizzaiola** *slices of cooked beef in tomato sauce, oregano, and anchovies*
**pizzoccheri alla Valtellinese** *pasta strips with vegetables and cheese*
**polenta** *boiled cornmeal left to set and sliced*
**polenta e osei** *polenta with small birds*
**polenta pasticciata** *layers of polenta, tomato sauce, and cheese*
**pollo** *chicken*
**pollo alla cacciatora** *chicken in white wine and mushroom sauce*
**pollo alla diavola** *deep-fried chicken pieces*
**polpette** *meatballs*
**polpettone** *meatloaf*
**pomodori** *tomatoes*
**pomodori ripieni** *stuffed tomatoes*
**pompelmo** *grapefruit*
**porri** *leeks*
**prezzemolo** *parsley*
**primi piatti** *first courses*
**prosciutto cotto** *cooked ham*
**prosciutto crudo** *type of cured ham*
**prugne** *plums*
**punte di asparagi all'agro** *asparagus tips in oil and lemon*
**purè di patate** *mashed potatoes*
**puttanesca** *tomato sauce with anchovies, capers, and black olives*

# Q, R

**quaglie** *quails*
**radicchio** *chicory*
**ragù** *meat-based sauce*
**rapanelli** *radishes*
**ravioli** *stuffed pasta parcels*
**ravioli al pomodoro** *meat ravioli in tomato sauce*
**razza** *skate*
**ricotta** *type of cottage cheese*
**risi e bisi** *risotto with peas and ham*
**riso** *rice*
**risotto** *rice cooked in stock*
**risotto alla castellana** *risotto with mushroom, ham, cream, and cheese*
**risotto alla milanese** *risotto with saffron*
**risotto al nero di seppia** *risotto with cuttlefish ink*
**risotto al tartufo** *truffle risotto*

**roast-beef all'inglese** *thinly sliced cold roast beef*
**robiola** *type of soft cheese from Lombardy*
**rognone trifolato** *kidney in garlic, oil, and parsley*
**rosatello/rosato** *rosé wine*
**rosmarino** *rosemary*

## S

**salame** *salami*
**sale** *salt*
**salmone affumicato** *smoked salmon*
**salsa cocktail/rosa** *mayonnaise and ketchup sauce for fish and seafood*
**salsa di pomodoro** *tomato sauce*
**salsa tartara** *tartar sauce*
**salsa vellutata** *white sauce made with clear broth instead of milk*
**salsa verde** *sauce for meat, with parsley and oil*
**salsiccia** *sausage*
**salsiccia di cinghiale** *wild boar sausage*
**salsiccia di maiale** *pork sausage*
**saltimbocca alla romana** *slices of veal stuffed with ham and sage and fried*
**salvia** *sage*
**sambuca (con la mosca)** *aniseed-flavour liqueur served with a coffee bean*
**sarde ai ferri** *grilled sardines*
**scaloppine** *veal escalopes*
**scaloppine al prezzemolo** *veal escalopes with parsley*
**scamorza alla griglia** *grilled soft cheese*
**scampi alla griglia** *grilled scampi*
**secco** *dry*
**secondi piatti** *second courses, main courses*
**sedano** *celery*
**selvaggina** *game*
**semifreddo** *dessert of ice cream and sponge fingers*
**senape** *mustard*
**seppie in umido** *stewed cuttlefish*
**servizio compreso** *service charge included*
**servizio escluso** *service charge excluded*
**Soave** *dry white wine from the Veneto region*
**sogliola** *sole*
**sogliola ai ferri** *grilled sole*
**sogliola al burro** *sole cooked in butter*

**sogliola alla mugnaia** *sole cooked in flour and butter*
**sorbetto** *sorbet, soft ice cream*
**soufflé al formaggio** *cheese soufflé*
**soufflé al prosciutto** *ham soufflé*
**speck** *cured, smoked ham*
**spezzatino di vitello** *veal stew*
**spiedini** *assorted chunks of spit-cooked meat or fish*
**spinaci** *spinach*
**spinaci all'agro** *spinach with oil and lemon*
**spremuta di ...** *freshly squeezed ... juice*
**spumante** *sparkling wine*
**stracchino** *soft cheese from Lombardy*
**stracciatella** *soup of beaten eggs in clear broth*
**strudel di mele** *apple strudel*
**succo di ...** *... juice*
**sugo al tonno** *tomato sauce with garlic, tuna, and parsley*

## T

**tacchino ripieno** *stuffed turkey*
**tagliata** *finely cut beef fillet cooked in the oven*
**tagliatelle** *thin pasta strips*
**tagliatelle rosse** *tagliatelle with chopped red peppers*
**tagliatelle verdi** *tagliatelle with spinach*
**tagliolini** *thin soup noodles*
**tartine** *small sandwiches*
**tartufo** *ice cream covered in cocoa or chocolate; truffle*
**tè** *tea*
**tiramisù** *dessert with coffee-soaked sponge, Marsala, Mascarpone, and cocoa powder*
**tonno** *tuna*
**torta** *tart, flan*
**torta di ricotta** *type of cheesecake*
**torta salata** *savoury flan*
**tortellini** *pasta shapes filled with minced pork, ham, Parmesan, and nutmeg*
**trancio di palombo** *smooth dogfish steak*
**trancio di pesce spada** *swordfish steak*
**trenette col pesto** *flat spaghetti with pesto sauce*
**triglie** *mullet (fish)*
**trippa** *tripe*
**trota** *trout*
**trota affumicata** *smoked trout*

**trota al burro** *trout cooked in butter*
**trota alle mandorle** *trout with almonds*
**trota bollita** *boiled trout*

## U

**uccelletti** *small birds wrapped in bacon, served on cocktail sticks*
**uova** *eggs*
**uova alla coque** *boiled eggs*
**uova al tegamino con pancetta** *fried eggs and bacon*
**uova farcite** *eggs with tuna, capers, and mayonnaise filling*
**uova sode** *hard-boiled eggs*
**uva** *grapes*
**uva bianca** *white grapes*
**uva nera** *black grapes*

## V

**vellutata di asparagi** *creamed asparagus with egg yolks*
**vellutata di piselli** *creamed peas with egg yolks*
**verdura** *vegetables*
**vermicelli** *very fine, thin pasta, often used in soups*
**vino** *wine*
**vino bianco** *white wine*
**vino da dessert** *dessert wine*
**vino da pasto** *table wine*
**vino da tavola** *table wine*
**vino rosso** *red wine*
**vitello** *veal*
**vitello tonnato** *sliced veal in tuna, anchovy, oil, and lemon sauce*
**vongole** *clams*

## W, Z

**würstel** *hot dog*
**zabaglione** *creamy dessert of eggs, sugar, and Marsala*
**zafferano** *saffron*
**zucca** *pumpkin*
**zucchine** *courgettes*
**zucchine al pomodoro** *courgettes in tomato, garlic, and parsley sauce*
**zucchine ripiene** *stuffed courgettes*
**zuccotto** *ice-cream cake with sponge fingers, cream, and chocolate*
**zuppa** *soup*
**zuppa di cipolle** *onion soup*
**zuppa di cozze** *mussel soup*
**zuppa di lenticchie** *lentil soup*
**zuppa di pesce** *fish soup*
**zuppa di verdura** *vegetable soup*
**zuppa inglese** *trifle*

# DICTIONARY
## English to Italian

The gender of an Italian noun is shown by the word for *the*: **il** or **lo** (masculine), **la** (feminine), and their plural forms **i** or **gli** (masculine) and **le** (feminine). When **lo** or **la** are abbreviated to **l'** in front of a vowel or **h**, the gender is shown by the abbreviations (m) or (f). Italian adjectives (adj) vary according to the gender and number of the word they describe, and the masculine form is shown here. In general, adjectives that end in **-o** adopt an **-a** ending in the feminine form, and those that end in **-e** usually stay the same. Plural endings are **-i** for masculine and **-e** for feminine.

### A

*a* **un/uno/una/un'**
*about:* about 16 **circa 16**; a book about Venice **un libro su Venezia**
*accelerator* **l'acceleratore** (m)
*accident* **l'incidente** (m)
*accommodation* **l'alloggio** (m), **il posto**
*accountant* **il ragioniere/la ragioniera**
*ache* **il dolore**
*adaptor* **il riduttore**
*address* **l'indirizzo** (m)
*admission charge* **il prezzo d'ingresso**
*advance* (on payment) **il anticipo**; in advance **anticipato**
*after* **dopo**
*afternoon* **il pomeriggio**
*aftershave* **il dopobarba**
*again* **di nuovo**
*against* **contro**
*agenda* **l'ordine del giorno** (m)
*AIDS* **l'Aids** (f)
*air* **l'aria** (f)
*air conditioning* **l'aria condizionata** (f)
*aircraft* **l'aereo** (m)
*airline* **la linea aerea**
*air mail* **via aerea**
*air mattress* **il materassino gonfiabile**
*airport* **l'aeroporto** (m)
*airport bus* **l'autobus navetta** (m)
*aisle* (in supermarket etc) **la fila**
*alarm clock* **la sveglia**
*alcohol* **l'alcol** (m)
*all* **tutto**; all the streets **tutte le strade**; that's all **questo è tutto**
*allergic* **allergico**
*allowed* **permesso**
*almost* **quasi**

*alone* **solo**
*Alps* **le Alpi**
*already* **già**
*always* **sempre**
*am:* I am (io) **sono**
*ambulance* **l'ambulanza** (f)
*America* **l'America** (f)
*American* **americano**
*and* **e**
*ankle* **la caviglia**
*anniversary* **il anniversario**
*another* **un altro, un'altra**
*answering machine* **la segreteria telefonica**
*antique shop* **l'antiquario** (m)
*antiseptic* **l'antisettico** (m)
*apartment* **l'appartamento** (m)
*aperitif* **l'aperitivo** (m)
*appetite* **l'appetito** (m)
*apple* **la mela**
*application form* **il modulo per la domanda**
*appointment* **l'appuntamento** (m)
*apricot* **l'albicocca** (f)
*April* **aprile**
*architecture* **l'architettura** (f)
*are:* you are (singular, formal) (Lei) **è**; (singular, informal) (tu) **sei**; (plural) (voi) **siete**; we are (noi) **siamo**; they are (loro) **sono**
*arm* **il braccio**
*armchair* **la poltrona**
*arrange* (appointment etc) **fissare**
*arrivals* **gli arrivi**
*arrive* **arrivare**
*art* **l'arte** (f)
*art gallery* **la pinacoteca, la galleria d'arte**
*artist* **l'artista** (m/f)
*as:* as soon as possible **(il) più presto possibile**
*ashtray* **il portacenere**
*asparagus* **gli asparagi**

*aspirin* **l'aspirina** (f)
*asthmatic* **asmatico**
*at:* at the post office **all'ufficio postale**; at night **di notte**; at 3 o'clock **alle tre**
*ATM* **il bancomat**
*attic* **la soffitta**
*attractive* **attraente**
*audience* **gli spettatori**
*August* **agosto**
*aunt* **la zia**
*Australia* **l'Australia** (f)
*Australian* **australiano** (-a)
*automatic* **automatico**
*autumn* **l'autunno** (m)
*away:* is it far away? **è lontano?**; go away! **vattene!**
*awful* **terribile, orribile**

### B

*baby* **il bambino/la bambina**
*back* (not front) **la parte posteriore**; (body) **la schiena**; to come back **tornare**
*backpack* **lo zaino**
*bacon* **la pancetta**
*bad* **cattivo**
*bag* **la borsa, il sacchetto**
*baggage claim* **il ritiro bagagli**
*bait* **l'esca** (f)
*bake* **cuocere (al forno)**
*bakery* **la panetteria**
*balcony* **il balcone**
*ball* (football etc) **la palla, il pallone**; (tennis etc) **la pallina**
*banana* **la banana**
*band* (musicians) **la banda**
*bandage* **la fascia**
*bank* **la banca**
*banknote* **la banconota**
*bar* (drinks) **il bar**; bar of chocolate **la tavoletta di cioccolata**

*barbecue* **il barbecue**; (occasion) **la grigliata all'aperto**

*barber's* (shop) **il barbiere**

*bargain* **l'affare** (m)

*basement* **il seminterrato**

*basket* **il cestino**; (in supermarket) **il cestello**

*bath* **il bagno**; (tub) **la vasca**; *to have a bath* **fare il bagno**

*bathing suit* **il costume da bagno**

*bathroom* **il bagno**

*battery* **la batteria**

*be* (verb) **essere**

*beach* **la spiaggia**

*beans* **i fagioli**

*beard* **la barba**

*beautiful* **bello**

*because* **perché**

*bed* **il letto**

*bed linen* **le lenzuola**

*bedroom* **la camera (da letto)**

*bedspread* **il copriletto**

*beef* **il manzo**

*beer* **la birra**

*before* **... prima di ...**

*beginner* **il/la principiante**

*beginners' slope* **la discesa per principianti**

*behind* **dietro**; *behind ...* **dietro a ...**

*beige* **beige**

*bell* (church) **la campana**; (door) **il campanello**

*below* **sotto**

*belt* **la cintura**

*beside ...* **vicino a ...**

*best* **il migliore**

*better* (than) **migliore (di)**

*between ...* **fra ...**

*bicycle* **la bicicletta**

*big* **grande**

*bikini* **il bikini**

*bill* **il conto**

*bird* **l'uccello** (m)

*birthday* **il compleanno**; *happy birthday!* **buon compleanno!**

*biscuit* **il biscotto**

*bite* (by dog) **il morso**; (by insect) **la puntura**; (verb: by dog) **mordere**; (verb: by insect) **pungere**

*bitter* **amaro**

*black* **nero**

*blackcurrant* **il ribes nero**

*blanket* **la coperta**

*bleach* **la varecchina**; (verb: hair) **ossigenare**

*blind* (cannot see) **cieco**; (on window) **la tenda avvolgibile**

*blond* (adj) **biondo/bionda**

*blood* **il sangue**; *blood test* **le analisi del sangue**

*blouse* **la camicetta**

*blue* **azzurro**; (navy blue) **blu**

*boarding pass* **la carta d'imbarco**

*boat* **la nave**; (small) **la barca**; (passenger) **il battello**

*body* **il corpo**

*boil* (verb: of water) **bollire**; (egg etc) **far bollire**

*boiled* **lesso**

*boiler* **la caldaia**

*bolt* (on door) **il catenaccio**; (verb) **chiudere con il catenaccio**

*bone* **l'osso** (m); (fish) **la lisca**

*bonnet* (car) **il cofano**

*book* **il libro**; (verb) **prenotare**

*booking office* **la biglietteria**

*bookshop* **la libreria**

*boot* (footware) **lo stivale**; (of car) **il bagagliaio**

*border* **il confine**

*boring* **noioso**; *that's boring!* **che noia!**

*born* **nato**; *I was born in 1965* **sono nato nel 1965**; *I was born in London* **sono nato a Londra**

*both of them* **tutti e due**; *both ... and ...* **sia ... che ...**

*bottle* **la bottiglia**

*bottle opener* **l'apribottiglie** (m)

*bottom* **il fondo**; *at the bottom (of)* **in fondo (a)**

*bowl* **la scodella, la ciotola**; (mixing bowl) **la terrina**

*box* **la scatola**; (of wood etc) **la cassetta**

*box office* **il botteghino**

*boy* **il ragazzo**

*bra* **il reggiseno**

*bracelet* **il braccialetto**

*brake* **il freno**; (verb) **frenare**

*branch* (of company) **la filiale**

*bread* **il pane**

*breakdown* (car) **il guasto**; (nervous) **l'esaurimento nervoso**

*breakfast* **la colazione**

*breathe* **respirare**

*bridge* **il ponte**

*briefcase* **la cartella**

*bring* **portare**

*British* **britannico**

*brochure* **l'opuscolo** (m)

*broken* **rotto**; *broken leg* **la gamba rotta**

*brooch* **la spilla**

*brother* **il fratello**

*brown* **marrone**

*bruise* **il livido**

*brush* (hair) **la spazzola**; (paint) **il pennello**; (cleaning) **la scopa**; (verb: hair) **spazzolare**

*bucket* **il secchio**

*budget* **il budget**

*builder* **il muratore**

*building* **l'edificio** (m)

*bumper* **il paraurti**

*bunker* (golf) **il bunker**

*burglar* **il ladro**

*burglary* **il furto**

*burn* **la bruciatura**; (verb) **bruciare**

*bus* **l'autobus** (m)

*business* **l'affare** (m); *it's none of your business* **non sono affari tuoi**; *business card* **il biglietto da visita**

*bus station* **la stazione degli autobus**

*bus stop* **la fermata dell'autobus**

*busy* (occupied) **occupato**; (bar etc) **animato**

*but* **ma**

*butcher's* (shop) **la macelleria**

*butter* **il burro**

*button* **il bottone**

*buy* **comprare**

*by*: *by the window* **vicino alla finestra**; *by Friday* **entro venerdì**; *by myself* **da solo**; *written by ...* **scritto da ...**

## C

*cabbage* **il cavolo**

*cable car* **la funivia**

*café* **il caffè, il bar**

*cage* **la gabbia**

*cake* **la torta**

*cake shop* **la pasticceria**

*calculator* **il calcolatore**

*call* **la chiamata**; *what's it called?* **come si chiama?**

*camera* **la macchina fotografica**

*camper van* **il camper**

*campfire* **il falò**

*camping gas* **il gas da campeggio**

*campsite* **il campeggio**

*camshaft* **l'albero a camme** (m)

*can* (vessel) **la lattina**; (verb: to be able) *can I have ...?* **posso avere ...?**; *can you ...?* **potreste ...?**; *he/she can't ...* **non può ...**
Canada **il Canada**
*Canadian* **canadese**
*canal* **il canale**
*candle* **la candela**
*canoe* **la canoa**
*can opener* **l'apriscatole** (m)
*cap* (bottle) **il tappo**; (hat) **il berretto**
*car* **l'auto** (m), **la macchina**
*caravan* **la roulotte**
*carburettor* **il carburatore**
*card* (greetings card) **il biglietto di auguri**; *playing cards* **le carte da gioco**
*careful* **attento**; *be careful!* **stia attento!**
*caretaker* **il portinaio/ la portinaia**
*car park* **il parcheggio**
*carpenter* **il falegname**
*carpet* **il tappeto**
*carrot* **la carota**
*carry out* (verb) **da portare via**
*car seat* (for a baby) **il seggiolino per macchina**
*case* (suitcase) **la valigia**
*cash* **il denaro, gli spicci**; (verb) **riscuotere**; *to pay cash* **pagare in contanti**
*cashier* **il cassiere**
*cash machine* **lo sportello automatico**
*cashpoint* **il bancomat**
*cassette* **la cassetta**
*cassette player* **il mangianastri**
*castle* **il castello**
*cat* **il gatto**
*cathedral* **il duomo, la cattedrale**
*Catholic* **cattolico**
*cauliflower* **il cavolfiore**
*cave* **la grotta**
*ceiling* **il soffitto**
*cellar* **la cantina**
*cemetery* **il cimitero**
*central heating* **il riscaldamento centrale**
*centre* **il centro**; *city centre* **il centro città**
*certificate* **il certificato**
*certainly* **certo**
*chair* **la sedia**; *swivel chair* **la sedia girevole**
*change* (money) **il cambio, gli spicci**; (verb: money,

trains) **cambiare**; (clothes) **cambiarsi**
*charger* **il caricabatterie**
*cheap* **economico, a buon mercato**
*check in* (verb) **fare il check-in**
*check-in* **il check-in**; *check-in desk* **lo sportello del check-in**
*check-out* **la cassa**
*cheers!* (toast) **alla salute!, cin cin!**
*cheese* **il formaggio**
*chemist* **la farmacia**
*cheque* **l'assegno** (m)
*chequebook* **il libretto degli assegni**
*cherry* **la ciliegia**
*chess* **gli scacchi**
*chest* (part of body) **il petto**; (furniture) **il baule**
*chest of drawers* **il cassettone**
*chewing gum* **il chewing-gum**
*chicken* **il pollo**
*child* **il bambino**; (female) **la bambina**
*children* **i bambini**; (own children) **i figli**; *children's ward* **il reparto di pediatria**
*chimney* **il comignolo**
*china* **la porcellana**
*chips* **le patatine fritte**
*chocolate* **la cioccolata**; *box of chocolates* **la scatola di cioccolatini**
*chop* (food) **la costoletta**; (verb) **tagliare (a pezzetti)**
*Christmas* **il Natale**
*church* **la chiesa**
*cigar* **il sigaro**
*cigarette* **la sigaretta**
*cinema* **il cinema**
*circle* (in theatre) **la galleria**
*city* **la città**
*city centre* **il centro città**
*class* **la classe**
*classical music* **la musica classica**
*clean* (adj) **pulito**; (verb) **pulire**
*cleaner* **la donna delle pulizie**
*clear* (obvious) **chiaro**; (water) **limpido**
*clever* **bravo, intelligente**
*client* **il cliente**
*clock* **l'orologio** (m)
*close* (near) **vicino (a)**; (stuffy) **soffocante**; (verb) **chiudere**
*closed* **chiuso**
*clothes* **i vestiti**
*clubs* (cards) **i fiori**

*clutch* **la frizione**
*coach* (long-distance bus) **il pullman**
*coat hanger* **l'attaccapanni** (m)
*coat* **il capotto**
*coffee* **il caffè**
*coin* **la moneta**
*cold* (illness) **il raffreddore**; (adj) **freddo**; *I have a cold* **ho un raffreddore**
*collar* **il colletto**; (for dog) **il collare**
*colleague* **il collega**
*collection* (stamps etc) **la collezione**; (postal) **la levata**
*colour* **il colore**
*colour film* **il rullino a colori**
*comb* **il pettine**; (verb) **pettinare**
*come* **venire**; *I come from ...* **sono di ...**; *come here!* (formal/informal) **vieni/ venga qui!**; *come with me* (formal/informal) **vieni/ venga con me**
*compact disc* **il compact disc**
*compartment* **lo scompartimento**
*complicated* **complicato**
*computer* **il computer**; *computer games* **i videogiochi**
*concert* **il concerto**
*concessionary rate* **la tariffa ridotta**
*conditioner* (hair) **il balsamo**
*condom* **il preservativo**
*conductor* (bus) **il bigliettaio**; (orchestra) **il direttore**
*conference* **la conferenza**; *conference room* **la sala conferenze**
*congratulations!* **congratulazioni!**
*connection* **la coincidenza**
*consulate* **il consolato**
*contact lenses* **le lenti a contatto**
*contraceptive* **il contraccettivo**
*contract* **il contratto**
*cook* **il cuoco/la cuoca**; (verb) **cucinare**
*cooker* **il cucina**
*cool* **fresco**
*cork* **il tappo**
*corkscrew* **il cavatappi**
*corner* **l'angolo** (m)
*corridor* **il corridoio**

cosmetics **i cosmetici**
cost (verb) **costare**; *what does it cost?* **quanto costa?**
cot **il lettino**
cotton **il cotone**
cotton wool **il cotone idrofilo**
cough **la tosse**; (verb) **tossire**
country (state) **il paese**; (not town) **la campagna**
course (educational) **il corso**
cousin **il cugino/la cugina**
crab **il granchio**
cramp **il crampo**
crayfish **il gambero**
crazy **pazzo**
cream (dairy) **la crema, la panna**; (lotion) **la crema**
credit card **la carta di credito**
crew **l'equipaggio** (m)
crisps **le patatine**
croissant **la brioche**
crowded **affollato**
cruise **la crociera**
crutches **le stampelle**
cry (to weep) **piangere**; (to shout) **gridare**
cucumber **il cetriolo**
cuff links **i gemelli**
cup **la tazza**
cupboard **l'armadio** (m)
curlers **i bigodini**
curls **i ricci**
curtain **la tenda**
cushion **il cuscino**
customs **la dogana**
cut **il taglio**; (verb) **tagliare**

## D

dad **il papà, il babbo**
dairy **la latteria**; *dairy products* **i latticini**
damp **umido**
dance **il ballo**; (verb) **ballare**
dangerous **pericoloso**
dark **scuro**
daughter **la figlia**
day **il giorno**
dead **morto**
deaf **sordo**
dear **caro**
debit card **la carta assegni**
December **dicembre**
decorator **l'imbianchino**
deep **profondo**
degree: *I have a degree in ...* **sono laureato in ...**
delayed **in ritardo**
deliberately **deliberatamente**
delicatessen **la salumeria**

delivery **la consegna**
dentist **il/la dentista**
dentures **la dentiera**
deodorant **il deodorante**
department **il reparto**
department store **il grande magazzino**
departure **la partenza**; *departures* **le partenze**; *departure lounge* **la sala d'attesa**
designer **il grafico/la grafica**
desk **la scrivania**
desserts **i dessert**
develop (film) **sviluppare**
diabetic **diabetico**
diamond (jewel) **il diamante**
diamonds (cards) **i quadri**
diarrhoea **la diarrea**
diary **l'agenda** (f)
dictionary **il dizionario**
die **morire**
diesel **il gasolio**
different **diverso**; *that's different!* **è diverso!**; *I'd like a different one* **ne vorrei un altro**
difficult **difficile**
dining room **la sala da pranzo**
dinner **la cena**
directory (telephone) **la guida telefonica**
dirty **sporco**
disabled (people) **i disabili**
discount **la riduzione**
dishtowel **lo strofinaccio**
dishwasher **la lavastoviglie**
dive **il tuffo**; (verb) **tuffarsi**
diving board **il trampolino**
divorced **divorziato**
do **fare**; *how do you do?* **piacere di conoscerla**; *what do you do?* **che lavoro fa?**
dock **il molo**
doctor (academic) **il dottore/la dottoressa**; (medical) **il medico**
document **il documento**
dog **il cane**; *dog basket* **la cuccia**; *dog bowl* **la ciotola del cane**
doll **la bambola**
dollar **il dollaro**
door **la porta**; (of car) **lo sportello**
double room **la matrimoniale, la camera doppia**
doughnut **il krapfen**
down **giù**

drawer **il cassetto**
drawing pin **la puntina da disegno**
dress **il vestito**
drink **la bibita**; (verb) **bere**; *would you like a drink?* **vorresti qualcosa da bere?**
drinking water **l'acqua potabile** (f)
drive (verb) **guidare**
driver **il guidatore/la guidatrice**; (of bus, truck etc) **l'autista** (m/f)
driveway **il viale**
driving licence **la patente (di guida)**
drops **le gocce**
drunk **ubriaco**
dry **asciutto**; (wine) **secco**
dry cleaner's **la lavanderia a secco**
dummy (for baby) **il ciuccio**
during **durante**
dustbin **la pattumiera**
duster **lo straccio per la polvere**
duvet **il piumino**

## E

each (every) **ogni**; *twenty euros each* **venti euro ciascuno**
ear **l'orecchio** (m); *ears* **le orecchie**
early **presto**; *see you soon* **a presto**
earphones **gli auricolari**
earrings **gli orecchini**
east **l'est** (m)
easy **facile**
eat **mangiare**
egg **l'uovo** (m)
eight **otto**
eighteen **diciotto**
eighty **ottanta**
either: *either of them* **l'uno o l'altro**
elastic **elastico**
elbow **il gomito**
electric **elettrico**; *electrical hook-up* **la presa di corrente**
electrician **il/la elettricista**
electricity **l'elettricità** (f)
eleven **undici**
else: *something else* **qualcos'altro**; *someone else* **qualcun'altro**; *somewhere else* **da qualche altra parte**

*e-mail* l'email (f), la posta elettronica
*e-mail address* l'indirizzo di posta elettronica (m)
*embarrassing* imbarazzante
*embassy* l'ambasciata (f)
*emergency* l'emergenza (f)
*emergency exit* l'uscita di sicurezza (f)
*emergency department* il pronto soccorso
*empty* vuoto
*end* la fine
*engaged* (to be married) fidanzato/fidanzata; (telephone, toilet) occupato
*engine* (car) il motore; (train) la locomotiva
*engineering* l'ingegneria
*England* l'Inghilterra (f)
*English* inglese
*enlargement* l'ampliamento (m)
*enough* abbastanza
*entrance* l'entrata (f)
*envelope* la busta
*epileptic* epilettico
*eraser* la gomma
*escalator* la scala mobile
*especially* particolarmente
*estate agent* l'agente immobiliare (m/f)
*estimate* il preventivo
*evening* la sera
*every* ogni; *every day* tutti i giorni
*everyone* ognuno, tutti
*everything* tutto
*everywhere* dappertutto
*example* l'esempio (m); *for example* per esempio
*excellent* ottimo, eccellente
*excess baggage* il bagaglio in eccesso
*exchange* (verb) scambiare
*exchange rate* il (tasso di) cambio
*excursion* l'escursione (f)
*excuse me!* (to get past) permesso!; (to get attention) mi scusi!; (when sneezing etc) scusate!
*executive* il dirigente
*exhaust* (car) la marmitta
*exhibition* la mostra
*exit* l'uscita (f)
*expensive* caro, costoso
*extension lead* la prolunga
*eye* l'occhio (m); *eyes* gli occhi
*eyebrow* il sopracciglio

## F

*face* la faccia
*faint* (unclear) indistinto; (verb) svenire
*fair* (funfair) il luna park; (trade) la fiera (commerciale); *it's not fair* non è giusto
*false teeth* la dentiera
*family* la famiglia
*fan* (ventilator) il ventilatore; (enthusiast) l'ammiratore (m)
*fan belt* la cinghia della ventola
*fantastic* fantastico
*far* lontano; *how far is it to …?* quanto dista da qui …?
*fare* il biglietto, la tariffa
*farm* la fattoria
*farmer* l'agricoltore (m)
*fashion* la moda
*fast* veloce
*fat* il grasso; (adj) grasso
*father* il padre
*February* febbraio
*feel* (touch) tastare; *I feel hot* ho caldo; *I feel like … ho* voglia di …; *I don't feel well* non mi sento bene
*fence* lo steccato
*fennel* il finocchio
*ferry* il traghetto
*fever* la febbre
*fiancé* il fidanzato
*fiancée* la fidanzata
*field* il campo
*fifteen* quindici
*fifty* cinquanta
*figures* le cifre
*filling* (in tooth) l'otturazione (f); (in sandwich, cake etc) il ripieno
*film* (for camera) la pellicola; (at the cinema) il film
*filter* il filtro
*financial consultant* il/la consulente finanziario
*fine!* benissimo!
*finger* il dito
*fire* il fuoco; (blaze) l'incendio (m)
*fire extinguisher* l'estintore (m)
*fireplace* il caminetto
*fireworks* i fuochi d'artificio
*first* primo; *first class* prima classe
*first aid* il pronto soccorso
*first floor* il primo piano

*first name* il nome di battesimo
*fish* il pesce
*fishing* la pesca; *to go fishing* andare a pesca
*fishmonger's* (shop) la pescheria
*five* cinque
*fizzy* frizzante
*fizzy water* l'acqua gassata (f)
*flag* la bandiera
*flash* (camera) il flash
*flat* (level) piatto; (apartment) l'appartamento
*flavour* il gusto
*flea* la pulce
*flight* il volo; *flight number* il numero del volo
*flip-flops* gli infradito
*flippers* le pinne
*floor* (ground) il pavimento; (storey) il piano
*Florence* Firenze
*flour* la farina
*flower* il fiore; *flower bed* l'aiuola (f)
*flute* il flauto
*fly* (insect) la mosca; (verb) volare; *I'm flying to London* vado a Londra in aereo
*flyover* il cavalcavia
*fly sheet* il telo protettivo
*fog* la nebbia
*folk music* la musica folk
*food* il cibo
*food poisoning* l'intossicazione alimentare (f)
*foot* il piede; *on foot* a piedi
*football* (game) il calcio; (ball) il pallone
*for* per; *for me* per me; *what for?* perché?
*forbidden* proibito
*foreigner* lo straniero, il forestiero
*forest* la foresta
*forget* dimenticare
*fork* (for food) la forchetta
*forty* quaranta
*four* quattro
*fourteen* quattordici
*fourth* quarto
*fracture* la frattura
*France* la Francia
*free* (not occupied) libero; (no charge) gratuito, gratis
*freezer* il congelatore
*French* francese
*Friday* venerdì
*fridge* il frigorifero
*fried* fritto

friend l'amico; (female)
l'amica
friendly cordiale
frightened: I'm frightened ho
paura
front: in front of you davanti
a te
frost il gelo
frozen foods i surgelati
fruit la frutta
fruit juice il succo di frutta
fry friggere
frying pan la padella
full pieno; I'm full (up) sono
sazio
full board la pensione
completa
funny divertente; (odd)
strano
furniture i mobili

# G

garage il garage
garden il giardino; garden
centre il vivaio
gardener il giardiniere
garlic l'aglio (m)
gas-permeable lenses le lenti
semi-rigide
gate il cancello; (at airport)
l'uscita (f)
gay (homosexual)
omosessuale, gay
gearbox (car) il cambio
gear stick la leva del
cambio
gel (hair) il gel
Genoa Genova
German tedesco
Germany la Germania
get (obtain) ricevere; (fetch:
person) chiamare;
(something) prendere;
have you got ...? ha ...?; to
get the train prendere il
treno
get back: we get back tomorrow
torniamo domani; to get
something back riavere
indietro qualcosa
get in entrare; (arrive)
arrivare
get off (bus etc) scendere (da)
get on (bus etc) salire (su)
get out uscire (da)
get up alzarsi
gift il regalo
gin il gin
ginger (spice) lo zenzero
girl la ragazza

give dare; give way dare
la precedenza
glad contento
glass (material) il vetro;
(for drinking) il bicchiere
glasses gli occhiali
gloves i guanti
glue la colla
go andare; (depart) partire
gold l'oro (m)
golf il golf
golfer il golfista
good buono; good! bene!
goodbye arrivederci
good day buongiorno
good evening buonasera
good night buonanotte
government il governo
granddaughter la nipote
grandfather il nonno
grandmother la nonna
grandparents i nonni
grandson il nipote
grapes l'uva (f)
grass l'erba (f)
great! benissimo!
Great Britain la Gran
Bretagna
Greece la Grecia
Greek greco
green verde
grey grigio
grill la griglia
grilled alla griglia
grocer's (shop) gli
alimentari
ground floor il pianterreno
ground sheet il telone
impermeabile
guarantee la garanzia; (verb)
garantire
guard la guardia
guest l'ospite (m/f)
guide (person) la guida
guidebook la guida
guitar la chitarra
gun (rifle) il fucile; (pistol)
la pistola
gutter la grondaia
guy rope la corda
gymnastics la palestra

# H

hair i capelli
haircut il taglio
hairdresser's il parrucchiere
hair dryer il fohn
hairspray la lacca per
i capelli
half metà; half an hour

mezz'ora; half board
mezza pensione; half past
... ... e mezza
ham il prosciutto
hamburger l'hamburger (m)
hammer il martello
hamster il criceto
hand brake il freno a mano
hand la mano; hand luggage
il bagaglio a mano
handle (door) la maniglia
handshake la stretta di mano
handsome bello, attraente
hangover i postumi della
sbornia
happy felice, contento
harbour il porto
hard duro; (difficult) difficile
hardware store la ferramenta
hat il cappello
have avere; I don't have ...
non ho ...; do you have ...?
ha ...?; I have to go now
devo andare adesso
he lui
head la testa
headache il mal di testa
headlights i fari
hear udire, sentire
hearing aid l'apparecchio
acustico (m)
heart il cuore
heart condition il disturbi
cardiaci
hearts (cards) i cuori
heater il termosifone
heating il riscaldamento
heavy pesante
hedge la siepe
heel (of foot) il tallone;
(of shoe) il tacco
hello ciao, buongiorno;
(on phone) pronto
help l'aiuto (m); (verb)
aiutare; can I help
you? dica?
her lei, lei, sua, sue, suoi;
it's for her è per lei; her
book il suo libro; her house
la sua casa; her shoes le
sue scarpe; her dresses i
suoi vestiti; it's hers è suo
herbal tea la tisana
here qui
here you are/here it is ecco
hi! Ciao!
high alto
hiking l'escursionismo
hill la collina
him: it's for him è per lui; give
it to him daglielo

his **suo, sua, sue, suoi**; *his book* **il suo libro**; *his house* **la sua casa**; *his shoes* **le sue scarpe**; *his socks* **i suoi calzini**; *it's his* **è suo**
history **la storia**
hitchhike **fare l'autostop**
HIV positive **HIV positivo**
hobby **il passatempo, il hobby**
holiday **la vacanza**; *public holiday* **il giorno festivo**
home: *at home* **a casa**
homeopathy **omeopatia**
honest **onesto**
honey **il miele**
honeymoon **la luna di miele**
horn (car) **il clacson**; (animal) **il corno**
horrible **orribile**
hose **il tubo**
hospital **l'ospedale** (m)
host **il padrone di casa**; *hostess* **la padrona di casa**
hot **caldo**
hour **l'ora** (f); *visiting hours* **l'orario di visita** (f)
house **la casa**
household *products* **gli articoli per la casa**
how? **come?**
how much? **quanto costa?**; *how much is that?* **quant'è?**
hundred **cento**; *three hundred* **trecento**
hungry: *I'm hungry* **ho fame**
hurry **affrettarsi**; *I'm in a hurry* **ho fretta**
hurry up! **sbrigati!**
hurt: *my ... hurts* **mi fa male il/la ...**; *will it hurt?* **farà male?**
husband **il marito**

## I

I **io**
ice **il ghiaccio**
ice cream **il gelato**
ice skates **i pattini da ghiaccio**
identification **il documento d'identità**
if **se**
ignition **l'accensione** (f)
ill **malato**
immediately **immediatamente**
impossible **impossibile**
in: *in English* **in inglese**; *in the hotel* **nell'albergo**; *in Venice* **a Venezia**
included **incluso**

indicator **la freccia, l'indicatore di direzione**
indigestion **l'indigestione** (f)
infection **l'infezione** (f)
information **le informazioni**; *information technology* **l'informatica** (f)
inhaler (for asthma etc) **l'inalatore** (m)
injection **l'iniezione** (m)
injury **la ferita**
ink **l'inchiostro** (m)
in-laws **i suoceri**
inner tube **la camera d'aria**
insect **l'insetto** (m)
insect repellent **l'insettifugo** (m)
insomnia **l'insonnia** (f)
instant *coffee* **il caffè solubile**
insurance **l'assicurazione** (f)
interesting **interessante**
internet **l'internet** (f)
interpret **interpretare**
interpreter **l'interprete** (m/f)
intravenous drip **la flebo**
invitation **l'invito** (m)
invoice **la fattura**
Ireland **l'Irlanda** (f)
Irish **irlandese**
iron (material) **il ferro**; (for clothes) **il ferro da stiro**; (verb) **stirare**
is: *he/she/it is ...* **(lui/lei/esso) è ...**
island **l'isola** (f)
it **esso**
Italian **italiano**
Italy **Italia**
its **suo**

## J

jacket **la giacca**
jam **la marmellata**
January **gennaio**
jazz **il jazz**
jeans **i jeans**
jellyfish **la medusa**
jeweller's (shop) **il gioielliere**
job **il lavoro**
jog (verb) **fare jogging**; *to go jogging* **andare a fare jogging**
jogging **il jogging**
joke **lo scherzo**
journey **il viaggio**
July **luglio**
junction **l'incrocio** (m)
June **giugno**
just (only) **solo**; *it's just arrived* **è appena arrivato**

## K

kettle **il bollitore**
key **la chiave**
keyboard **la tastiera**
kidney **il rene**
kilo **il chilo**
kilometre **il chilometro**
kitchen **la cucina**
knee **il ginocchio**
knife **il coltello**
knit **lavorare a maglia**
knitwear **la maglieria**
know **sapere**; (person) **conoscere**; *I don't know* **non so**

## L

label **l'etichetta** (f)
lace **il pizzo**
laces (of shoe) **i lacci**
lady **la signora**
lake **il lago**
lamb **l'agnello** (m)
lamp **la lampada**
lampshade **il paralume**
land **la terra**; (verb) **atterrare**
language **la lingua**
laptop (computer) **il computer portatile**
large **grande**
last (final) **ultimo**; *last week* **la settimana scorsa**; *at last!* **finalmente!**
last name **il cognome**
late: *it's getting late* **si sta facendo tardi**; *the bus is late* **l'autobus è in ritardo**
later **più tardi**
laugh **ridere**
laundry (place) **la lavanderia**; (dirty clothes) **la biancheria**
law **la legge**
lawn **il prato**; *lawnmower* **il tosaerba**
lawyer **l'avvocato**
laxative **il lassativo**
lazy **pigro**
lead (for dog) **il guinzaglio**
leaf **la foglia**
leaflet **il volantino**
learn **imparare**
leather **la pelle, il cuoio**; *leather goods shop* **la pelletteria**
lecture theatre **l'aula delle lezioni** (f)
left (not right) **sinistra**; *there's nothing left* **non c'è rimasto più nulla**

left luggage locker
  **il desposito bagagli**
leg **la gamba**
lemon **il limone**
lemonade **la limonata**
length **la lunghezza**
lens **la lente**
less **meno**
lesson **la lezione**
letter **la lettera**
lettuce **la lattuga**
library **la biblioteca**
licence **la patente**
life **la vita**
lift **l'ascensore** (m)
light **la luce**; (not heavy)
  **leggero**; (not dark)
  **chiaro**
light bulb **la lampadina**
lighter **l'accendino** (m)
lighter fuel **il gas per
  accendini**
light meter **l'esposimetro**
  (m)
like: I like ... **mi piace ...**;
  it's like ... **assomiglia a ...**;
  like this one **come
  questo**
lime (fruit) **il limoncello**
line (telephone etc) **la linea**;
  outside line **la linea
  esterna**
lipstick **il rossetto**
liqueur **il liquore**
list **l'elenco** (m)
literature **la letteratura**
litre **il litro**
litter (bin) **i rifiuti**
little (small) **piccolo**; it's a little
  big **è un po' grande**; just a
  little **solo un po'**
liver **il fegato**
living room **il soggiorno**
lollipop **il lecca lecca**
long **lungo**; how long does it
  take? **quanto ci vuole?**
long-distance (call)
  **interurbana**
lost: I'm lost **mi sono persa**
lost property **l'ufficio oggetti
  smarriti** (m)
lot: a lot **molto**
loud **forte**
love (verb) **amare**
low **basso**
luck **la fortuna**; good luck!
  **buona fortuna!**
luggage **i bagagli**
luggage rack **la reticella (per
  i bagagli)**
lunch **il pranzo**

# M

madam **signora**
magazine **la rivista**
maid **la cameriera**
main courses **i secondi piatti**
make **fare**
makeup **il trucco**
man **l'uomo**; men **gli uomini**
manager **il direttore/la
  direttrice**
many **molti**; not many **non
  molti**
map **la carta (geografica)**;
  (of town) **la pianta**
marble **il marmo**
March **marzo**
margarine **la margarina**
market **il mercato**
marmalade **la marmellata
  d'arance**
married **sposato**
mascara **il mascara**
mass (church) **la messa**
mast **l'albero** (m)
match (light) **il fiammifero**;
  (sport) **l'incontro** (m)
material (cloth) **la stoffa**
matter: it doesn't matter **non
  importa**; what's the matter
  **cosa c'è?**
mattress **il materasso**
May **maggio**
maybe **forse**
me: it's me **sono io**; it's for me
  **è per me**
meal **il pasto**
mean: what does this mean?
  **che cosa significa?**
meat **la carne**
mechanic **il meccanico**
medicine **la medicina**
Mediterranean **il Mediterraneo**
meeting **la riunione,
  l'incontro** (m)
melon **il melone**
menu **il menù**
message **il messaggio**
microwave **il forno a
  microonde**
middle: in the middle of the
  square **in mezzo alla
  piazza**; in the middle of the
  night **nel cuore della notte**
midnight **mezzanotte**
Milan **Milano**
milk **il latte**
million **milione**
mine: it's mine **è mio**
mineral water **l'acqua
  minerale** (f)

minute **il minuto**
mirror **lo specchio**
Miss **Signorina**
mistake **l'errore** (m)
mobile phone **il cellulare,
  il telefonino**
modem **il modem**
Monday **lunedì**
money **i soldi**
monitor (computer)
  **il monitor**
month **il mese**
monument **il monumento**
moon **la luna**
moped **il motorino**
more **più**; more than ...
  **più di ...**
morning **la mattina**; in the
  morning **di mattina**
mosaic **il mosaico**
mosquito **la zanzara**
mother **la madre**
motorboat **il motoscafo**
motorcycle **la motocicletta**
motorway **l'autostrada** (f)
mountain **la montagna**
mountain bike **il mountain
  bike**
mouse (animal) **il topo**;
  (computer) **il mouse**
mousse (for hair) **la
  schiuma**
moustache **i baffi**
mouth **la bocca**
move **muovere**; don't move!
  **non muoverti!**
move house **traslocare**
Mr **Signor**
Mrs **Signora**
much **molto**; much better
  **molto meglio**; much slower
  **molto più lentamente**;
  not much **non molto**
mug **il tazzone**
mum **mamma**
museum **il museo**
mushroom **il fungo**
music **la musica**
musical instrument **lo
  strumento musicale**
musician **il musicista**
music system **lo stereo**
mussels **le cozze**
must (to have to) **devore**;
  I must **devo**
mustard **la senape**
my **mio, mia, mie, miei**; my
  book **il mio libro**; my bag
  **la mia borsa**; my keys
  **le mie chiavi**; my dresses
  **i miei vestiti**

# N

nail (metal) **il chiodo**; (finger) **l'unghia** (f)
nail clippers **il tagliaunghie**
nailfile **la limetta per le unghie**
nail polish **lo smalto per le unghie**
name **il nome**; what's your name? **come si chiama/ti chiami?** (formal/informal); my name's ... **mi chiamo...**
napkin **il tovagliolo**
Naples **Napoli**
nappies **i pannolini**
narrow **stretto**
near **vicino**; near to ... **vicino a ...**
necessary **necessario, obbligatorio**
neck **il collo**
necklace **la collana**
need **avere bisogno**; I need ... **ho bisogno di ...**; there's no need **non c'è bisogno**
needle **l'ago** (m)
negative (photo) **la negativa**; (adj) **negativo**
nephew **il nipote**
never **mai**
new **nuovo**
news **le notizie**; (on radio) **il notiziario**
newsagent's (shop) **il giornalaio**
newspaper **il giornale**
New Zealand **la Nuova Zelanda**
New Zealander **neozelandese**
next **prossimo**; next week **la settimana prossima**; what next? **e poi?**; who's next? **a chi tocca?**
nice (attractive) **carino, bello**; (pleasant) **simpatico**; (to eat) **buono**
niece **la nipote**
night **la notte**
nightclub **il night**
nightdress **la camicia da notte**
nine **nove**
nineteen **diciannove**
ninety **novanta**
no (negative response) **no**; I have no money **non ho soldi**
nobody **nessuno**
no entry **divieto di accesso**
noisy **rumoroso**
noon **il mezzogiorno**

north **il nord**
Northern Ireland **l'Irlanda del Nord**
nose **il naso**
not **non**; he's not ... **non è ...**
notebook **il quaderno**
notepad **il bloc-notes**
nothing **niente**
novel **il romanzo**
November **novembre**
now **ora, adesso**
nowhere **da nessuna parte**
number **il numero**
number plate **la targa**
nurse **il infermiere/la infermiera**
nut **la noce, la nocciola**; (for bolt) **il dado**

# O

oars **i remi**
occasionally **ogni tanto**
occupied **occupato**
o'clock: one o'clock **l'una**; two o'clock **le due**
October **ottobre**
octopus **la piovra, il polipo**
of **di**
office **l'ufficio** (m), **la direzione**; office worker **l'impiegato/a**; head office **la sede centrale**
often **spesso**
oil **l'olio** (m)
ointment **la pomata, l'unguento** (m)
OK **OK**
old **vecchio**; how old are you? **quanti anni hai?**
olive **l'oliva** (f)
olive oil **l'olio d'oliva** (m)
omelette **l'omelette** (f)
on **su**; a book on Venice **un libro su Venezia**; on Monday **di lunedì**
one **uno**
one way **senso unico**
onion **la cipolla**
only **solo**
open (adj) **aperto**; (verb) **aprire**
opera **l'opera** (f)
operating theatre **la sala operatoria**
operation **l'operazione** (f)
operator **l'operatore/ l'operatrice** (m/f)
opposite **davanti a**
optician **l'ottico** (m)
or **o**

orange (fruit) **l'arancia** (f); (colour) **arancione**
orange juice **il succo d'arancia**
orchestra **l'orchestra** (f)
order (for goods) **l'ordinativo** (m), **l'ordine** (m)
ordinary **normale**
organ (music) **l'organo** (m)
other: the other (one) **l'altro**
our: our hotel **il nostro albergo**; our car **la nostra macchina**; it's ours **è nostro**
out: he's out **è uscito**
outside **fuori**
oven **il forno**
over (above) **su, sopra**; over 100 **più di cento**; over the river **al di là del fiume**; it's over (finished) **è finito**; over there **laggiù**

# P

pack (of cards) **il mazzo di carte**
package, packet **il pacchetto**
padlock **il lucchetto**
Padua **Padova**
page **la pagina**
pain **il dolore**
paint **la vernice**
painting **la pittura**
pair **il paio**
palace **il palazzo**
pale **pallido**
paper **la carta**; (newspaper) **il giornale**
paraffin **la paraffina**
parcel **il pacco**
pardon? **prego?**
parents **i genitori**
park **il parco**; (verb) **parcheggiare**; no parking **sosta vietata**
parking lights **le luci di posizione**
parsley **il prezzemolo**
parting (hair) **la riga**
party (celebration) **la festa**; (group) **il gruppo**; (political) **il partito**
pass (driving) **sorpassare**
passenger **il passeggero**; (female) **la passeggera**
passport **il passaporto**; passport control **il controllo passaporti**
password **la password**
pasta **la pasta**
path **il vialetto, il sentiero**
pavement **il marciapiede**

pay **pagare**
payment **il pagamento**
peach **la pesca**
peanuts **le arachidi**
pear **la pera**
pearl **la perla**
peas **i piselli**
pedestrian **il pedone**
pedestrian zone **la zona pedonale**
peg (clothes) **la molletta**; (tent) **il picchetto**
pen **la penna**
pencil **la matita**
pencil sharpener **il temperamatite**
pen friend **il/la corrispondente**
penicillin **la penicillina**
penknife **il temperino**
people **la gente**
pepper (spice)**il pepe**; (vegetable) **il peperone**
peppermint **la menta piperita**
per: per person **a persona**; per annum **all'anno**
perfect **perfetto**
perfume **il profumo**
perhaps **magari, forse**
perm **la permanente**
petrol **la benzina**
petrol station **il benzinaio, la stazione di servizio**
phonecard **la scheda telefonica**
photocopier **la fotocopiatrice**
photograph **la fotografia**; (verb) **fotografare**
photographer **il fotografo**
phrase book **il vocabolarietto**
pickpocket **il borsaiolo**
picnic **il picnic**
piece **il pezzo**
pillow **il guanciale**
PIN **il pin, il codice segreto**
pin **lo spillo**
pineapple **l'ananas** (m)
pink **rosa**
pipe (for smoking) **la pipa**; (for water) **il tubo**
piston **il pistone**
pitch (in campsite, etc) **la piazzola**
place **il posto**; at your place **a casa tua**
plans **le piante**
plant **la pianta**
plaster (sticking) **il cerotto**
plastic **la plastica**
plastic bag **il sacchetto di plastica**

plate **il piatto**
platform **il binario**
play (theatre) **la commedia**; (verb) **giocare**
please **per favore**
pleased to meet you **piacere**
plug (electrical) **la spina**; (sink) **il tappo**
plumber **l'idraulico**
pocket **la tasca**
poison **il veleno**
police **la polizia**
police officer **il poliziotto**
police report **il rapporto di polizia**
police station **la stazione di polizia**
politics **la politica**
poor **povero**
poor quality **di cattiva qualità**
pop music **la musica pop**
Pope **il Papa**
pork **la carne di maiale**
port **il porto**
porter (hotel) **il portiere**
possible **possibile**
post **la posta**; (verb) **spedire per posta**
post box **la cassetta delle lettere**
postcard **la cartolina**
postman **il postino**
post office **l'ufficio postale** (m)
potato **la patata**
poultry **il pollame**
pound (weight) **la libbra**; (currency) **la sterlina**
pram **la carrozzina**
prefer **preferire**
pregnant **incinta**
prescription **la ricetta**
presentation **la conferenza**
pretty (beautiful) **grazioso, carino**; (quite) **piuttosto**
price **il prezzo**
priest **il prete**
printer **la stampante**
private **privato**
problem **il problema**; no problem **non c'è problema**
profits **i profitti**
public **pubblico**
pull **tirare**
puncture **la foratura**
purple **viola**
purse **il borsellino**
push **spingere**
pushchair **il passegino**
put **mettere**
pyjamas **il pigiama**

## Q

quality **la qualità**
quarter **il quarto**; quarter past ... ... **e un quarto**
question **la domanda**
queue **la fila**; (verb) **fare la fila**
quick **veloce**
quiet **tranquillo**
quite (fairly) **abbastanza**; (fully) **molto**

## R

rabbit **il coniglio** (m)
radiator **il radiatore**
radio **la radio**
radish **il ravanello**
railway **la ferrovia**
rain **la pioggia**
raincoat **l'impermeabile** (m)
raisins **l'uvetta** (f)
rake **il rastrello**
rare (uncommon) **raro**; (meat) **al sangue**
rash **il arrossamento**
raspberry **il lampone**
rat **il ratto**
razor blades **le lamette**
read **leggere**
reading lamp **la lampada da studio**
ready **pronto**; ready meals **i piatti pronti**
rear lights **i fari posteriori**
receipt (restaurants, hotels) **la ricevuta**; (shops, bars) **lo scontrino**
reception (party) **il rinfresco**; (hotel) **la reception**
receptionist **il/la receptionist**
record (music) **il disco**; (sports etc) **il record**
record shop **il negozio di dischi**
red **rosso**
refreshments **i rinfreschi**
registered (post) **raccomandata**
relax **rilassarsi**
relief: what a relief! **che sollievo!**
religion **la religione**
remember **ricordare**; I don't remember **non ricordo**
rent (verb) **affittare, noleggiare**
repair **riparare**
report **la relazione**
research **la ricerca**
reservation **la prenotazione**
rest (noun: remainder) **il resto**; (verb: to relax) **riposarsi**

restaurant il ristorante

return ritornare; (give back) restituire

return ticket il biglietto di andata e ritorno

rice il riso

rich ricco

right (correct) giusto, esatto; (not left) destro

ring (jewellery) l'anello (m)

ripe maturo

river il fiume

road la strada

roasted arrosto

rock (stone) la roccia; (music) il rock

roll (bread) il panino

Rome Roma

roof il tetto

room la stanza, la camera; (space) lo spazio; room service il servizio in camera

rope la corda

rose la rosa

round (circular) rotondo

roundabout la rotatoria

row remare

rubber band l'elastico (m)

rubbish le immondizie, la spazzatura

rubbish bag il sacchetto per la pattumiera

ruby (gem) il rubino

rug (mat) il tappeto

rugby il rugby

ruins le rovine, i resti

ruler (for drawing) la riga

rum il rum

run (verb) correre

## S

sad triste

safe (not dangerous) sicuro

safety pin la spilla di sicurezza

sailing la vela

salad l'insalata (f)

salami il salame

sale (at reduced prices) i saldi

sales (of goods etc) le vendite

salmon il salmone

salt il sale

same: the same dress lo stesso vestito; same again, please un altro, per favore

sand la sabbia

sandals i sandali

sand dunes le dune

sandwich il panino

sanitary towels gli assorbenti (igienici)

Sardinia la Sardegna

Saturday sabato

sauce la salsa

saucepan la pentola

saucer il piattino

sauna la sauna

sausage la salsiccia

say dire; what did you say? che cosa ha detto?; how do you say ...? come si dice ...?

scarf la sciarpa; (head) il foulard

school la scuola

science la scienza

scissors le forbici

Scotland la Scozia

Scotsman lo scozzese

Scotswoman la scozzese

Scottish scozzese

screen lo schermo

screw la vite

screwdriver il cacciavite

sea il mare

seafood i frutti di mare

seat il posto

seat belt la cintura di sicurezza

second secondo; second class seconda classe

secretary il segretario/la segretaria

see vedere; I can't see non vedo; I see (understand) capisco, vedo

self-employed libero professionista

sell vendere

seminar il seminario

send mandare

separate (adj) separato

separated (couple) separati

September settembre

serious serio; (illness) grave

seven sette

seventeen diciassette

seventy settanta

several diversi

sew cucire

shampoo lo shampoo

shave (verb) radersi

shaving cream la schiuma da barba

shawl lo scialle

she lei

sheers le cesoie

sheet il lenzuolo

shell la conchiglia

shellfish (crabs etc) i crostacei; (molluscs) i molluschi

sherry lo sherry

ship la nave

shirt la camicia

shoelaces i lacci per le scarpe

shoe polish il lucido per le scarpe

shoe repairer il calzolaio

shoes le scarpe

shop il negozio

shopkeeper il/la commerciante

shopping lo shopping, la spesa; to go shopping andare a fare acquisti; (for food) andare a fare la spesa

short basso, corto

shorts gli short

shoulder la spalla

shower la doccia; (rain) l'acquazzone (m)

shower gel la docciaschiuma (f)

shutter (camera) l'otturatore (m); (window) l'imposta (f), le persiane

Sicily la Sicilia

side (edge) il lato

sign (in station etc) il cartello; (road, etc) l'insegna (f)

sign (verb) firmare

silk la seta

silver (colour) d'argento; (metal) l'argento (m)

simple semplice

sing cantare

single (one) solo; (unmarried: man) celibe; (woman) nubile

single room la camera singola

single ticket il biglietto di sola andata

sink il lavabo, il lavandino; (kitchen) il lavello

sir signore

sister la sorella

six sei

sixteen sedici

sixty sessanta

size (clothes) la taglia; (shoe) il numero

skid slittare

skiing: to go skiing andare a sciare

skin cleanser il latte detergente

ski resort la località sciistica

skirt la gonna

skis gli sci

sky il cielo

*sleep* **il sonno**; (verb) **dormire**

*sleeping bag* **il sacco a pelo**

*sleeping car* **il vagone letto**

*sleeping pill* **il sonnifero**

*sleeve* **la manica**

*slippers* **le pantofole**

*slow* **lento**

*small* **piccolo**

*smell* **l'odore** (m); (verb: to stink) **puzzare**

*smile* **il sorriso**; (verb) **sorridere**

*smoke* **il fumo**; (verb) **fumare**

*smoking* (section) **fumatori**; *non-smoking* **non fumatori**

*snack* **lo spuntino**

*snorkel* **il boccaglio**

*snow* **la neve**

*so* **così**; *so good* **così bene**; *not so much* **non così tanto**

*soaking solution* (for contact lenses) **il liquido per lenti**

*soap* **il sapone**

*socks* **i calzini**

*soda water* **l'acqua di seltz** (f)

*sofa* **il divano**

*soft* **morbido**

*soil* **la terra**

*somebody* **qualcuno**

*somehow* **in qualche modo**

*something* **qualcosa**

*sometimes* **qualche volta**

*somewhere* **da qualche parte**

*son* **il figlio**

*song* **la canzone**

*sorry!* **scusi!**; *I'm sorry* **mi dispiace, spiacente**; *sorry?* (pardon) **come?, scusi?**

*soup* **la minestra, la zuppa**

*south* **il sud**

*souvenir* **il souvenir**

*spade* (shovel) **la vanga**

*spades* (cards) **le picche**

*Spain* **la Spagna**

*Spanish* **spagnolo**

*spare parts* (car) **i pezzi di ricambio**

*spark plug* **la candela**

*speak* **parlare**; *do you speak ...?* **parla ...?**; *I don't speak ...* **non parlo ...**

*speed* **la velocità**

*SPF* (sun protection factor) **il fattore di protezione**

*spider* **il ragno**

*spinach* **gli spinaci**

*spoon* **il cucchiaio**

*sport* **lo sport**

*spring* (mechanical) **la molla**; (season) **la primavera**

*square* (noun: in town) **la piazza**; (adj: shape) **quadrato**

*staircase* **la scala**

*stairs* **le scale**

*stalls* (in theatre) **la platea**

*stamp* **il francobollo**

*stapler* **la cucitrice, la spillatrice**

*star* **la stella**; (film) **la star**

*start* **l'inizio** (m); (verb) **cominciare**

*starters* **i primi piatti**

*statement* (to police) **la denuncia**

*station* **la stazione**

*statue* **la statua**

*steal* **rubare**; *it's been stolen* **è stato rubato**

*steamed* **a vapore**

*steamer* (boat) **la nave a vapore**; (for cooking) **la pentola a pressione**

*still water* **l'acqua naturale** (f)

*stockings* **le calze**

*stomach* **lo stomaco**

*stomachache* **il mal di pancia**

*stop* (noun: bus) **la fermata dell'autobus**; (verb) **fermare**; *stop!* **alt!, fermo!**

*storm* **la tempesta**

*straight on* **sempre dritto**

*strawberry* **la fragola**

*stream* **il ruscello**

*street* **la strada**

*string* (cord) **lo spago**; (guitar etc) **la corda**

*strong* **forte**

*student* **lo studente/la studentessa** (m/f)

*stupid* **stupido**

*suburbs* **la periferia**

*sugar* **lo zucchero**

*suit* **il completo**; *it suits you* **ti sta bene**

*suitcase* **la valigia**

*summer* **l'estate** (f)

*sun* **il sole**

*sunbathe* **prendere il sole**

*sunburn* **l'eritema solare** (m)

*Sunday* **domenica**

*sunglasses* **gli occhiali da sole**

*sunny: it's sunny* **c'è il sole**

*sunshade* **l'ombrellone** (m)

*suntan: to get a suntan* **abbronzarsi**

*suntan lotion* **la lozione solare**

*suntanned* **abbronzato**

*supermarket* **il supermercato**

*supper* **la cena**

*supplement* **il supplemento**

*suppository* **la supposta**

*sure* **sicuro**; *are you sure?* **sei sicuro?**

*sweat* **il sudore**; (verb) **sudare**

*sweater* **il maglione**

*sweatshirt* **la felpa**

*sweet* **la caramella**; (not sour) **dolce**

*swim* (verb) **nuotare**

*swimming* **il nuoto**

*swimming pool* **la piscina**

*swimming trunks* **il costume da bagno (per uomo)**

*Swiss* **lo svizzerola/la svizzera**; (adj) **svizzero**

*switch* **l'interruttore** (m)

*Switzerland* **la Svizzera**

*synagogue* **la sinagoga**

*syrup* **lo sciroppo**

**T**

*table* **il tavolo**; *bedside table* **il comodino**

*tablet* **la compressa**

*take* **prendere**

*takeoff* **il decollo**

*talcum powder* **il talco**

*talk* **la conversazione**; (verb) **parlare**

*tall* **alto**

*tampons* **i tamponi**

*tangerine* **il mandarino**

*tap* **il rubinetto**

*tapestry* **l'arazzo** (m)

*taxi* **il taxi**

*taxi rank* **il posteggio dei taxi**

*tea* **il tè**; *tea with milk* **il tè con latte**

*teach* **insegnare**

*teacher* **l'insegnante**

*technician* **il tecnico**

*telephone* **il telefono**; (verb) **telefonare**

*telephone booth* **la cabina telefonica**

*telephone call* **la telefonata**

*telephone number* **il numero di telefono**

*television* **la televisione**

*temperature* **la temperatura**; (fever) **la febbre**

*ten* **dieci**

*tennis* **il tennis**

*tent* **la tenda**

*tent pole* **il palo della tenda**

*terminal* (airport) **il terminale**

*terrace* **il patio**

*test* **il controllo**

*than* **di**

thank (verb) ringraziare; thank you/thanks grazie

that: that one quello; that country quel paese; that man quell'uomo; that woman quella donna; what's that? cos'è quello?; I think that ... penso che ...; that'll be all basta così

the il/lo (m); la (f); i/gli (m pl); le (f pl)

theatre il teatro

their: their room la loro stanza; their friend il loro amico; their books i loro libri; their pens le loro penne; it's theirs è per loro

them: it's for them è per loro; give it to them dallo a loro

then poi, allora

there là; there is/are ... c'è/ci sono ...; is/are there ...? c'è/ci sono ...?

these: these things queste cose; these boys questi ragazzi

they loro

thick spesso

thief il ladro

thin magro

think pensare; I think so penso di sì; I'll think about it ci penserò

third terzo

thirsty: I'm thirsty ho sete

thirteen tredici

thirty trenta

this: this one questo; this picture questo quadro; this man quest'uomo; this woman questa donna; what's this? cos'è questo?; this is Mr ... (questo è) il signor ...

those: those things quelle cose; those boys quei ragazzi

thousand mille

three tre

throat la gola

throat pastilles le pasticche per la gola

through attraverso

thunderstorm il temporale

Thursday giovedì

Tiber il Tevere

ticket il biglietto

ticket office la biglietteria

tide la marea

tie la cravatta; (verb) legare

tight (clothes) stretto

tights (sheer) i collant; (wool) la calzamaglia

tile la piastrella

time il tempo; what's the time? che ore sono?; opening times l'orario di apertura (m); leisure time il tempo libero

timetable l'orario (m)

tin la scatola

tip (money) la mancia; (end) la punta

tired stanco

tissues i fazzolettini di carta

to: to England in Inghilterra; to the station alla stazione; to the doctor dal dottore; to the centre in centro

toast il pane tostato

tobacco il tabacco

tobacconist's (shop) il tabaccaio

today oggi

together insieme

toilet il bagno, la toilette

toilet paper la carta igienica

tomato il pomodoro

tomato juice il succo di pomodoro

tomorrow domani; see you tomorrow a domani

tongue la lingua

tonic l'acqua tonica (f)

tonight stasera

too (also) anche; (excessively) troppo

tooth il dente

toothache il mal di denti

toothbrush lo spazzolino da denti

toothpaste il dentifricio

torch la torcia (elettrica)

tour il giro; guided tour la visita guidata

tourist il/la turista

tourist information l'azienda turistica (f); (office) l'ufficio turistico (m)

towel l'asciugamano (m)

tower la torre; Leaning Tower of Pisa la Torre di Pisa

town la città

town hall il municipio

toy il giocattolo

toy shop il negozio di giocattoli

track suit la tuta da ginnastica

tractor il trattore

tradition la tradizione

traffic il traffico

traffic jam l'ingorgo (m)

traffic lights il semaforo

trailer il rimorchio, la roulotte

train il treno

trainers le scarpe da ginnastica

translate tradurre

translator il traduttore/ la traduttrice

travel viaggiare

travel agent l'agenzia di viaggio (f)

tray il vassoio

tree l'albero (m)

trolley il carrello

trousers i pantaloni

truck il camion

true vero

try provare

Tuesday martedì

tunnel il tunnel

Turin Torino

turn: turn left/right giri a sinistra/destra

Tuscany la Toscana

tweezers le pinzette

twelve dodici

twenty venti

twin room la camera a due letti

two due

typewriter la macchina da scrivere

tyre la gomma; flat tyre la gomma a terra

# U

ugly brutto

umbrella l'ombrello (m)

uncle lo zio

under ... sotto ...

underground la metro(politana)

underpants le mutande

underskirt la sottoveste

understand capire; I don't understand non capisco

underwear la biancheria intima

university l'università (f)

university lecturer il professore universitario/ la professoressa universitaria

unleaded senza piombo

until fino a

unusual insolito

up su; (upward) verso l'alto; up there lassù

urgent urgente

us noi; it's for us è per noi

use l'uso (m); (verb) usare; it's no use non serve a niente

*useful* **utile**
*usual* **solito**
*usually* **di solito**

# V

*vacancy* (room) **la stanza libera**
*vacation* **la vacanza**
*vaccination* **la vaccinazione**
*valley* **la valle**
*valuables* **gli oggetti di valore**
*valve* **la valvola**
*vanilla* **la vaniglia**
*vase* **il vaso**
*Vatican* **il Vaticano**; *Vatican City* **la Città del Vaticano**
*VCR* **il videoregistratore**
*veal* **la carne di vitello**
*vegetables* **la verdura**
*vegetarian* **vegetariano**
*vehicle* **il veicolo**
*Venice* **Venezia**
*very* **molto**; *very much* **moltissimo**
*vest* **la canottiera**
*vet* **il veterinario**
*video* (tape/film) **il video cassetta**; *video games* **i videogiochi**
*view* **la vista**
*viewfinder* **il mirino**
*villa* **la villa**
*village* **il paese, il villaggio**
*violin* **il violino**
*visit* **la visita**; (verb) **andare a trovare**
*visitor* (guest) **l'ospite**
*vitamin pill* **la compressa di vitamine**
*vodka* **la vodka**
*voice* **la voce**; *voicemail* **la segreteria telefonica**

# W

*wait* **aspettare**; *wait!* **aspetta!**
*waiter* **il cameriere**
*waiting room* **la sala d'aspetto**
*waitress* **la cameriera**
*Wales* **il Galles**
*walk* **la passeggiata**; (verb) **camminare**; *to go for a walk* **andare a fare una passeggiata**
*wall* **il muro**
*wallet* **il portafoglio**
*want* **volere**; *I want* (io) **voglio**
*war* **la guerra**

*wardrobe* **il guardaroba, l'armadio** (m)
*warm* **caldo**
*was: I was* (io) **ero**; *he/she/it was* (lui/lei/esso) **era**
*wash* (verb) **lavare**
*washbasin* **il lavandino**
*washing machine* **la lavatrice**
*washing powder* **il detersivo (per bucato)**
*washing-up liquid* **il detersivo per i piatti**
*wasp* **la vespa**
*watch* **l'orologio** (m); (verb) **guardare**
*water* **l'acqua** (f)
*water heater* **lo scaldabagno**
*waterfall* **la cascata**
*wave* **l'onda** (f); (verb: with hand) **salutare**
*wavy: wavy hair* **i capelli ondulati**
*we* **noi**
*weather* **il tempo**
*web site* **il sito internet**
*wedding* **il matrimonio**
*Wednesday* **mercoledì**
*weed* **l'erbaccia** (f)
*week* **la settimana**
*welcome* **benvenuto**; *you're welcome* **di niente, prego**
*well done* (food) **ben cotta**
*Wellington boots* **gli stivali do gomma**
*Welsh* **gallese**
*Welshman* **il gallese**
*Welshwoman* **la gallese**
*were: you were* (Lei) **era**; (singular, familiar) (tu) **eri**; (plural) (voi) **eravate**; *we were* (noi) **eravamo**; *they were* (loro) **erano**
*west* **l'ovest** (m)
*wet* **bagnato**
*what?* **cosa?**
*wheel* **la ruota**; *wheel brace* **il girabacchino**
*wheelchair* **la sedia a rotelle**
*when?* **quando?**
*where?* **dove?**; *where are you from?* **di dov'è?/di dove sei?** (formal/informal)
*whether* **se**
*which?* **quale?**
*white* **bianco**
*who?* **chi?**
*why?* **perchè?**
*wide* **ampio**
*wife* **la moglie**
*wind* **il vento**
*window* **la finestra**

*windscreen* **il parabrezza**
*wine* **il vino**; *wine list* **la lista dei vini**; *wine shop* **l'enoteca** (f)
*wing* **l'ala** (f)
*winter* **l'inverno** (m)
*with* **con**
*withdraw* (money) **prelevare**
*without* **senza**
*witness* **il/la testimone**
*woman* **la donna**
*wood* (material) **il legno**
*wool* **la lana**
*word* **la parola**
*work* **il lavoro**; (verb) **lavorare**; (machine) **funzionare**
*worktop* **il piano di lavoro**
*worry: don't worry* **non si preoccupi**
*worse* **peggiore**
*worst* **il peggiore**
*wrapping paper* **la carta da imballaggio**; (for presents) **la carta da regalo**
*wrench* **la chiave fissa**
*wrist* **il polso**
*writing paper* **la carta da scrivere**
*wrong* **sbagliato**

# X, Y, Z

*x-ray* **la radiografia**
*year* **l'anno** (m)
*yellow* **giallo**
*yes* **sì**
*yesterday* **ieri**
*yet* **ancora**; *not yet* **non ancora**
*yoghurt* **lo yogurt**
*you:* (singular, formal) **Lei**; (singular, informal) **tu**; (plural) **voi**
*young* **giovane**
*your:* (singular, formal) *your book* **il suo libro**; *your shirt* **la sua camicia**; *your shoes* **le sue scarpe**; (singular, informal) *your book* **il tuo libro**; *your shirt* **la tua camicia**; *your shoes* **le tue scarpe**
*yours: is this yours?* (singular, formal) **è suo?**; (singular, informal) **è tuo?**
*youth hostel* **l'ostello della gioventù** (m)
*zip* **la chiusura lampo**
*zoo* **lo zoo**

# DICTIONARY
## Italian to English

The gender of Italian nouns listed here is indicated by the abbreviations (m) and (f), for masculine and feminine. Plural nouns are followed by the abbreviations (m pl) or (f pl). Italian adjectives (adj) vary according to the gender and number of the word they describe, and the masculine form is shown here. In general, adjectives that end in **-o** adopt an **-a** ending in the feminine form, and those that end in **-e** usually stay the same. Plural endings are **-i** for masculine and **-e** for feminine.

## A

**a** *in, at, per;* **a casa** *at home;* **a Venezia** *in Venice;* **all'ufficio postale** *at the post office;* **alla stazione** *to the station;* **alle tre** *at 3 o'clock;* **a persona** *per person;* **all'anno** *per annum*
**abbastanza** *enough, quite (fairly)*
**abbronzarsi** *to get a suntan*
**abbronzato** *suntanned*
**acceleratore** (m) *accelerator*
**accendino** (m) *lighter*
**accensione** (f) *ignition*
**acqua** (f) *water;* **l'acqua di seltz** *soda water;* **l'acqua gassata** *fizzy water;* **l'acqua minerale** *mineral water;* **l'acqua naturale** *still water;* **l'acqua potabile** *drinking water;* **l'acqua tonica** *tonic water*
**acquazzone** (m) *shower (rain)*
**adesso** *now*
**aereo** (m) *aircraft*
**aeroporto** (m) *airport*
**affare** (m) *business, bargain;* **non sono affari tuoi** *it's none of your business*
**affittare** *to rent*
**affollato** *crowded*
**agenda** (f) *diary*
**agente immobiliare** (m/f) *estate agent*
**agenzia di viaggio** (f) *travel agent*
**aglio** (m) *garlic*
**agnello** (m) *lamb*
**ago** (m) *needle*
**agosto** *August*
**agricoltore** (m) *farmer*
**Aids** *AIDS*
**aiuola** (f) *flowerbed*
**aiutare** *to help*
**aiuto** (m) *help*

**ala** (f) *wing*
**albero** (m) *tree, mast;* **l'albero a camme** *camshaft*
**albicocca** (f) *apricot*
**alcol** (m) *alcohol*
**alimentari** (m pl) *grocer's*
**alla salute!** *cheers! (toast)*
**allergico** *allergic*
**alloggio** (m) *accommodation*
**allora** *then*
**le Alpi** *the Alps*
**al sangue** *rare (steak)*
**alt!** *stop!*
**alto** *high, tall*
**altro** *other;* **l'altro** *the other (one);* **un altro, un'altra** *another;* **l'uno o l'altro** *either of them;* **un altro, per favore** *same again, please;* **qualcos'altro** *something else;* **qualcun'altro** *someone else;* **da qualche altra parte** *somewhere else*
**alzarsi** *get up*
**amare** *to love*
**amaro** *bitter*
**ambasciata** (f) *embassy*
**ambulanza** (f) *ambulance*
**America** (f) *America*
**americano** *American*
**amico/amica** (m/f) *friend*
**ammiratore** (m) *fan (enthusiast)*
**ampio** *wide*
**ampliamento** (m) *enlargement*
**ananas** (m) *pineapple*
**anche** *too (also)*
**ancora** *yet;* **non ancora** *not yet*
**andare** *to go;* **andare a trovare** *to visit*
**anello** (m) *ring (jewellery)*
**angolo** (m) *corner*
**animato** *busy (bar)*
**anniversario** (m) *anniversary*
**anno** (m) *year*

**anticipo** (m) *advance (on payment etc);* **anticipato** *in advance*
**antiquario** (m) *antique shop*
**antisettico** (m) *antiseptic*
**aperitivo** (m) *aperitif*
**aperto** *open (adj)*
**apparecchio acustico** (m) *hearing aid*
**appartamento** (m) *apartment*
**appetito** (m) *appetite*
**appuntamento** (m) *appointment*
**apribottiglie** (m) *bottle opener*
**aprile** *April*
**aprire** *to open*
**apriscatole** (m) *can opener*
**arachidi** (m pl) *peanuts*
**arancia** (f) *orange (fruit)*
**arancione** *orange (colour)*
**arazzo** (m) *tapestry*
**architettura** (f) *architecture*
**argento** (m) *silver (colour);* **d'argento** *silver (metal)*
**aria** (f) *air*
**aria condizionata** (f) *air conditioning*
**armadio** (m) *cupboard, wardrobe*
**arrivare** *to arrive*
**arrivederci** *goodbye*
**arrivi** *arrivals*
**arrossamento** (m) *rash*
**arrosto** *roasted*
**arte** (f) *art*
**articoli per la casa** (m pl) *household products*
**artista** (m/f) *artist*
**ascensore** (m) *lift*
**asciugamano** (m) *towel*
**asciutto** *dry*
**asmatico** *asthmatic*
**asparagi** (m) *asparagus*
**aspettare** *wait;* **aspetta!** *wait!*

**aspirina** (f) *aspirin*
**assegno** (m) *cheque*
**assicurazione** (f) *insurance*
**assomiglia a ...** *it's like ...*
**assorbenti (igienici)** (m pl)
    *sanitary towels*
**attaccapanni** (m) *coat hanger*
**attento** *careful*; **stia attento!**
    *be careful!*
**atterrare** *to land*
**attraente** *attractive*
**attraverso** *through*
**aula delle lezioni** (f) *lecture
    theatre*
**auricolari** (m pl) *earphones*
**l'Australia** (f) *Australia*
**australiano** *Australian*
**autista** (m/f) *driver* (of bus,
    truck etc)
**auto** (m) *car*
**autobus** (m) *bus*; **la stazione
    degli autobus** *bus station*;
    **la fermata dell'autobus**
    *bus stop*
**automatico** *automatic*
**autostop: fare l'autostop** *to
    hitchhike*
**autostrada** (f) *motorway*
**autunno** (m) *autumn*
**a vapore** *steamed*
**avere** *to have*; **non ho ...** *I
    don't have ...*; **ha ...?**; *do you
    have ...?*
**avvocato** (m) *lawyer*
**azienda turistica** (f) *tourist
    informaion*
**azzurro** *blue*

# B

**babbo** (m) *dad*
**baffi** (m pl) *moustache*
**bagagli** (m pl) *luggage*
**bagagliaio** (m) *boot* (of car)
**bagaglio a mano** (m) *hand
    luggage*
**bagaglio in eccesso** (m)
    *excess baggage*
**bagnato** *wet*
**bagno** (m) *bath, bathroom*;
    **fare il bagno** *to have a
    bath*; **i bagni** *toilets*
**balcone** (m) *balcony*
**ballare** *to dance*
**ballo** (m) *dance*
**balsamo** (m) *conditioner* (hair)
**bambino** (m), **bambina** (f)
    *baby, child*
**bambola** (f) *doll*
**banana** (f) *banana*
**banca** (f) *bank*

**bancomat** (m) *cashpoint,
    ATM*
**banconota** (f) *banknote*
**banda** (f) *band* (musicians)
**bandiera** (f) *flag*
**bar** (m) *bar* (drinks)
**barba** (f) *beard*
**barbiere** (m) *barber's*
**barca** (f) *boat* (small)
**basso** *low, short*
**basta!** *enough!*; **basta così**
    *that'll be all*
**battello** (m) *boat* (passenger)
**batteria** (f) *battery*
**baule** (m) *chest* (furniture)
**beige** *beige*
**bello** *beautiful, handsome, nice*
**bene** *good, well*; **bene!** *good!*;
    **benissimo!** *great!*; **ben
    cotta** *well done* (food); **non
    mi sento bene** *I don't feel
    well*; **ti sta bene** *it suits you*
**benvenuto** *welcome*
**benzina** (f) *petrol*
**benzinaio** (m) *petrol station*
**bere** *to drink*
**berretto** (m) *cap* (hat)
**biancheria** (f) *laundry* (dirty
    clothes)
**biancheria intima** (f)
    *underwear*
**bianco** *white*
**bibita** (f) *drink*
**biblioteca** (f) *library*
**bicchiere** (m) *glass* (for
    drinking)
**bicicletta** (f) *bicycle*
**bigliettaio** (m) *conductor*
    (bus)
**biglietteria** (f) *ticket office,
    booking office*
**biglietto** (m) *ticket, card*;
    **il biglietto di andata
    e ritorno** *return ticket*; **il
    biglietto di sola andata**
    *single ticket*; **il biglietto
    da visita** *business card*;
    **il biglietto di auguri**
    *greetings card*
**bigodini** (m pl) *curlers*
**bikini** (m) *bikini*
**binario** (m) *platform*
**biondo** *blond*
**birra** (f) *beer*
**biscotto** (m) *biscuit*
**bisogno** (m) *need*; **ho
    bisogno di ...** *I need ...*;
    **non c'è bisogno** *there's
    no need*
**bloc-notes** (m) *notepad*
**blu** *navy blue*

**bocca** (f) *mouth*
**boccaglio** (m) *snorkel*
**bollire** *to boil* (water);
    (egg etc) **far bollire**
**bollitore** (m) *kettle*
**borsa** (f) *bag*
**borsaiolo** (m) *pickpocket*
**borsellino** (m) *purse*
**botteghino** (m) *box office*
**bottiglia** (f) *bottle*
**bottone** (m) *button*
**braccialetto** (m) *bracelet*
**braccio** (m) *arm*
**brandy** (m) *brandy*
**bravo** *clever*
**brioche** (f) *croissant*
**britannico** *British*
**bruciare** *to burn*
**bruciatura** (f) *burn*
**brutto** *ugly*
**budget** (m) *budget*
**bunker** (m) *bunker* (golf)
**buonanotte** *good night*
**buonasera** *good evening*
**buongiorno** *good day, hello*
**buono** *good, nice* (to eat); **a
    buon mercato** *cheap*
**burro** (m) *butter*; **il burro
    di cacao** *lip balm*
**busta** (f) *envelope*

# C

**c'è ...** *there is ...*; **c'è ...?**
    *is there ...?*
**cabina telefonica** (f)
    *telephone booth*
**cacciavite** (m) *screwdriver*
**caffè** (m) *coffee, café*; **il caffè
    solubile** *instant coffee*
**calcio** (m) *football* (game)
**calcolatore** (m) *calculator*
**caldaia** (f) *boiler*
**caldo** *hot, warm*; **ho caldo**
    *I feel hot*
**calzamaglia** (f) *tights* (wool)
**calze** (f pl) *stockings*
**calzini** (m pl) *socks*
**calzolaio** (m) *shoe repairer*
**cambiare** *to change* (money,
    trains)
**cambiarsi** *to change* (clothes)
**cambio** (m) *change* (money),
    *gear* (car); **il (tasso di)
    cambio** *exchange rate*
**camera** (f) *(bed)room*; **la
    camera a due letti** *twin
    room*; **la camera doppia**
    *double room*; **la camera
    singola** *single room*
**camera d'aria** (f) *inner tube*

**cameriera** (f) *waitress, maid*
**cameriere** (m) *waiter*
**camicetta** (f) *blouse*
**camicia** (f) *shirt;* **la camicia da notte** *nightdress*
**caminetto** (m) *fireplace*
**camion** (m) *truck*
**camminare** *to walk*
**campagna** (f) *country (not town)*
**campana** (f) *bell (church)*
**campanello** (m) *bell (door)*
**campeggio** (m) *campsite*
**camper** (m) *camper van*
**campo** (m) *field*
**il Canada** *Canada*
**canadese** *Canadian*
**canale** (m) *canal*
**cancello** (m) *gate*
**candela** (f) *candle, spark plug*
**cane** (m) *dog*
**canoa** (f) *canoe*
**canottiera** (f) *vest*
**cantare** *to sing*
**cantina** (f) *cellar*
**canzone** (f) *song*
**capelli** (m pl) *hair*
**capire** *to understand;* **non capisco** *I don't understand*
**capotto** (m) *coat*
**cappello** (m) *hat*
**caramella** (f) *sweet*
**carburatore** (m) *carburettor*
**caricabatterie** (m) *charger*
**carino** *nice, pretty*
**carne** (f) *meat*
**caro** *expensive*
**carota** (f) *carrot*
**carrello** (m) *trolley*
**carrozzina** (f) *pram*
**carta** (f) *paper, card;* **la carta (geografica)** *map;* **la carta assegni** *debit card;* **la carta d'imbarco** *boarding card;* **la carta da imballaggio** *wrapping paper;* **la carta da regalo** *wrapping paper (for presents);* **la carta da scrivere** *writing paper;* **la carta di credito** *credit card;* **la carta igienica** *toilet paper;* **le carte da gioco** *playing cards*
**cartello** (m) *sign (in station etc)*
**cartella** (f) *briefcase*
**cartolina** (f) *postcard*
**casa** (f) *house, home*
**cascata** (f) *waterfall*
**cassa** (f) *check-out*

**cassetta** (f) *box (of wood), cassette;* **la cassetta delle lettere** *post box*
**cassetto** (m) *drawer*
**cassettone** (m) *chest of drawers*
**cassiere** (m) *cashier*
**castello** (m) *castle*
**catenaccio** (m) *bolt (on door)*
**cattedrale** (f) *cathedral*
**cattivo** *bad*
**cattolico** *Catholic*
**cavalcavia** (m) *flyover*
**cavatappi** (m) *corkscrew*
**caviglia** (f) *ankle*
**cavolfiore** (m) *cauliflower*
**cavolo** (m) *cabbage*
**celibe** *single (unmarried)*
**cellulare** (m) *mobile phone*
**cena** (f) *supper, dinner*
**cento** *hundred*
**centro** (m) *centre;* **il centro città** *city centre*
**cerotto** (m) *plaster (sticking)*
**certificato** (m) *certificate*
**certo** *certainly*
**cesoie** (f pl) *shears*
**cestello** (m) *basket (in supermarket)*
**cestino** (m) *basket*
**cetriolo** (m) *cucumber*
**check-in** (m) *check-in;* **lo sportello del check-in** *check-in desk;* **fare il check-in** *to check in*
**chewing gum** (m) *chewing gum*
**chi?** *who?*
**chiamare** *to call*
**chiaro** *light (not dark), clear (obvious)*
**chiave** (f) *key;* **la chiave fissa** *wheel brace, wrench*
**chiesa** (f) *church*
**chilo** (m) *kilo*
**chilometro** (m) *kilometre*
**chiodo** (m) *nail (metal)*
**chitarra** (f) *guitar*
**chiudere** *to close;* **chiudere con il catenaccio** *to bolt*
**chiuso** *closed*
**chiusura lampo** (f) *zip*
**ciao** *hello, hi*
**ciascuno** *each;* **venti euro ciascuno** *twenty euros each*
**cibo** (m) *food*
**cieco** *blind (cannot see)*
**cielo** (m) *sky*
**cifre** (f pl) *figures*
**ciliegia** (f) *cherry*
**cimitero** (m) *cemetery*

**cin cin!** *cheers! (toast)*
**cinema** (m) *cinema*
**cinghia della ventola** (f) *fan belt*
**cinquanta** *fifty*
**cinque** *five*
**cintura** (f) *belt;* **la cintura di sicurezza** *seat belt*
**cioccolata** (f) *chocolate;* **la scatola di cioccolatini** *box of chocolates*
**ciotola** (f) *bowl;* **la ciotola del cane** *dog bowl*
**cipolla** (f) *onion*
**cipria** (f) *powder (cosmetic)*
**circa 16** *about 16*
**ci sono** *there are ...;* **ci sono?** *are there ...?*
**città** (f) *city, town*
**ciuccio** (m) *dummy (for baby)*
**clacson** (m) *horn (car)*
**classe** (f) *class*
**cliente** (m) *client*
**codice segreto** (m) *PIN*
**cofano** (m) *bonnet (car)*
**cognome** (m) *last name*
**coincidenza** (f) *connection*
**colazione** (f) *breakfast*
**colla** (f) *glue*
**collana** (f) *necklace*
**collant** (m pl) *tights (sheer)*
**collare** (m) *collar (for dog)*
**collega** (m/f) *colleague*
**colletto** (m) *collar*
**collezione** (f) *collection (stamps etc)*
**collina** (f) *hill*
**collo** (m) *neck*
**colore** (m) *colour*
**coltello** (m) *knife*
**come** *like;* **come questo** *like this one*
**come?** *how?, sorry? (pardon);* **come si chiama/ti chiami?** *what's your name? (formal/informal);* **come si chiama?** *what's it called?*
**comignolo** (m) *chimney*
**cominciare** *to start*
**commedia** *play (theatre)*
**commerciante** (m/f) *shopkeeper*
**comodino** (m) *bedside table*
**compact disc** (m) *compact disc*
**compleanno** (m) *birthday;* **buon compleanno!** *happy birthday!*
**completo** (m) *suit*
**complicato** *complicated*
**comprare** *buy*

**compressa** (f) *tablet*;
**la compressa di vitamine** *vitamin pill*
**computer** (m) *computer*;
**il computer portatile** *laptop (computer)*
**con** *with*
**concerto** (m) *concert*
**conchiglia** (f) *shell*
**conferenza** (f) *lecture, conference*; **la sala conferenze** *conference room*
**confine** (m) *border*
**congelatore** (m) *freezer*
**congratulazioni!** *congratulations!*
**coniglio** (m) *rabbit*
**conoscere** *to know (person)*
**consegna** (f) *delivery*
**consolato** (m) *consulate*
**consulente finanziario** (m/f) *financial consultant*
**contento** *glad, happy*
**conto** (m) *bill*
**contraccettivo** (m) *contraceptive*
**contratto** (m) *contract*
**contro** *against*
**controllo** (m) *test*
**conversazione** (f) *talk*
**coperta** (f) *blanket*
**copriletto** (m) *bedspread*
**corda** (f) *rope, guy rope, string (guitar etc)*
**cordiale** *friendly*
**corno** (m) *horn (animal)*
**corpo** (m) *body*
**correre** *to run*
**corridoio** (m) *corridor*
**corrispondente** (m/f) *pen friend*
**corso** (m) *course (educational)*
**corto** *short*
**cosa?** *what?*; **cosa c'è?** *what's the matter*
**cosmetici** (m pl) *cosmetics*
**costare** *to cost* ; **quanto costa?** *what does it cost?*
**costoletta** (f) *chop (food)*
**costoso** *expensive*
**costume da bagno** (m) *bathing suit, swimming trunks*
**cotone** (m) *cotton*; **il cotone idrofilo** *cotton wool*
**cozze** (f pl) *mussels*
**crampo** (m) *cramp*
**cravatta** (f) *tie*
**crema** (f) *cream, lotion*
**criceto** (m) *hamster*
**crociera** (f) *cruise*

**crostacei** (m pl) *shellfish (crabs etc.)*
**cucchiaio** (m) *spoon*
**cuccia** (f) *dog basket*
**cucina** (f) *kitchen, cooker*
**cucinare** *to cook*
**cucire** *to sew*
**cucitrice** (f) *stapler*
**cugino/cugina** *cousin*
**cuocere (al forno)** *to bake*
**cuoco/cuoca** (m/f) *cook*
**cuoio** (m) *leather*
**cuore** (m) *heart*; **nel cuore della notte** *in the middle of the night*
**cuori** (m pl) *hearts (cards)*
**curry** (m) *curry*
**cuscino** (m) *cushion*

## D

**dado** (m) *nut (for bolt)*
**dappertutto** *everywhere*
**dare** *to give*; **dare la precedenza** *to give way*
**davanti a** *opposite, in front of*
**decollo** (m) *takeoff*
**deliberatamente** *deliberately*
**denaro** (m) *cash*
**dente** (m) *tooth*
**dentiera** (f) *dentures, false teeth*
**dentifricio** (m) *toothpaste*
**dentista** (m/f) *dentist*
**denuncia** (f) *statement (to police)*
**deodorante** (m) *deodorant*
**desposito bagagli** (m) *left luggage locker*
**dessert** (m pl) *desserts*
**destro** *right (not left)*
**detersivo** (m) *detergent*; **il detersivo (per bucato)** *washing powder*; **il detersivo per i piatti** *washing-up liquid*
**devo** *I must*; **devo andare adesso** *I must go now*
**di** *of, from, than, on, at*: **più di** *more than*; **di dov'è?/di dove sei?** *where are you from? (formal/informal)*; **di lunedì** *on Monday*; **di notte** *at night*
**diabetico** *diabetic*
**diamante** (m) *diamond (gem)*
**diarrea** (f) *diarrhoea*
**dica?** *can I help you?*
**dicembre** *December*
**diciannove** *nineteen*
**diciassette** *seventeen*
**diciotto** *eighteen*

**dieci** *ten*
**dietro** *behind*; **dietro a ... behind ...**
**difficile** *difficult*
**dimenticare** *to forget*
**dire** *to say*; **che cosa ha detto?** *what did you say?*; **come si dice ...?** *how do you say ...?*
**direttore** (m) *conductor (orchestra)*
**direttore/direttrice** *manager*
**direzione** (f) *office*
**dirigente** (m) *executive*
**disabili** (m pl) *the disabled*
**discesa per principianti** (f) *beginners' slope*
**disco** (m) *record (music)*
**dito** (m) *finger*
**divano** (m) *sofa*
**diversi** *several*
**diverso**; **è diverso!** *that's different!*
**divertente** *funny*
**divieto di accesso** *no entry*
**divorziato** *divorced*
**dizionario** (m) *dictionary*
**doccia** (f) *shower*
**docciaschiuma** (f) *shower gel*
**documento** (m) *document*; **il documento d'identità** *identification*
**dodici** *twelve*
**dogana** (f) *customs*
**dolce** *sweet (not sour)*
**dollaro** (m) *dollar*
**dolore** (m) *ache, pain*
**domanda** (f) *question*
**domani** *tomorrow*; **a domani** *see you tomorrow*
**domenica** *Sunday*
**donna** (f) *woman*; **la donna delle pulizie** *cleaner*
**dopo** *after*
**dopobarba** (m) *aftershave*
**dormire** *to sleep*
**dottore** (m) *doctor*
**dove?** *where?*
**due** *two*; **le due** *two o'clock*
**dune** (f pl) *sand dunes*
**duomo** (m) *cathedral*
**durante** *during*
**duro** *hard*
**duty free** (m) *duty-free*

## E

**e** *and*; **e poi?** *what next?*
**è** *he/she/it is*
**eccellente** *excellent*

**ecco** *here you are, here it is*
**economico** *cheap*
**edificio** (m) *building*
**elastico** (m) *elastic, rubber band*
**elettricista** (m/f) *electrician*
**elettricità** (f) *electricity*
**elettrico** *electric*
**email** (f) *e-mail*
**emergenza** (f) *emergency*
**enoteca** (f) *wine shop*
**entrare** *to enter*
**entrata** (f) *entrance*
**entro (venerdì)** *by (Friday)*
**epilettico** *epileptic*
**equipaggio** (m) *crew*
**era: (Lei) era** *you were (singular, formal);* **(lui/lei/ esso) era** *he/she/it was*
**erano** *they were*
**eravamo** *we were*
**eravate** *you were* (plural)
**erba** (f) *grass*
**erbaccia** (f) *weed*
**eri** *you were (singular, informal)*
**eritema solare** (m) *sunburn*
**ero** *I was*
**errore** (m) *mistake*
**esatto** *right* (correct)
**esaurimento nervoso** (m) *nervous breakdown*
**esca** (f) *bait*
**escursione** (f) *excursion*
**escursionismo** (m) *hiking*
**esempio** (m) *example;* **per esempio** *for example*
**esposimetro** (m) *light meter*
**esso** *it*
**est** (m) *east*
**estate** (f) *summer*
**estintore** (m) *fire extinguisher*
**etichetta** (f) *label*

# F

**faccia** (f) *face*
**facile** *easy*
**fagioli** (m pl) *beans*
**falegname** (m) *carpenter*
**falò** (m) *campfire*
**fame: ho fame** *I'm hungry*
**famiglia** (f) *family*
**fantastico** *fantastic*
**fare** *to do, to make;* **che lavoro fa?** *what (work) do you do?*
**fare jogging** *to jog;* **andare a fare jogging** *to go jogging*
**fare la fila** *to queue*

**fari** (m pl) *lights, headlights;* **i fari posteriori** *rear lights*
**farina** (f) *flour*
**farmacia** (f) *chemist (shop)*
**fascia** (f) *bandage*
**fattore di protezione** (m) *SPF (sun protection factor)*
**fattoria** (f) *farm*
**fattura** (f) *invoice*
**favore: per favore** *please*
**fazzolettini di carta** (m pl) *tissues*
**febbraio** *February*
**febbre** (f) *fever, temperature*
**fegato** (m) *liver*
**felice** *happy*
**felpa** (f) *sweatshirt*
**ferita** (f) *injury*
**fermare** *to stop ;* **fermo!** *stop!*
**fermata dell'autobus** (f) *bus stop*
**ferramenta** (f) *hardware store*
**ferro** (m) *iron* (material); *(for clothes)* **il ferro da stiro**
**ferrovia** (f) *railway*
**festa** (f) *party (celebration)*
**fiammifero** (m) *match (light)*
**fidanzata** (f) *fiancée, (adj) engaged*
**fidanzato** (m) *fiancé, (adj) engaged*
**fiera (commerciale)** (f) *fair (trade)*
**figlia** (f) *daughter*
**figlio** (m) *son*
**fila** (f) *queue, aisle (in supermarket etc)*
**filiale** (f) *branch (of company)*
**film** (m) *film (cinema)*
**filtro** (m) *filter*
**finalmente!** *at last!*
**fine** (f) *end*
**finestra** (f) *window*
**finito** *finished*
**fino a** *until*
**finocchio** (m) *fennel*
**fiore** (m) *flower*
**fiori** *clubs (cards)*
**Firenze** *Florence*
**firmare** *to sign*
**fissare** *to arrange (appointments etc)*
**fiume** (m) *river*
**flash** (m) *flash (camera)*
**flauto** (m) *flute*
**flebo** (f) *intravenous drip*
**foglia** (f) *leaf*
**fohn** (m) *hair dryer*
**fondo** (m) *bottom;* **in fondo (a)** *at the bottom (of)*

**foratura** (f) *puncture*
**forbici** (f pl) *scissors*
**forchetta** (f) *fork (for food)*
**foresta** (f) *forest*
**forestiero** (m) *foreigner*
**formaggio** (m) *cheese*
**forno** (m) *oven;* **il forno a microonde** *microwave*
**forse** *maybe, perhaps*
**forte** *loud, strong*
**fortuna** (f) *luck;* **buona fortuna!** *good luck!*
**fotocopiatrice** (f) *photocopier*
**fotografare** *to photograph*
**fotografia** (f) *photograph*
**fotografo** (m) *photographer*
**foulard** (m) *headscarf*
**fra ... between ...**
**fragola** (f) *strawberry*
**francese** *French*
**la Francia** *France*
**francobollo** (m) *stamp*
**fratello** (m) *brother*
**frattura** (f) *fracture*
**freccia** (f) *indicator*
**freddo** *cold* (adj)
**frenare** *to brake*
**freno** (m) *brake;* **il freno a mano** *hand brake*
**fresco** *cool*
**fretta: ho fretta** *I'm in a hurry*
**friggere** *to fry*
**frigorifero** (m) *fridge*
**fritto** *fried*
**frizione** (f) *clutch*
**frizzante** *fizzy*
**frutta** (f) *fruit*
**frutti di mare** (m pl) *seafood*
**fucile** (m) *gun (rifle)*
**fumare** *to smoke*
**fumatori** *smoking (section);* **non fumatori** *non-smoking*
**fumo** (m) *smoke*
**fungo** (m) *mushroom*
**funivia** (f) *cable car*
**funzionare** *to work (machine)*
**fuochi d'artificio** (m pl) *fireworks*
**fuoco** (m) *fire*
**fuori** *outside*
**furto** (m) *burglary*

# G

**gabbia** (f) *cage*
**galleria** (f) *gallery, circle (in theatre);* **la galleria d'arte** *art gallery*
**il Galles** *Wales*
**gallese** *Welsh*
**gamba** (f) *leg*

**gambero** (m) *crayfish*
**garage** (m) *garage*
**garantire** *to guarantee*
**garanzia** (f) *guarantee*
**gas** *gas, fuel;* **il gas da campeggio** *camping gas;* **il gas per accendini** *lighter fuel*
**gatto** (m) *cat*
**gay** *gay (homosexual)*
**gasolio** (m) *diesel*
**gel** (m) *gel (hair)*
**gelato** (m) *ice cream*
**gelo** (m) *frost*
**gemelli** (m pl) *cuff links*
**genitori** (m pl) *parents*
**gennaio** *January*
**Genova** *Genoa*
**gente** (f) *people*
**la Germania** *Germany*
**ghiaccio** (m) *ice*
**già** *already*
**giacca** (f) *jacket*
**giallo** *yellow*
**giardiniere** (m) *gardener*
**giardino** (m) *garden*
**gin** (m) *gin*
**ginocchio** (m) *knee*
**giocare** *to play*
**giocattolo** (m) *toy*
**gioielliere** (m) *jeweller's (shop)*
**giornalaio** (m) *newsagent's (shop)*
**giornale** (m) *newspaper*
**giorno** (m) *day;* **il giorno festivo** *public holiday*
**giovane** *young*
**giovedì** *Thursday*
**girabacchino** (m) *wheel brace*
**giri a sinistra/destra** *turn left/right*
**giro** *tour*
**giù** *down*
**giugno** *June*
**giusto** *right (correct);* **non è giusto** *it's not fair*
**gli** *the (m pl)*
**gocce** (f pl) *drops*
**gola** (f) *throat*
**golf** (m) *golf*
**golfista** (m) *golfer*
**gomito** (m) *elbow*
**gomma** (f) *eraser, tyre;* **la gomma a terra** *flat tyre*
**gonna** (f) *skirt*
**governo** (m) *government*
**grafico/grafica** (m/f) *designer*
**la Gran Bretagna** *Great Britain*
**granchio** (m) *crab*
**grande** *big, large*

**grande magazzino** (m) *department store*
**grasso** (m) *fat;* *fat (adj)*
**gratis** *free (no charge)*
**gratuito** *free (no charge)*
**grave** *serious (illness)*
**grazie** *thank you/ thanks*
**grazioso** *pretty (beautiful)*
**la Grecia** *Greece*
**greco** *Greek*
**gridare** *to shout*
**grigio** *grey*
**griglia** (f) *grill;* **alla griglia** *grilled*
**grondaia** (f) *gutter*
**grotta** (f) *cave*
**gruppo** (m) *group*
**guanciale** (m) *pillow*
**guanti** (m pl) *gloves*
**guardare** *to watch*
**guardaroba** (m) *wardrobe*
**guardia** (f) *guard*
**guasto** *breakdown (car)*
**guerra** (f) *war*
**guida** (f) *guide, guidebook;* **la guida telefonica** *telephone directory*
**guidare** *to drive*
**guidatore/guidatrice** (m/f) *driver (car)*
**guinzaglio** (m) *lead (for dog)*
**gusto** (m) *flavour*

## H

**ha ...?** *do you have ...?*
**hamburger** (m) *hamburger*
**HIV positivo** *HIV positive*
**ho ...** *I have ...*
**hobby** (m) *hobby*

## I

**i** *the (m pl)*
**idraulico** (m) *plumber*
**ieri** *yesterday*
**il** *the (m)*
**imbarazzante** *embarrassing*
**imbianchino** (m) *decorator*
**immediatamente** *immediately*
**immondizie** (f pl) *rubbish*
**imparare** *to learn*
**impermeabile** (m) *raincoat*
**impiegato/impiegata** (m/f) *office worker*
**importa: non importa** *it doesn't matter*
**impossibile** *impossible*
**imposta** (f) *shutter (window)*

**in** *in, to:* **in inglese** *in English;* **in Inghilterra** *to England;* **in mezzo alla piazza** *in the middle of the square;* **in centro** *to the centre;* **in ritardo** *delayed*
**inalatore** (m) *inhaler (for asthma etc)*
**incendio** (m) *fire (blaze)*
**inchiostro** (m) *ink*
**incidente** (m) *accident*
**incinta** *pregnant*
**incluso** *included*
**incontro** (m) *meeting, match (sport)*
**incrocio** (m) *junction*
**indicatore di direzione** (m) *indicator*
**indigestione** (f) *indigestion*
**indirizzo** (m) *address;* **l'indirizzo di posta elettronica** *e-mail address*
**indistinto** *faint (unclear)*
**infermiere/infermiera** (m/f) *nurse*
**infezione** (f) *infection*
**informatica** (f) *information technology*
**informazioni** (f pl) *information*
**infradito** (m pl) *flip-flops*
**ingegneria** (f) *engineering*
**l'Inghilterra** (f) *England*
**inglese** *English*
**ingorgo** (m) *traffic jam*
**iniezione** (m) *injection*
**inizio** (m) *start*
**insalata** (f) *salad*
**insegna** (f) *sign (road etc)*
**insegnante** (m/f) *teacher*
**insegnare** *to teach*
**insettifugo** (m) *insect repellent*
**insetto** (m) *insect*
**insieme** *together*
**insolito** *unusual*
**insonnia** (f) *insomnia*
**intelligente** *clever*
**interessante** *interesting*
**internet** (f) *internet*
**interpretare** *interpret*
**interprete** (m/f) *interpreter*
**interruttore** (m) *switch*
**interurbana** *long-distance (call)*
**intossicazione alimentare** (f) *food poisoning*
**inverno** (m) *winter*
**invito** (m) *invitation*
**io** *I*

l'**Irlanda** (f) *Ireland*; l'**Irlanda del Nord** *Northern Ireland*
**irlandese** *Irish*
**isola** (f) *island*
**Italia** *Italy*
**italiano** *Italian*

## J, K

**jazz** (m) *jazz*
**jeans** (m pl) *jeans*
**jogging** (m) *jogging*
**krapfen** (m) *doughnut*

## L

**la** *the* (f)
**là** *there*
**lacca per i capelli** (f) *hairspray*
**lacci** (m pl) *laces* (of shoe)
**ladro** (m) *burglar, thief*
**laggiù** *over there*
**lago** (m) *lake*
**lamette** (f pl) *razor blades*
**lampada** (f) *lamp*; **la lampada da studio** *reading lamp*
**lampadina** (f) *light bulb*
**lampone** (m) *raspberry*
**lana** (f) *wool*
**lassativo** (m) *laxative*
**lassù** *up there*
**lato** (m) *side* (edge)
**latte** (m) *milk*; **il latte detergente** *skin cleanser*
**latteria** (f) *dairy*
**latticini** (m pl) *dairy products*
**lattina** (f) *can* (vessel)
**lattuga** (f) *lettuce*
**laureato: sono laureato in ...** *I have a degree in ...*
**lavabo** (m) *sink*
**lavanderia** (f) *laundry* (place); **la lavanderia a secco** *dry cleaner's*
**lavandino** (m) *sink, wash basin*
**lavastoviglie** (f) *dishwasher*
**lavatrice** (f) *washing machine*
**lavello** (m) *sink* (kitchen)
**lavorare** *to work*
**lavorare a maglia** *knit*
**lavoro** (m) *job, work*
**le** *the* (f pl)
**lecca lecca** (m) *lollipop*
**legare** *to tie*
**legge** (f) *law*
**leggere** *to read*
**leggero** *light* (not heavy)

**legno** (m) *wood* (material)
**lei** *she*
**Lei** *you* (singular, formal)
**lente** (f) *lens*; **le lenti a contatto** *contact lenses*; **le lenti semi-rigide** *gaspermeable lenses*
**lento** *slow*
**lenzuola** (f pl) *bed linen*
**lenzuolo** (m) *sheet*
**lesso** *boiled*
**lettera** (f) *letter*
**letteratura** (f) *literature*
**lettino** (m) *cot*
**letto** (m) *bed*
**leva del cambio** (f) *gear stick*
**levata** (f) *collection* (postal)
**lezione** (f) *lesson*
**libbra** (f) *pound* (weight)
**libero** *free* (not occupied)
**libero professionista** *self-employed*
**libreria** (f) *bookshop*
**libretto degli assegni** (m) *chequebook*
**libro** (m) *book*
**limetta per le unghie** (f) *nailfile*
**limonata** (f) *lemonade*
**limoncello** (m) *lime* (fruit)
**limone** (m) *lemon*
**limpido** *clear* (water)
**linea** (f) *line* (telephone etc); **la linea aerea** (f) *airline*; **la linea esterna** *outside line*
**lingua** (f) *language, tongue*
**liquido per lenti** (m) *soaking solution* (for contact lenses)
**liquore** (m) *liqueur*
**lisca** (f) *fishbone*
**litro** (m) *litre*
**livido** (m) *bruise*
**lo** *the* (m)
**località sciistica** (f) *ski resort*
**locomotiva** (f) *engine* (train)
**lontano** *far*; **è lontano?** *is it far away?*
**loro** *they, their, them*; **la loro stanza** *their room*; **il loro amico** *their friend*; **i loro libri** *their books*; **le loro penne** *their pens*; **è loro** *it's theirs*; **è per loro** *it's for them*; **dallo a loro** *give it to them*
**lozione solare** (f) *suntan lotion*
**lucchetto** (m) *padlock*
**luce** (f) *light*
**luci di posizione** (f pl) *parking lights*

**lucido per le scarpe** (m) *shoe polish*
**luglio** *July*
**lui** *he, him*; **è per lui** *it's for him*
**luna** (f) *moon*; **la luna di miele** (f) *honeymoon*
**luna park** (m) *fair* (funfair)
**lunedì** *Monday*
**lunghezza** (f) *length*
**lungo** *long*

## M

**ma** *but*
**macchina** (f) *car*
**macchina da scrivere** (f) *typewriter*
**macchina fotografica** (f) *camera*
**macelleria** (f) *butcher's* (shop)
**madre** (f) *mother*
**magari** *perhaps*
**maggio** *May*
**maglieria** (f) *knitwear*
**maglione** (m) *sweater*
**magro** *thin*
**mai** *never*; **non fumo mai** *I never smoke*
**mal di denti** (m) *toothache*
**mal di pancia** (m) *stomachache*
**mal di testa** (m) *headache*
**malato** *ill*
**male: mi fa male il/la ...** *my ... hurts*; **farà male?** *will it hurt?*
**mamma** *mum*
**mancia** (f) *tip* (money)
**mandare** *to send*
**mandarino** (m) *tangerine*
**mangianastri** (m) *cassette player*
**mangiare** *to eat*
**manica** (f) *sleeve*
**maniglia** (f) *handle* (door)
**mano** (f) *hand*
**manzo** (m) *beef*
**marciapiede** (m) *pavement*
**mare** (m) *sea*
**marea** (f) *tide*
**margarina** (f) *margarine*
**marito** (m) *husband*
**marmellata** (f) *jam*; **la marmellata d'arance** *marmalade*
**marmitta** (f) *exhaust* (car)
**marmo** (m) *marble*
**marrone** *brown*
**martedì** *Tuesday*
**martello** (m) *hammer*

**marzo** *March*
**mascara** (m) *mascara*
**materassino gonfiabile** (m) *air mattress*
**materasso** (m) *mattress*
**matita** (f) *pencil*
**matrimoniale** (f) *double room*
**matrimonio** (m) *wedding*
**mattina** (f) *morning;* **di mattina** *in the morning*
**maturo** *ripe*
**meccanico** (m) *mechanic*
**medicina** (f) *medicine*
**medico** (m) *doctor*
**il Mediterraneo** *the Mediterranean*
**medusa** (f) *jellyfish*
**mela** (f) *apple*
**melone** (m) *melon*
**meno** *less*
**menta piperita** (f) *peppermint*
**menù** (m) *menu*
**mercato** (m) *market*
**mercoledì** *Wednesday*
**mese** (m) *month*
**messa** (f) *mass (church)*
**messaggio** (m) *message*
**metà** *half*
**metro(politana)** (f) *underground*
**mettere** *to put*
**mezzanotte** *midnight*
**mezzo** (m) *half:* **... e mezzo** *half past ...;* **mezz'ora** *half an hour;* **mezzo pensione** *half board*
**mezzogiorno** *noon*
**mia** *my;* **la mia borsa** *my bag*
**mi chiamo... ** *my name's ...*
**mi dispiace** *I'm sorry*
**mie** *my;* **le mie chiavi** *my keys*
**miei** *my;* **i miei vestiti** *my dresses*
**miele** (m) *honey*
**migliore** (m) *best, better;* **migliore di** *better than*
**Milano** *Milan*
**milione** *million*
**mille** *thousand*
**minestra** (f) *soup*
**minuto** (m) *minute*
**mio** *my, mine;* **il mio libro** *my book;* **è mio** *it's mine*
**mirino** (m) *viewfinder*
**mi scusi!** *excuse me! (to get attention)*
**mobili** (m pl) *furniture*
**moda** (f) *fashion*

**modem** (m) *modem*
**modulo per la domanda** (m) *application form*
**moglie** (f) *wife*
**molla** (f) *spring (mechanical)*
**molletta** (f) *peg (clothes)*
**molluschi** (m pl) *shellfish (molluscs)*
**molo** (m) *dock*
**molto** *a lot;* **molto meglio** *much better;* **molto più lentamente** *much slower;* **non molto** *not much*
**moltissimo** *very much*
**moneta** (f) *coin*
**monitor** (m) *monitor (computer)*
**montagna** (f) *mountain*
**monumento** (m) *monument*
**mora** (f) *blackberry*
**morbido** *soft*
**mordere** *bite (verb: by dog)*
**morire** *to die*
**morso** (m) *bite (noun: by dog)*
**morto** *dead*
**mosaico** (m) *mosaic*
**mosca** (f) *fly (insect)*
**mostra** (f) *exhibition*
**motocicletta** (f) *motorcycle*
**motore** (m) *engine (car)*
**motorino** (m) *moped*
**motoscafo** (m) *motorboat*
**mountain bike** (m) *mountain bike*
**mouse** (m) *mouse (computer)*
**municipio** (m) *town hall*
**muovere** *to move;* **non muoverti!** *don't move!*
**muratore** (m) *builder*
**muro** (m) *wall*
**museo** (m) *museum*
**musica** (f) *music;* **la musica classica** *classical music;* **la musica folk** *folk music;* **la musica pop** *pop music*
**musicista** (m) *musician*
**mutande** (f pl) *underpants*

# N

**Napoli** *Naples*
**naso** (m) *nose*
**Natale** (m) *Christmas*
**nato: sono nato nel 1975** *I was born in 1975*
**nave** (f) *boat, ship;* **la nave a vapore** *steamer (boat)*
**nebbia** (f) *fog*
**necessario** *necessary*
**negativa** (f) *negative (photo);* (adj) **negativo**

**negozio** (m) *shop;* **il negozio di dischi** *record shop;* **il negozio di giocattoli** (m) *toy shop*
**neozelandese** (m/f) *New Zealander;* (adj) *New Zealand*
**nero** *black*
**nessuno** *nobody;* **da nessuna parte** *nowhere*
**neve** (f) *snow*
**niente** *nothing;* **di niente** *you're welcome;* **non serve a niente** *it's no use*
**night** (m) *nightclub*
**nipote** (f) *granddaughter, niece*
**nipote** (m) *grandson, nephew*
**no** *no (negative response)*
**nocciola** (f) *nut*
**noce** (f) *nut*
**noi** *we, us;* **è per noi** *it's for us*
**noioso** *boring;* **che noia!** *that's boring!*
**noleggiare** *to rent*
**nome** (m) *name;* **il nome di battesimo** *first name*
**non** *not;* **non è ...** *he's not ...*
**nonna** (f) *grandmother*
**nonni** (m pl) *grandparents*
**nonno** (m) *grandfather*
**nord** (m) *north*
**normale** *ordinary*
**nostro/a** *our;* **il nostro albergo** *our hotel;* **la nostra macchina** *our car;* **è nostro** *it's ours*
**notizie** (f pl) *news;* (on radio) **il notiziario**
**notte** (f) *night*
**novanta** *ninety*
**nove** *nine*
**novembre** *November*
**nubile** *single (unmarried: woman)*
**numero** (m) *number, shoe size;* **il numero di telefono** *telephone number*
**nuotare** *to swim*
**nuoto** (m) *swimming*
**la Nuova Zelanda** *New Zealand*
**nuovo** *new;* **di nuovo** *again*

# O

**o** *or;* **o ... o ...** *either ... or ...*
**obbligatorio** *necessary*
**occhiali** (m pl) *glasses*
**occhiali da sole** (m pl) *sunglasses*
**occhio** (m) *eye;* **gli occhi** *eyes*

**occupato** busy, occupied
**odore** (m) smell
**oggetti di valore** (m pl) valuables
**oggi** today
**ogni** each, every; **ogni tanto** occasionally
**ognuno** everyone
**olio** (m) oil; **olio d'oliva** (m) olive oil
**oliva** (f) olive
**ombrello** (m) umbrella
**ombrellone** (m) sunshade
**omelette** (f) omelette
**omeopatia** homeopathy
**omosessuale** gay (homosexual)
**onda** (f) wave; **i capelli ondulati** (m pl) wavy hair
**onesto** honest
**opera** (f) work (of art), opera
**operatore/operatrice** (m/f) operator
**operazione** (f) operation
**opuscolo** (m) brochure
**ora** (f) hour; **ora sono occupato** I'm busy now
**orario** (m) timetable; **l'orario di apertura** opening times; **l'orario di visita** (m) visiting hours
**orchestra** (f) orchestra
**ordinativo** (m) order (for goods)
**ordine del giorno** (m) agenda
**ore: che ore sono?** what's the time?
**orecchini** (m pl) earrings
**orecchio** (m) ear; **le orecchie** ears
**organo** (m) organ (music)
**oro** (m) gold
**orologio** (m) clock, watch
**orribile** awful, horrible
**ospedale** (m) hospital
**ospite** (m/f) guest
**ossigenare** to bleach (hair)
**osso** (m) bone
**ostello della gioventù** (m) youth hostel
**ottanta** eighty
**ottico** (m) optician
**ottimo** excellent
**otto** eight
**ottobre** October
**otturatore** (m) shutter (camera)
**otturazione** (f) filling (in tooth)
**ovest** (m) west

## P

**pacchetto** (m) package, packet
**pacco** (m) parcel
**padella** (f) frying pan
**Padova** Padua
**padre** (m) father
**padrona di casa** (f) hostess
**padrone di casa** (m) host
**paese** (m) country (state), village
**pagamento** (m) payment
**pagare** to pay; **pagare in contanti** to pay cash
**pagina** (f) page
**paio** (m) pair
**palazzo** (m) palace
**palestra** (f) gymnastics
**palla** (f) ball (football etc)
**pallido** pale
**pallina** (f) ball (tennis etc)
**pallone** (m) ball, football
**palo della tenda** (m) tent pole
**pancetta** (f) bacon
**pane** (m) bread; **il pane tostato** (m) toast
**panetteria** (f) bakery
**panino** (m) sandwich; rock (music)
**panna** (f) cream (dairy)
**pannolini** (m pl) nappies
**pantaloncini corti** (m pl) shorts
**pantaloni** (m pl) trousers
**pantofole** (m pl) slippers
**papà** (m) dad
**Papa: il Papa** Pope
**parabrezza** (m) windscreen
**paraffina** (f) paraffin
**paralume** (f) lampshade
**paraurti** (m) bumper
**parcheggiare** to park
**parcheggio** (m) car park
**parco** (m) park
**parlare** to talk, speak; **parla ...?** do you speak ...?; **non parlo ...** I don't speak ...
**parola** (f) word
**parrucchiere** (m) hairdresser's
**parte posteriore** (f) back (not front)
**partenza** (f) departure; **le partenze** departures
**particolarmente** especially
**partire** to depart, leave
**partito** (m) party (political)
**passaporto** (m) passport; **il controllo passaporti** passport control

**passatempo** (m) hobby
**passeggero/passeggera** (m/f) passenger
**passeggiata** (f) walk; **andare a fare una passeggiata** to go for a walk
**passegino** (m) pushchair
**password** (f) password
**pasta** (f) pasta
**pasticceria** (f) cake shop
**pasticche per la gola** (f pl) throat pastilles
**pasto** (m) meal
**patata** (f) potato
**patatine** (f pl) crisps
**patatine fritte** (f) chips
**patente** (f) licence; **patente di guida** driving licence
**patio** (m) terrace
**pattini da ghiaccio** (m pl) ice skates
**pattumiera** (f) dustbin
**paura: ho paura** I'm frightened
**pavimento** (m) floor (ground)
**pazzo** crazy
**pedone** (m) pedestrian; **la zona pedonale** pedestrian zone
**peggiore** worst, worse
**pelle** (f) leather
**pelletteria** (f) leather goods shop
**pellicola** (f) film (for camera)
**penicillina** (f) penicillin
**penna** (f) pen
**pennello** (m) paintbrush
**pensare** to think; **penso di sì** I think so; **ci penserò** I'll think about it
**pensione completa** (f) full board
**pentola** (f) saucepan; **la pentola a pressione** steamer (for cooking)
**pepe** (m) pepper (spice)
**peperone** (m) pepper (red, green)
**per** for; **per me** for me
**pera** (f) pear
**perché** because
**perché?** why?, what for?
**perfetto** perfect
**pericoloso** dangerous
**periferia** (f) suburbs
**perla** (f) pearl
**permanente** (f) perm
**permesso** allowed; **permesso!** excuse me! (to get past)

**persiane** (f pl) *shutters (window)*
**pesante** *heavy*
**pesca** (f) *peach*, *fishing*; **andare a pesca** *to go fishing*
**pesce** (m) *fish*
**pescheria** (f) *fishmonger's (shop)*
**pettinare** *to comb*
**pettine** (m) *comb*
**petto** (m) *chest (part of body)*
**pezzi di ricambio** (m pl) *spare parts (car)*
**pezzo** (m) *piece*
**piace: mi piace ...** *I like ...*; **mi piace nuotare** *I like swimming*
**piacere** *pleased to meet you*
**piacere di conoscerla** *how do you do?*
**piangere** *cry (verb: weep)*
**piano** (m) *floor (storey)*; **piano di lavoro** *worktop*
**pianta** (f) *map (of town)*, *plan*; *plant*
**pianterreno** (m) *ground floor*
**piastrella** (f) *tile*
**piattino** (m) *saucer*
**piatto** (m) *plate*, *meal*; **i piatti pronti** *ready meals*
**piatto** *flat (level)*
**piazza** (f) *square*
**piazzola** (f) *pitch (in campsite etc)*
**picche** (m pl) *spades (cards)*
**picchetto** (m) *tent peg*
**piccolo** *little*, *small*
**picnic** (m) *picnic*
**piede** (m) *foot*; **a piedi** *on foot*
**pieno** *full*
**pigiama** (m) *pyjamas*
**pigro** *lazy*
**pin** (m) *PIN*
**pinacoteca** (f) *art gallery*
**pinne** (f pl) *flippers*
**pinzette** (f pl) *tweezers*
**pioggia** (f) *rain*
**piovra** (f) *octopus*
**pipa** *pipe (for smoking)*
**piscina** (f) *swimming pool*
**piselli** (m pl) *peas*
**pistola** (f) *gun (pistol)*
**pistone** (m) *piston*
**pittura** (f) *painting*
**più** *more*; **più di ...** *more than ...*; **più presto possibile** *as soon as possible*
**piumino** (m) *duvet*
**piuttosto** *pretty*, *quite*

**pizzo** (m) *lace*
**plastica** (f) *plastic*
**platea** (f) *stalls (in theatre)*
**po'** *a little*; **è un po' grande** *it's a little big*; **solo un po'** *just a little*
**poi** *then*
**polipo** (m) *octopus*
**politica** (f) *politics*
**polizia** (f) *police*
**poliziotto** (m) *police officer*
**pollame** (m) *poultry*
**pollo** (m) *chicken*
**polso** (m) *wrist*
**poltrona** (f) *armchair*
**pomata** (f) *ointment*
**pomeriggio** (m) *afternoon*
**pomodoro** (m) *tomato*
**ponte** (m) *bridge*
**porcellana** (f) *china*
**porta** (f) *door*
**portacenere** (m) *ashtray*
**portafoglio** (m) *wallet*
**portare** *to bring*; **da portare via** *to carry out*
**portiere** (m) *porter (hotel)*; **il portiere di notte** *night porter*
**portinaio/portinaia** *caretaker*
**porto** (m) *harbour*, *port*
**possibile** *possible*
**posso avere ...?** *can I have ...?*
**posta** (f) *post*; **la posta elettronica** *email*
**posteggio dei taxi** (m) *taxi rank*
**postino** (m) *postman*
**posto** (m) *place*, *accommodation*, *seat*
**postumi della sbornia** (m pl) *hangover*
**potreste ...?** *can you ...?*
**povero** *poor*
**pranzo** (m) *lunch*
**prato** (m) *lawn*
**preferire** *to prefer*
**prego** *you're welcome*; **prego?** *pardon?*
**prelevare** *to withdraw (money)*
**prendere** *to fetch (something)*
**prendere** *to take*; **prendere il sole** *to sunbathe*; **prendere il treno** *to catch the train*
**prenotare** *to book*
**prenotazione** (f) *reservation*
**preoccupi: non si preoccupi** *don't worry*

**presa di corrente** (f) *electrical hook-up*
**preservativo** (m) *condom*
**presto** *early*; **a presto** *see you soon*
**prete** (m) *priest*
**preventivo** (m) *estimate*
**prezzemolo** (m) *parsley*
**prezzo** (m) *price*; **il prezzo d'ingresso** *admission charge*
**prima di ...** *before ...*
**primavera** (f) *spring (season)*
**primi piatti** (m pl) *starters*
**primo** *first*; **il primo piano** *first floor*; **la prima classe** *first class*
**principiante** (m/f) *beginner*
**privato** *private*
**problema** (m) *problem*; **non c'è problema** *no problem*
**professore/professoressa** (m/f) *teacher*; **il professore universitario** *university lecturer*
**profitti** (m pl) *profits*
**profondo** *deep*
**profumo** (m) *perfume*
**proibito** *forbidden*
**prolunga** (f) *extension lead*
**pronto** *ready*, *hello (on phone)*
**pronto soccorso** (m) *emergency department*, *first aid*
**prosciutto** (m) *ham*
**prossimo** *next*; **la settimana prossima** *next week*
**provare** *to try*
**pubblico** *public*
**pulce** (f) *flea*
**pulire** *to clean*
**pulito** *clean (adj)*
**pullman** (m) *coach (long-distance bus)*
**pungere** *to bite (by insect)*
**punta** (f) *tip (end)*
**puntina da disegno** (f) *drawing pin*
**puntura** (f) *bite (by insect)*
**può** *he/she can*; **non può ...** *he/she can't ...*
**puzzare** *to smell (stink)*

## Q

**quaderno** (m) *notebook*
**quadrato** *square (adj: shape)*
**quadri** (m pl) *diamonds (cards)*
**qualche modo** *somehow*

**qualche parte** *somewhere*
**qualche volta** *sometimes*
**qualcosa** *something*
**qualcuno** *somebody*
**quale?** *which?*
**qualità** (f) *quality*
**quando?** *when?*
**quant'è?** *how much is that?*
**quanti anni hai?** *how old are you?*
**quanto ci vuole?** *how long does it take?*
**quanto costa?** *how much?*
**quanto dista da qui ...?** *how far is it to ...?*
**quaranta** *forty*
**quarto** (m) *quarter;* **... e un quarto** *quarter past ...*
**quarto** *fourth*
**quasi** *almost*
**quattordici** *fourteen*
**quattro** *four*
**quei** *those;* **quei ragazzi** *those boys*
**quella** *that;* **quella donna** *that woman*
**quelle** *those;* **quelle cose** *those things*
**quelli** *those;* **prendo quelli** *I'll take those*
**quello** *that;* **quell'uomo** *that man;* **cos'è quello?** *what's that?*
**questa** *this;* **questa donna** *this woman*
**queste** *these;* **queste cose** *these things*
**questi** *these;* **questi ragazzi** *these boys*
**questo** *this;* **questo quadro** *this picture;* **quest'uomo** *this man;* **cos'è questo?** *what's this?;* **questo è il signor ...** *this is Mr ...*
**quindici** *fifteen*

## R

**raccomandata** *registered (post)*
**radersi** *to shave*
**radiatore** (m) *radiator*
**radio** (f) *radio*
**radiografia** (f) *x-ray*
**raffreddore** (m) *cold (illness);* **ho un raffreddore** *I have a cold*
**ragazza** (f) *girl*
**ragazzo** (m) *boy*

**ragioniere/ragioniera** (m/f) *accountant*
**ragno** (m) *spider*
**rapporto di polizia** (m) *police report*
**raro** *rare (uncommon)*
**rastrello** (m) *rake*
**ratto** (m) *rat*
**ravanello** (m) *radish*
**reception** (f) *reception (hotel)*
**receptionist** (m/f) *receptionist*
**record** (m) *record (sports etc)*
**regalo** (m) *gift*
**reggiseno** (m) *bra*
**relazione** (f) *report*
**religione** (f) *religion*
**remare** *to row*
**remi** (m pl) *oars*
**rene** (m) *kidney*
**reparto** (m) *department, ward;* **il reparto di pediatria** *children's ward*
**respirare** *to breathe*
**resti** (m pl) *ruins*
**restituire** *to return (give back)*
**resto** (m) *rest (noun: remainder)*
**reticella (per i bagagli)** (f) *luggage rack*
**riavere indietro qualcosa** *to get something back*
**ribes nero** (m) *blackcurrant*
**ricci** (m pl) *curls*
**ricco** *rich*
**ricerca** (f) *research*
**ricetta** (f) *prescription*
**ricevere** *to get (obtain)*
**ricevuta** (f) *receipt (restaurants, hotels)*
**ricordare** *to remember;* **non ricordo** *I don't remember*
**ridere** *to laugh*
**riduttore** (m) *adaptor*
**riduzione** (f) *discount*
**rifiuti** (m pl) *litter (bin)*
**riga** (f) *ruler (for drawing)*
**rilassarsi** *to relax*
**rimorchio** (m) *trailer*
**rinfreschi** (m pl) *refreshments*
**rinfresco** *reception (party)*
**ringraziare** *to thank*
**riparare** *to repair*
**ripieno** (m) *filling (in sandwich, cake etc)*
**riposarsi** *to rest*
**riscaldamento** (m) *heating;* **il riscaldamento centrale** *central heating*
**riscuotere** *to cash*

**riso** (m) *rice*
**ristorante** (m) *restaurant*
**ritardo: l'autobus è in ritardo** *the bus is late*
**ritiro bagagli** (m) *baggage claim*
**ritornare** *to return*
**riunione** (f) *meeting*
**rivista** (f) *magazine*
**roccia** *rock (stone)*
**Roma** *Rome*
**romanzo** (m) *novel*
**rosa** (f) *rose; pink (colour)*
**rossetto** (m) *lipstick*
**rosso** *red*
**rotatoria** (f) *roundabout*
**rotondo** *round (circular)*
**rotto** *broken;* **la gamba rotta** *broken leg*
**roulotte** (f) *trailer, caravan*
**rovine** (f pl) *ruins*
**rubare** *steal;* **è stato rubato** *it's been stolen*
**rubinetto** (m) *tap*
**rubino** (m) *ruby (gem)*
**rugby** (m) *rugby*
**rullino a colori** (m) *colour film*
**rum** (m) *rum*
**rumoroso** *noisy*
**ruota** (f) *wheel*
**ruscello** (m) *stream*

## S

**sabato** *Saturday*
**sabbia** (f) *sand*
**sacchetto** (m) *bag;* **il sacchetto di plastica** (m) *plastic bag;* **il sacchetto per la pattumiera** (m) *rubbish bag*
**sacco a pelo** (m) *sleeping bag*
**sala** (f) *room;* **la sala d'aspetto** *waiting room;* **la sala da pranzo** *dining room;* **la sala operatoria** *operating theatre*
**salame** (m) *salami*
**saldi** (m pl) *sale (at reduced prices)*
**sale** (m) *salt*
**salire** *to go up;* **salire su** *to get on (bus etc)*
**salmone** (m) *salmon*
**salsa** (f) *sauce*
**salsiccia** (f) *sausage*
**salumeria** (f) *delicatessen*
**salutare** *to wave*
**sandali** (m pl) *sandals*

**sangue** (m) *blood*; **le analisi del sangue** *blood test*

**sapere** *know* (fact); *I don't know* **non so**

**sapone** (m) *soap*

**la Sardegna** *Sardinia*

**sauna** (f) *sauna*

**sazio** *full (up)*: **sono sazio** *I'm full (up)* (after a meal)

**sbagliato** *wrong*

**sbrigati!** *hurry up!*

**scacchi** (m pl) *chess*

**scala** (f) *staircase*; **le scale** *stairs*; **la scala mobile** *escalator*

**scaldabagno** (m) *water heater*

**scambiare** *to exchange*

**scarpe** (f pl) *shoes*; **le scarpe da ginnastica** *trainers*

**scatola** (f) *box, tin*

**scendere** *to go down*; **scendere da** *to get off* (bus etc)

**scheda telefonica** (f) *phonecard*

**schermo** (m) *screen*

**scherzo** (m) *joke*

**schiena** (f) *back* (body)

**schiuma** (f) *foam, mousse, cream* (for hair); **la schiuma da barba** *shaving cream*

**sci** (m pl) *skis*

**scialle** (m) *shawl*

**sciare: andare a sciare** *to go skiing*

**sciarpa** (f) *scarf*

**scienza** (f) *science*

**sciroppo** (m) *syrup*

**scodella** (f) *bowl*

**scompartimento** (m) *compartment*

**scontrino** (m) *receipt* (shops, bars)

**scopa** (f) *brush* (cleaning)

**la Scozia** *Scotland*

**scozzese** *Scottish*

**scritto da ...** *written by ...*

**scrivania** (f) *desk*

**scuola** (f) *school*

**scuro** *dark*

**scusate!** *excuse me!* (when sneezing etc)

**scusi!** *sorry!*; **scusi?** *pardon?*

**se** *if, whether*

**secchio** (m) *bucket*

**secco** *dry* (wine)

**secondi piatti** (m pl) *main courses*

**secondo** *second*; **seconda classe** *second class*

**sede centrale** (f) *head office*

**sedia** (f) *chair*; **la sedia girevole** *swivel chair*; **la sedia a rotelle** *wheelchair*

**sedici** *sixteen*

**seggiolino per macchina** (m) *car seat* (for a baby)

**segretario/segretaria** (m/f) *secretary*; **la segreteria telefonica** *answering machine*; **la segreteria telefonica** *voicemail*

**sei** *six*

**sei** *you are* (singular, informal)

**semaforo** (m) *traffic lights*

**seminario** (m) *seminar*

**seminterrato** (m) *basement*

**semplice** *simple*

**sempre** *always*; **sempre dritto** *straight on*

**senape** (f) *mustard*

**senso unico** *one way*

**sentiero** (m) *path*

**sentire** *to hear*

**senza** *without*; **senza piombo** *unleaded*

**separati** *separated* (couple)

**separato** *separate* (adj)

**sera** (f) *evening*

**serio** *serious*

**servizio in camera** (m) *room service*

**sessanta** *sixty*

**seta** (f) *silk*

**sete** *thirsty*; **ho sete** *I'm thirsty*

**settanta** *seventy*

**sette** *seven*

**settembre** *September*

**settimana** (f) *week*; **la settimana scorsa** *last week*

**shampoo** (m) *shampoo*

**sherry** (m) *sherry*

**shopping** *shopping*

**short** (m pl) *shorts*

**sì** *yes*

**sia ... che ...** *both ... and ...*

**siamo** *we are*

**la Sicilia** *Sicily*

**sicuro** *safe* (not dangerous); *sure* (certain); **sei sicuro?** *are you sure?*

**siepe** (f) *hedge*

**siete** *you are* (plural, informal)

**sigaretta** (f) *cigarette*

**sigaro** (m) *cigar*

**significa: che cosa significa?** *what does this mean?*

**Signor** *Mr*

**signora** (f) *lady, madam*; **Signora** *Mrs*

**signore** *sir*

**Signorina** *Miss*

**simpatico** *nice* (pleasant)

**sinagoga** (f) *synagogue*

**sinistra** *left* (not right)

**sito internet** (m) *web site*

**slittare** *to skid*

**smalto per le unghie** (m) *nail polish*

**soffitta** (f) *attic*

**soffitto** (m) *ceiling*

**soffocante** *close* (stuffy)

**soggiorno** (m) *living room*

**soldi** (m pl) *money*

**sole** (m) *sun*; **c'è il sole** *it's sunny*

**solito** *usual*; **di solito** *usually*

**sollievo: che sollievo!** *what a relief!*

**solo** *alone, single* (one), *only*; **da solo** *by oneself*

**sonnifero** (m) *sleeping pill*

**sonno** (m) *sleep*

**sono** *I am*; **sono di ...** *I come from ...*

**sopra** *over* (above)

**sopracciglio** (m) *eyebrow*

**sordo** *deaf*

**sorella** (f) *sister*

**sorpassare** *to pass* (driving)

**sorridere** *to smile*

**sorriso** (m) *smile*

**sosta vietata** *no parking*

**sotto** *below, under*

**sottoveste** (f) *underskirt*

**souvenir** (m) *souvenir*

**la Spagna** *Spain*

**spagnolo** *Spanish*

**spago** *string* (cord)

**spalla** (f) *shoulder*

**spazio** (m) *room* (space)

**spazzatura** (f) *rubbish*

**spazzola** (f) *hairbrush*

**spazzolare** *to brush* (hair)

**spazzolino da denti** (m) *toothbrush*

**specchio** (m) *mirror*

**spedire per posta** *to post*

**spesa** (f) *shopping*; **andare a fare la spesa** *to go shopping*

**spesso** *often; thick*

**spettatori** *audience*

**spiacente** *I'm sorry*

**spiaggia** (f) *beach*

**spicci** (m pl) *cash, change*

**spilla** (f) *brooch*; **la spilla di sicurezza** *safety pin*

**spillatrice** (f) *stapler*

**spillo** (m) *pin*

**spina** *plug* (electrical)

**spinaci** (m pl) *spinach*

**spingere** *to push*

**sporco** *dirty*

**sport** (m) *sport*

**sportello** (m) *door* (of car); **lo sportello automatico** *cash machine*

**sposato** *married*

**spuntino** (m) *snack*

**stampante** (f) *printer*

**stampelle** (f pl) *crutches*

**stanco** *tired*

**stanza** (f) *room*; **stanza libera** *vacancy* (room)

**star** (f) *star* (film)

**stasera** *tonight*

**statua** (f) *statue*

**stazione** (f) *station*; **la stazione di polizia** *police station*; **la stazione di servizio** (f) *petrol station*

**steccato** (m) *fence*

**stella** (f) *star*

**stereo** (m) *music system*

**sterlina** (f) *pounds sterling*

**stesso** *same*; **lo stesso vestito** *the same dress*

**stirare** *to iron*

**stivale** (m) *boot* (footwear); **gli stivali do gomma** *Wellington boots*

**stoffa** (f) *fabric*

**stomaco** (m) *stomach*

**storia** (f) *history*

**straccio per la polvere** (m) *duster*

**strada** (f) *road, street*

**straniero** (m) *foreigner*

**strano** *odd, funny*

**stretta di mano** (f) *handshake*

**stretto** *narrow, tight* (clothes)

**strofinaccio** (m) *dishcloth*

**strumento musicale** (m) *musical instrument*

**studente/studentessa** (m/f) *student*

**stupido** *stupid*

**su** *on, over* (above); **sul tavolo** *on the table*; **un libro su Venezia** *a book on Venice*

**succo** (m) *juice*; **il succo d'arancia** *orange juice*; **il succo di frutta** *fruit juice*;

**il succo di pomodoro** *tomato juice*

**sud** (m) *south*

**sudare** *to sweat*

**sudore** (m) *sweat*

**suo** *her/his/your* (singular, formal)**: il suo libro** *her/his/ your book*; **la sua casa** *her/ his/your house*; **le sue scarpe** *her/his/your shoes*; **i suoi vestiti** *her/his/ your dresses*; **è suo** *it's hers/ his/yours*

**suoceri** (m pl) *in-laws*

**supermercato** (m) *supermarket*

**supplemento** *supplement*

**supposta** (f) *suppository*

**surgelati** (m pl) *frozen foods*

**sveglia** (f) *alarm clock*

**svenire** *to faint*

**sviluppare** *to develop* (film)

**la Svizzera** *Switzerland*

**svizzero** *Swiss*

## T

**tabaccaio** (m) *tobacconist's* (shop)

**tabacco** (m) *tobacco*

**tacco** (m) *heel* (of shoe)

**taglia** (f) *size* (clothes)

**tagliare** *to cut, chop*

**tagliaunghie** (m) *nail clippers*

**taglio** (m) *cut, haircut*

**talco** (m) *talcum powder*

**tallone** (m) *heel* (of foot)

**tamponi** (m pl) *tampons*

**tappeto** (m) *carpet, rug*

**tappo** (m) *cap* (bottle), *cork, plug* (sink)

**tardi** *late*; **si sta facendo tardi** *it's getting late*; **più tardi** *later*

**targa** (f) *number plate*

**tariffa** (f) *fare, rate*; **la tariffa ridotta** (f) *concessionary rate*

**tasca** (f) *pocket*

**tastare** *to feel* (touch)

**tastiera** (f) *keyboard*

**tavoletta di cioccolata** (f) *bar of chocolate*

**tavolo** (m) *table*

**taxi** (m) *taxi*

**tazza** (f) *cup*

**tazzone** (m) *mug*

**tè** (m) *tea*; **il tè con latte** *tea with milk*

**teatro** (m) *theatre*

**tecnico** (m) *technician*

**tedesco** *German*

**telefonare** *to telephone*

**telefonata** (f) *telephone call*

**telefonino** (m) *mobile phone*

**telefono** (m) *telephone*

**televisione** (f) *television*

**telo protettivo** (m) *fly sheet*

**telone impermeabile** (m) *ground sheet*

**temperamatite** (m) *pencil sharpener*

**temperatura** (f) *temperature*

**temperino** (m) *penknife*

**tempesta** (f) *storm*

**tempo** (m) *time, weather*; **il tempo libero** *leisure time*

**temporale** (m) *thunderstorm*

**tenda** (f) *curtain, tent*; **la tenda avvolgibile** *blind* (on window)

**tennis** (m) *tennis*

**terminale** (m) *terminal* (airport)

**termosifone** (m) *heater*

**terra** (f) *soil, land*

**terribile** *awful, terrible*

**terrina** (f) *mixing bowl*

**terzo** *third*

**testa** (f) *head*

**testimone** (m/f) *witness*

**tetto** (m) *roof*

**il Tevere** *the Tiber*

**tirare** *to pull*

**tisana** (f) *herbal tea*

**toilette** (f) *toilet*; (men's) **la toilette degli uomini**; (women's) **la toilette delle donne**

**topo** (m) *mouse* (animal)

**torcia (elettrica)** (f) *torch*

**Torino** *Turin*

**tornare** *to come back*

**torre** (f) *tower*

**torta** (f) *cake*

**tosaerba** (m) *lawnmower*

**la Toscana** *Tuscany*

**tosse** (f) *cough*

**tossire** *to cough*

**tovagliolo** (m) *napkin*

**tradizione** (f) *tradition*

**tradurre** *to translate*

**traduttore/traduttrice** (m/f) *translator*

**traffico** (m) *traffic*

**traghetto** (m) *ferry*

**trampolino** (m) *diving board*

**tranquillo** *quiet*

**traslocare** *to move house*

**trattore** (m) *tractor*

**tre** *three*

**trecento** *three hundred*

**tredici** *thirteen*
**treno** (m) *train*
**trenta** *thirty*
**triste** *sad*
**troppo** *too (excessively)*
**trucco** (m) *makeup*
**tu** *you (singular, informal)*
**tubo** (m) *hose, pipe (for water)*
**tuffarsi** *to dive*
**tuffo** (m) *dive (noun*
**tunnel** (m) *tunnel*
**tuo** *your (singular, informal);*
  **il tuo libro** *your book;*
  **la tua camicia** *your shirt;*
  **le tue scarpe** *your shoes;*
  **è tuo?** *is this yours?*
**turista** (m/f) *tourist*
**tuta da ginnastica** (f) *track
  suit*
**tutto** *all;* **tutto** *everything;*
  **tutte le strade** *all the
  streets;* **questo è tutto**
  *that's all;* **tutti** *everyone;*
  **tutti i giorni** *every day*
**TV cavo** *cable TV*
**TV satellite** *satellite TV*

## U

**ubriaco** *drunk*
**uccello** (m) *bird*
**udire** *to hear*
**ufficio** (m) *office;* **l'ufficio
  oggetti smarriti** *lost
  property office;* **l'ufficio
  postale** *post office;* **l'ufficio
  turistico** *tourist office*
**ultimo** *last (final)*
**umido** *damp*
**un/uno/una/un'** *a*
**undici** *eleven*
**unghia** (f) *nail (finger)*
**unguento** (m) *ointment*
**università** (f) *university*
**uno** *one;* **l'una** *one o'clock*
**uomo** (m) *man;* **gli uomini**
  *men*
**uovo** (m) *egg*
**urgente** *urgent*
**usare** *to use*
**uscire** *to go out*
**uscita** (f) *exit, gate (at airport)*

**uso** (m) *use*
**utile** *useful*
**uva** (f) *grapes*
**uvetta** (f) *raisins*

## V

**vacanza** (f) *holiday, vacation*
**vaccinazione** (f) *vaccination*
**vagone letto** (m) *sleeping car*
**valigia** (f) *case, suitcase*
**valle** (f) *valley*
**valvola** (f) *valve*
**vanga** (f) *spade (shovel)*
**vaniglia** (f) *vanilla*
**varecchina** (f) *bleach*
**vasca** (f) *bath (tub)*
**vaso** (m) *vase*
**vassoio** (m) *tray*
**vattene!** *go away!*
**il Vaticano** *Vatican;* **la Città
  del Vaticano** *Vatican City*
**vecchio** *old*
**vedere** *to see*
**vegetariano** *vegetarian*
**veicolo** (m) *vehicle*
**vela** (f) *sailing*
**veleno** (m) *poison*
**veloce** *fast, quick*
**velocità** (f) *speed*
**vendere** *to sell*
**vendite** (f pl) *sales (of goods,
  etc)*
**venerdì** *Friday*
**Venezia** *Venice*
**venga qui!** *come here!
  (informal);* **venga con me**
  *come with me (informal)*
**venire** *to come*
**venti** *twenty*
**ventilatore** (m) *fan
  (ventilator)*
**vento** (m) *wind*
**verde** *green*
**verdura** (f) *vegetables*
**vernice** (f) *paint*
**vero** *true*
**vespa** (f) *wasp*
**vestito** (m) *dress;* **i vestiti**
  *clothes*
**veterinario** (m) *vet*
**vetro** (m) *glass (material)*

**via aerea** *air mail*
**viaggiare** *to travel*
**viaggio** (m) *journey*
**viale** (m) *driveway*
**vialetto** (m) *path*
**vieni qui!** *come here!* (formal);
  **vieni con me** *come with
  me* (formal)
**vicino (a)** *close, near (to);*
  **vicino alla finestra** *near
  the window;* **vicino alla
  porta** *near the door*
**video cassetta** (m) *video
  (tape/film)*
**videogiochi** (m pl) *video games*
**videoregistratore** (m) *VCR*
**villa** (f) *villa*
**villaggio** (m) *village*
**vino** (m) *wine;* **la lista
  dei vini** *wine list*
**viola** *purple*
**violino** (m) *violin*
**visita** (f) *visit;* **la visita
  guidata** *guided tour*
**vista** (f) *view*
**vita** (f) *life, screw*
**vivaio** (m) *garden centre*
**vocabolarietto** (m) *phrase
  book*
**voce** (f) *voice*
**vodka** (f) *vodka*
**voi** *you (plural)*
**volantino** (m) *leaflet*
**volare** *to fly*
**volere** *to want*
**volo** (m) *flight;* **il numero
  del volo** *flight number*
**vorrei** *I'd like*
**vuoto** *empty*

## W, Y, Z

**whisky** (m) *whisky*
**yogurt** (m) *yoghurt*
**zaino** (m) *backpack*
**zanzara** (f) *mosquito*
**zenzero** (m) *ginger (spice)*
**zia** (f) *aunt*
**zio** (m) *uncle*
**zoo** (m) *zoo*
**zucchero** (m) *sugar*
**zuppa** (f) *soup*

# Acknowledgments

The publisher would like to thank the following for their help in the preparation of this book: Fiorella Elviri and Anna Mazzotti for the organization of location photography in Italy; Farmacia Gaoni, Rome; La Taverna dei Borgia, Rome; Treni Italia, Tuscolana, Rome; Coolhurst Tennis Club, London; Magnet Showroom, Enfield, MyHotel, London; Kathy Gammon; Juliette Meeus and Harry.

*Language content for Dorling Kindersley by* **g-and-w publishing**
*Managed by* **Jane Wightwick**
*Editing and additional input:* **Paula Tite**

*Additional design assistance:* **Phil Gamble, Lee Riches, Fehmi Cömert, Sally Geeve**
*Additional editorial assistance:* **Kajal Mistry, Paul Docherty, Nikki Sims, Lynn Bresler**
*Picture research:* **Louise Thomas**

## Picture credits

Key: t=top; b=bottom; l=left; r=right; c=centre; A=above; B=below

p2 **DK Images:** *Demetrio Carrasco;* p4/5 **DK Images:** *Max Alexander trl Demetrio Carrasco bl;* p6/7 **Laura Knox:** *cl;* p10/11 **Alamy:** *BananaStock cAr; RubberBall cBl, bl;* **Ingram Image Library:** *bl;* p12/13 **Alamy:** *John Foxx cl, cAr; RubberBall br;* **DK Images:** *Steve Shott cBr;* **Ingram Image Library:** *tr, cr;* p14/15 **Alamy:** *Comstock Images tcr; Think Stock bcl;* **Dreamstime.com:** *Slobodan Mračina (cl);* **Ingram Image Library:** *cAl, cl, cBl, cAr, cBr, bcr;* p16/17 **Alamy:** *Think Stock crA;* **Getty:** *Taxi / James Day bcr;* **Ingram Image Library:** *tr;* p18/19 **DK Images:** *David Murray tr;* p22/23 **DK Images:** *cl, Andy Crawford cAr; Susanna Price br; Magnus Rew tcrB;* **Ingram Image Library:** *bcl, tcr;* p24/25 **DK Images:** *clA, Dave King tcr;* p26/27 **Ingram Image Library:** *cl;* p28/29 **DK Images:** *John Bulmer tcr; Dave King cr; Matthew Ward bclA;* **Ingram Image Library:** *bcrA, bcr;* p30/31 **Alamy:** *Comstock Images bcl;* **DK Images:** *cl;* 34/35 **Dreamstime.com:** *Slobodan Mračina (cb);* p36/37 **DK Images:** *bcl, bcr; Magnus Rew cl;* **Dreamstime.com:** *Slobodan Mračina (cla);* **Ingram Image Library:** *bl;* **iStockphoto.com:** *nicolas_ (cla/sim card);* p38/39 **Alamy:** *Imageshop / Zefa Visual Media cl;* p40/41 **DK:** *Sean Hunter cl;* p42/43 **DK:** *Demetrio Carrasco cAAr; Mike Dunning tcr;* p44/45 **Courtesy of Renault:** *c;* p46/47 **Alamy:** *Imageshop / Zefa Visual Media br;* **DK Images:** *Sean Hunter bcl;* **Ingram Image Library:** *tclB;* **Courtesy of Renault:** *tcr;* p48/49 **Alamy:** *CuboImages cAl;* **DK Images:** *Kim Sayer c, cl;* p50/51 **Alamy:** *Robert Harding Picture Library c; Peter Titmuss cr;* p52/53 **Alamy:** *Image Farm Inc cAr;* **DK Images:** *cl;* p54/55 **Alamy:** *Frank Herholdt bcl; Jackson Smith cBl;* **Alamy:** *BananaStock cl; John Foxx c; Image Source cAr; ThinkStock tcr;* **DK Images:** *Andy Crawford bclA;* p56/57 **Alamy:** *CuboImages tcll;* **Alamy:** *Max Alexander clAA; Kim Sayer cAl, c;* **Courtesy of Renault:** *bc;* p58/59 **Alamy:** *Michael Juno tcr;* **Alamy:** *Brand X Pictures cBl, cBBl; Image Source cAAl;* **DK Images:** *cAl;* p60/61 **123RF.com:** *shutswis (cb);* **Alamy:** *Robert Harding Picture Library bcr;* **Alamy:** *Image Source cAr; Barry Mason bl;* **DK Images:** *Steve Gorton tcrB; Pia Tryde cAAr;* **Ingram Image Library:** *cr;* p62/63 **DK Images:** *Stephen Whitehorn c;* p64/65 **Alamy:** *Arcaid bcrA;* **Alamy:** *GKPhotography cBr; Goodshoot cAAr; Justin Kase tcrB;* **DK Images:** *Roger Moss c; Steve Tanner cAl;* **Ingram Image Library:** *tcr; p66/67* **Alamy:** *Arcaid tl;* **Alamy:** *Image Source cAr;* **DK Images:** *tr; Stephen Whitehorn bl;* **Ingram Image Library:** *bl;* p68/69 **Alamy:** *Balearic Pictures cr;* p72/73 **Alamy:** *imagebroker tcrB; Image Source cAr; Comstock Images tcr;* **Avery Weight-Tronix:** *bl;* p74/75 **Alamy RF:** *Doug Norman bl;* **Ingram Image Library:** *c;* p76/77 **Alamy:** *Balearic Pictures cBl;* p78/79 **Alamy:** *Think Stock bcr;* p80/81 **Getty:** *Taxi / Rob Melnychuk bc;* **Ingram Image Library:** *cAr;* **Xerox UK Ltd:** *tcr;* p82/83 **Alamy:** *wildphotos.com tcr;* **Alamy:** *FogStock cAAl; Momentum Creative Group cAl; Shoosh / Up the Res cBl;* **Ingram Image Library:** *cl;* p84/85 **Alamy:** *Brand X Pictures cr; f1 Online c;* **Alamy RF:** *BananaStock bl; SuperStock tr;* **Ingram Image Library:** *crB;* p86/87 **Alamy:** *Luca DiCecco bcl;* **Getty:** *Taxi / Rob Melnychuk tc;* p90/91 **Alamy:** *Brand X Pictures tcr;* **DK Images:** *cl; David Jordan cAr; Stephen Oliver cr;* **Ingram Image Library:** *cBr;* p82/93 **Alamy:** *Pixland cr;* **DK Images:** *cl; Guy Ryecart cr;* p94/95 **Alamy:** *David Kamm cl; Phototake Inc bcl;* **Alamy:** *Comstock Images cr; ImageState Royalty Free bcr;* **DK Images:** *Stephen Oliver tcr;* p96/97 **Alamy:** *Pixland bc;* **DK Images:** *tl;* **Ingram Image Library:** *tr;* p98/99 **Alamy:** *Shotfile cr;* **Alamy:** *Bildagentur Franz Waldhaeusl bl; Keith Levit c; ThinkStock br;* **Dreamstime.com:** *Alexandre Dvihally (tl);* p100/101 **DK Images:** *Steve Gorton tcr;* p102/103 **Alamy:** *Hortus b; D Hurst tcrB;* **Alamy:** *image100 tcr;* **DK Images:** *Geoff Brightling cAAr;* **Ingram Image Library:** *cAr;* p104/105 **DK Images:** *Paul Bricknell cl(6); Jane Burton bcl; Geoff Dann cl(2); Max Gibbs cl(4); Frank Greenaway cl(3); Dave King cl(1), cAr, Tracy Morgan cl(5);* p106/107 **Alamy:** *Shotfile cr;* **DK Images:** *Geoff Brightling br;* p110/111 **Alamy:** *RubberBall cr;* **DK Images:** *Andy Crawford cl;* p112/113 **Alamy RF:** *BananaStock tcr; Image Source bl;* **DK Images:** *cl;* **Ingram Image Library:** *bcrA;* p114/115 **Alamy:** *FogStock tcr;* **Alamy:** *Image Source cAr; Index Stock cAl;* p116/117 **Alamy:** *image100 cAl;* p118/119 **Alamy RF:** *Pixland tcr;* **GettyNews:** *Giuseppe Cacace c;* p120/121 **Alamy:** *ImageState / Pictor International cl;* **Alamy:** *Sarkis Images tcr;* **DK Images:** *cBl, bcl;* p122/123 **Alamy:** *BananaStock cA;* **Ingram Image Library:** *cl;* p124/125 **Alamy:** *ImageState / Pictor International bclA;* **DK Images:** *cBl, bcl; Paul Bricknell tc(5); Geoff Dann tc(3); Max Gibbs tc(1); Frank Greenaway tc(2); Dave King tc(4); Tracy Morgan tc(6);* p126/127 **Alamy:** *Image Farm Inc bl;* p128 **DK Images:** *Neil Mersh.*

All other images **Mike Good**.